How to Keep Your Research Project on Track

How to Keep Your Research Project on Track

Track

Insights from When Things Go Wrong

Edited by

Keith Townsend

Associate Professor of Employment Relations, Griffith Business School, Griffith University, Australia

Mark N.K. Saunders

Professor of Business Research Methods, Birmingham Business School, University of Birmingham, UK

Cheltenham, UK • Northampton, MA, USA

Cover image: The Horse and Groom, Bourton-on-the-Hill, UK.
© Mark N.K. Saunders.

Published by
Edward Elgar Publishing Limited
The Lypiatts
15 Lansdown Road
Cheltenham
Glos GL50 2JA
UK

Edward Elgar Publishing, Inc.
William Pratt House
9 Dewey Court
Northampton
Massachusetts 01060
USA

Paperback edition 2018

A catalogue record for this book
is available from the British Library

Library of Congress Control Number: 2017950460

This book is available electronically in the **Elgar**online
Business subject collection
DOI 10.4337/9781786435767

ISBN 978 1 78643 575 0 (cased)
ISBN 978 1 78643 576 7 (eBook)
ISBN 978 1 78897 414 1 (paperback)

Typeset by Servis Filmsetting, Stockport, Cheshire
Printed and bound by CPI Group (UK) Ltd, Croydon, CR0 4YY

Contents

About the editors   ix
List of contributors   xi

1 Shit happens, but you have a job to do!   1
   Keith Townsend and Mark N.K. Saunders

PART I GETTING STARTED

2 Developing research ideas   11
   Bill Lee

3 On the path to enlightenment? Reviewing the literature
   systematically – or not   20
   Céline Rojon

4 The master and apprentice: lessons from two PhD supervisors
   and a recent PhD graduate   28
   Jillian Cavanagh, Hannah Meacham and Timothy Bartram

5 'Finders, keepers, losers, weepers!' A doctoral candidate's reality
   of changing thesis advisors   36
   Polly Black

6 Reply all, tweets and social media: technological friends for
   developing a professional identity that need to be treated with
   care   44
   Hugh T.J. Bainbridge

7 Coming up with a research question: opinions, feedback and
   networking   46
   Deisi Yunga

PART II GETTING DATA

8 Finding epistemology   51
   Neve Isaeva

9   Bounce back, firewalls and legal threats: reaching respondents
    using Internet questionnaires   59
    Mark N.K. Saunders and David E. Gray

10 Finding the truth amongst conflicting evidence   67
    Heather Short

11 Rolling with the punches   77
    Sharyn Rundle-Thiele, Julia Carins and Christiane Stock

12 Access, involvement and interference: encounters and
    experiences of case studies   87
    Kenneth Cafferkey

13 Is a pilot necessary?   98
    Polly Black

14 The precarious nature of access   100
    Wojciech Marek Kwiatkowski

15 The diminishing dissertation: seven cases to three+   101
    Ashlea Kellner

16 So, I guess we're probably finished then   103
    Keith Townsend

17 Your incentives are too lucrative: caution in rewarding
    interview participants   104
    Catheryn Khoo-Lattimore

18 Sales skills for researchers   106
    Colin Hughes

19 Being flexible in interviews: make sure that you account for
    power imbalance   109
    Qian Yi Lee

PART III   GETTING IT TOGETHER

20 '. . . Just one goat': the importance of interpretation in
    qualitative data analysis   113
    Keith Townsend and Rebecca Loudoun

21 Analysing quantitative data   121
    Sameer Qaiyum and Catherine L. Wang

22 When the words just won't come   129
    Dawn C. Duke

23 I'm a paper person or maybe not?   138
    Ilenia Bregoli

24 A mug of stress   140
    Rohit Talwar

25 Excuse me . . . should that comma be there? Dealing with
    awkward questions   142
    Kenneth Cafferkey

26 Finding the time to progress your research, and the big lie that
    you are part of!   144
    Jennifer Kilroy

PART IV GETTING FINISHED

27 Authorship in action   149
    Kate L. Daunt and Aoife M. McDermott

28 'They think I'm stupid': dealing with supervisor feedback   157
    Amanda Lee

29 Grasping roses or nettles? Losing and finding ourselves in
    research projects   164
    Kiran Trehan, Alex Kevill and Jane Glover

30 Using social media to enhance your research   174
    Angelique Gatsinzi

31 Organisations, clients and feminists: getting in, coming back
    and having fun   184
    Marian Baird

32 Born to . . . write, rewrite and rewrite again   194
    Mark N.K. Saunders

33 'I'm over it . . .'   197
    Peter J. Jordan

Index   199

Editors

Keith Townsend is Associate Professor at Griffith University, Australia. His research spans a wide range of areas including a focus on line managers (including frontline managers), employee involvement and participation in decision-making, industrial relations and human resource management and work–life balance. These broad themes are brought together with an overarching approach to better understanding the complexities of managing people within the modern workplace. His research has been published in journals including *Human Resource Management Journal, Work, Employment and Society* and *British Journal of Management*. He has also published a number of research methods books, including *Method in the Madness: Research Stories You Won't Read in Textbooks* and *Handbook of Qualitative Research Methods on Human Resource Management: Innovative Techniques*.

Mark N.K. Saunders is Professor of Business Research Methods and Director of PhD Programmes at Birmingham Business School, University of Birmingham, UK. His research interests include research methods (in particular participant selection, and methods of understanding organisational relationships) and human resource aspects of the management of change (in particular trust, and organisational learning). He also has an emerging interest in small and medium-sized enterprises. His research has been published in journals including the *British Journal of Management, Human Relations, Journal of Small Business Management* and *Social Science and Medicine*. He is co-editor of the Sage book series Understanding Research Methods for Business and Management Students and editor of the Edward Elgar Handbooks of Research Methods series. He has also co-authored a number of research methods books including *Research Methods for Business Students* (currently in its 7th edition), *Handbook of Research Methods on Trust* (currently in its 2nd edition) and *Handbook of Research Methods on Human Resource Development*.

Contributors

Hugh T.J. Bainbridge is a Senior Lecturer in the School of Management, University of New South Wales, Australia. His research interests focus on workforce diversity with a specialisation in the experience of employees who, in addition to their job, also provide informal unpaid care to family members with disabilities.

Marian Baird AO is Professor of Gender and Employment Relations and Chair of Work and Organisational Studies at the University of Sydney Business School, Australia. Marian is a policy-focused and action-oriented academic.

Timothy Bartram is a Professor of Human Resource Management in the Business School at La Trobe University, Australia. His research is in the area of HRM in healthcare, Indigenous Men's Sheds and disability in the workplace. Tim is currently the Co-editor of the *Asia Pacific Journal of Human Resources*, Australia's leading management journal.

Polly Black is Visiting Professor of Practice in Communications and Entrepreneurship at Wake Forest University, USA. Her research focuses on consumer behaviour and consumer trust.

Ilenia Bregoli is a Senior Lecturer in Marketing at the University of Lincoln, UK. She considers herself a pragmatist and in her research she uses mixed methods.

Kenneth Cafferkey is currently an Assistant Professor at the Graduate School of Business, Universiti Tun Abdul Razak, Malaysia. His research interests include high-performance work systems, ideological orientations towards HRM, organisational climate, and employee perspectives and experiences of HRM.

Julia Carins is a Researcher at Griffith University, Australia and a Defence Food and Nutrition Scientist. Julia takes a social marketing approach to improve eating behaviour for individual and societal benefit.

Jillian Cavanagh is the Business School Graduate Research Co-ordinator and Senior Lecturer in Human Resource Management at La Trobe University, Australia. She has undertaken commission research on Men's

Sheds and Indigenous Men's Groups, and she researches disability in the workplace.

Kate L. Daunt is a Reader in Marketing and Deputy Director of Postgraduate Studies at Cardiff Business School, Cardiff University, UK.

Dawn C. Duke is the Head of Researcher Development within the University of Surrey's Doctoral College, UK. She leads the team that supports the transferable/employability skills of researchers across all disciplines.

Angelique Gatsinzi is a final-year doctoral student at the University of Surrey researching child labour in artisanal and small-scale mining in sub-Saharan Africa.

Jane Glover is a Research Fellow at the University of Birmingham, UK. Her research interests lie in small family firms with a particular focus on rural firms. Jane conducts qualitative research using multiple approaches including interviews, participant observation and documentary analysis.

David E. Gray is Professor of Leadership and Organisational Behaviour at the University of Greenwich, UK. His research interests include research methods, management learning (particularly coaching and mentoring), professional identity, action learning, reflective learning, management learning in SMEs and the factors that contribute to SME success.

Colin Hughes is a Department Head at the College of Business, Dublin Institute of Technology, Republic of Ireland. His PhD research at the University of Birmingham focuses on trust building in virtual sales teams.

Neve Isaeva is a doctoral researcher at the University of Birmingham, UK. Her research interests include, but are not limited to, trust and distrust, research philosophy and methodology, and culture.

Peter J. Jordan is a Professor of Organizational Behaviour at the Griffith Business School, Griffith University, Australia. Peter's research interests include emotions in organizations, team performance and psychological entitlement in organizations.

Ashlea Kellner is a Research Fellow at Griffith University's Centre for Work, Organisation and Wellbeing, Australia. She completed her doctoral thesis in 2012, and is currently involved in research relating to HRM systems and high performance, people management in healthcare, and HR control in the franchise relationship.

Alex Kevill is Lecturer in Enterprise at the University of Leeds, UK. His research interests include dynamic capabilities, micro-enterprises and social entrepreneurship. Alex completed his doctoral research, 'Dynamic Capabilities in Micro-Organizations: Understanding Key Micro-Foundations', at Lancaster University in 2015.

Catheryn Khoo-Lattimore is a Senior Lecturer in Tourism and Hospitality at Griffith University, Australia. Her research focuses on women travellers and family tourism, and often, qualitatively, from an Asian perspective.

Jennifer Kilroy completed her PhD at NUI Galway, Republic of Ireland, while working full time in a HRM position in a multinational firm. She continues her practitioner life while publishing from her PhD findings.

Wojciech Marek Kwiatkowski is a Doctoral Researcher at Alliance Manchester Business School, University of Manchester, UK.

Amanda Lee is a Senior Lecturer in Human Resource Management at the University of Derby, UK and Chartered Fellow of the CIPD. Prior to a career in academia she worked in retail, construction and the NHS.

Bill Lee is Professor of Accounting at Sheffield University Management School, UK. He has a long-term interest in research methods and is an editor of Sage's Mastering Business Research Methods series.

Qian Yi Lee is a PhD candidate at Griffith University, Australia, exploring performance management in the public sector. She has an honours degree also from Griffith and an MBA from Korea University.

Rebecca Loudoun is Senior Lecturer at Griffith University, Australia. Her research and teaching focuses in the areas of human resource management, industrial relations, and health and safety management.

Aoife M. McDermott is a Reader in Human Resource Management and coordinator of the Cardiff Health Organisation and Policy Studies (CHOPS) group at Cardiff Business School, Cardiff University, UK.

Hannah Meacham recently completed her PhD at La Trobe University, Australia. She completed in two and a half years on the topic of disability in the workplace. Hannah has already published three refereed journal articles in the area of HR and disability.

Sameer Qaiyum is a Senior Lecturer in Strategic Management at Liverpool Business School, Liverpool John Moores University, UK. His research interests are in the areas of strategic management and innovation.

Céline Rojon is a Lecturer in Human Resource Management at the University of Edinburgh Business School, UK. Her research interests include work performance, assessment, selection and development, research methods and cross-cultural studies.

Sharyn Rundle-Thiele is Director, Social Marketing at Griffith, Griffith University, Australia. Drawing on her commercial marketing background Sharyn's research focuses on applying marketing tools and techniques to change behaviour for the better.

Mark N.K. Saunders is Professor of Business Research Methods in the Birmingham Business School at the University of Birmingham, UK

Heather Short lectures in business and management at Portsmouth University, UK and is Managing Editor of *Human Resource Development Quarterly*. Having worked in multinational organisations and run her own small and medium enterprise (SME), her research interests include e-learning and SMEs.

Christiane Stock is an Associate Professor at the University of Southern Denmark. Her research focuses on young people's health and health behaviour and on intervention research for behaviour change.

Rohit Talwar is a Teaching Fellow in marketing at the University of Birmingham, UK. His research focuses on consumer experiences generated by interactive installations in public spaces with a postmodern lens.

Keith Townsend is Associate Professor of Employment Relations in the Griffith Business School at Griffith University, Australia.

Kiran Trehan is Professor of Leadership and Enterprise Development at the University of Birmingham, UK. Kiran is a key contributor to debates on critical approaches to enterprise development, leadership and diversity and how it can be applied in a variety of small business and policy domains.

Catherine L. Wang is a Professor of Entrepreneurship and Strategy at Brunel Business School, Brunel University London, UK. Her research interests are in the areas of entrepreneurship and strategic management.

Deisi Yunga is an Early Stage Researcher on the European Doctorate in Teacher Education Programme (EdiTE) at Eötvös Loránd University in Budapest, Hungary. She is interested in topics related to adult learning.

1. Shit happens, but you have a job to do!

Keith Townsend and Mark N.K. Saunders

The *Horse and Groom* is a friendly Cotswolds country pub that has consistently won UK 'best public house' awards since 2009.[1] The quality of this Bourton-on-the-Hill pub is hence a perfect starting point for this unusual research offering. We sat in this country pub after a day of working through a significant and important revision of a research methods article. As we enjoyed a pint of beer, an award-winning dinner and exceptional service, we discussed the differences between textbook research methods and the realities that all of us in the field face on a day-to-day basis. Previously, we had both embarked on publications that drew on the realities (see for example, Townsend and Burgess 2009; and Saunders and Lewis 1997), but felt that there was scope for something new. Something that was both practical but based in experiences.

As a fellow researcher we are sure you can appreciate the excitement that grew throughout the course of the evening as we discussed the possibilities that would become this edition. 'There's so much that goes unwritten', we would lament; 'we're doing our students a disservice by not telling them', we would declare. 'So let's do something', we agreed. It was then that we embarked upon a journey that started the same way that many top research publications start . . . on the back of beer mats (see Figure 1.1).

As you can see from the photograph, our plan was *literally* written on the back of what Mark (being British) calls 'beer mats' and Keith (being Australian) 'beer coasters', with the key final stage 'Talk to Fran tomorrow' as one of us had a meeting the next day with Francine O'Sullivan, our commissioning editor at Edward Elgar Publishing.

One might be forgiven for thinking pubs, beer mats (or coasters!), chats with publishers – doesn't sound all that 'scientific' or high-brow. Perhaps not, but it does reflect the broad experience of reality while not paying enough attention to the many hours of subsequent planning, discussions, reviewing and commenting on drafts that we were about to face.

The chapters in this book are written with a starting point of realising that research projects do not always go smoothly. In fact, we would argue

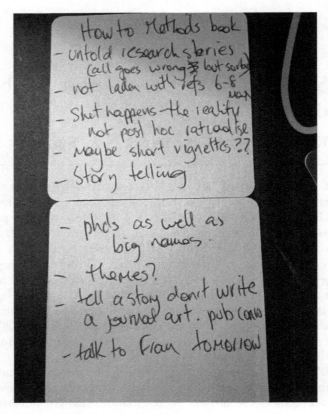

Figure 1.1   Horse and Groom *research proposal*

that they rarely go smoothly. But we are employed to perform research from conceptualisation of worthwhile projects to the completion of these projects including dissemination to a range of different audiences.

We are not suggesting that 'doing research' is particularly difficult, nor are we suggesting that it is easy – it just is what it is. And we as researchers must find ways to jump through a myriad of invisible hoops and over a plethora of hurdles of unknown heights. So planning is important and the knowledge and understandings we can glean from textbooks and journal articles on research methods are an important part of that planning. But, and this is an important 'but': these textbooks and journal articles rarely are of help regarding what do you do when your research project goes off track, usually offering only sanitised accounts. This book we hope will address this important, and usually hidden, aspect of research.

Our contributors have provided their own inside accounts in the form of 19 chapters and 14 vignettes offering revealing insights and highlighting their own lessons. We believe these will give hope to the early career researcher, the PhD or Masters student, and at the same time provide the 'old timers' such as ourselves with some reinvigoration.

Contributors were given strict instructions. This is not to be a theory driven, literature soaked piece of work. Much like the book's inception, we would tell the authors to imagine you were at a pub or a coffee shop and relaying a story to a friend. Keep it informal, keep it light, but tell it as it actually was and have some lessons for the reader to take away.

We have divided the book into four sections. Maintaining the informal theme, the sections are 'Getting started', 'Getting data', 'Getting it together', and 'Getting finished'. Within each section we have chapters followed by short vignettes, all of which tell tales of researchers facing real-world problems or not quite getting things right in the first instance.

In the first section, 'Getting started', we draw on expert experiences in the 'not-so-straightforward' manner in which research projects develop and progress. Bill Lee leads the book with his chapter (2) 'Developing research ideas' and recounts an experience with research on flexible manufacturing systems where the expectations that were drawn from the literature and theory were not aligned with what he was finding empirically. The research project obviously became much more difficult, but indeed, much more interesting! So what does this say about literature reviews? Céline Rojon gives some insights in Chapter 3. There are many 'types' of literature reviews, and her chapter, whilst focusing on the use of systematic literature reviews, also offers insights into traditional narrative reviews, providing some important insights to keep the researcher on track.

The next two chapters in this section focus on the interactions between PhD supervisors and students. In Chapter 4 Jillian Cavanagh, Hannah Meacham and Timothy Bartram explore a number of important themes where all parties within a PhD team must be working together to ensure the success of the research project and in particular successful completion. As part of this they reflect on a few different matters, for example: the differences between the literature review and a theoretical framework; academic writing styles; and key challenges in different supervision styles. Polly Black then, in Chapter 5, outlines a supervision saga that happens all too often: when a supervisor and student are forced to go separate ways, but the PhD and research project must go on and a new supervisor found! New supervisors, indecision, uncertainty, and a completely different approach to feedback . . . all at a time when the PhD student is at their most vulnerable.

We round out the first section of the book with two vignettes. The first of these (vignette 6) is from Hugh Bainbridge, explaining why a researcher with career development in mind needs to differentiate between 'reply' and 'reply all' in an email [editor's note: Keith feels Hugh's pain here having engaged in a similar faux pas]. Our final vignette (7) in this 'getting started' section comes from Deisi Yunga who explores a number of issues in coming up with a research question, including the importance of communication and evaluating rather than acting immediately on every piece of advice.

Once a research project moves from the 'getting started' phase, 'getting data' is often the next hurdle where researchers and research projects can come unstuck. Neve Isaeva opens this section with Chapter 8, titled 'Finding epistemology', offering what she refers to as a journey of self-discovery 'from clueless despair to confident revelation'. Ideally, researchers should have some sense of their epistemology prior to collecting data because this drives many of the decisions around the data that will be collected. However, as Neve illustrates through her story, an epistemological position is something that emerges over time and may not fit neatly into the typologies offered by textbooks.

In Chapter 9 Mark Saunders and David Gray provide us with the first of four chapters focusing on the realities of data collection. Theirs is a panicked description of an online data collection process that began to spiral into desperate territory as questionnaires were not returned and email requests to respondents did not meet the intended people. Not only were their numbers not flowing back in, but the legal threats were arriving! However, as you will read, their research was eventually completed successfully, and lessons were learned. Next, in Chapter 10, Heather Short offers insights about undertaking interviews and, reflecting on her experiences, asks why research participants may be less than truthful. Heather questions whether she was either willing or able to hear the truth and, quoting George Bernard Shaw, asks whether she and her research participants were 'separated by a common language'?

Sharyn Rundle-Thiele, Julia Carins and Christiane Stock's chapter offers insights from a project where data were to be collected using observation. Theirs was an interesting research agenda, looking at the eating and alcohol consumption habits of people within and outside the workplace. What could possibly go wrong? Read Chapter 11 and you'll discover a few things as well as real insights regarding the need to be flexible and roll with the punches! The fourth chapter (Chapter 12) in this section comes from Kenneth Cafferkey, who demonstrates through his experiences using case studies that access and data collection do not come without the difficulties of interference from practitioners. He reveals how practitioners may prefer researchers to ask the questions the managers want, not the theoretically derived research agendas that we seek to deliver, emphasising the importance of having the right access for the right question.

Getting data is one thing, but in the business-related fields of applied research we are often reliant upon collecting data from people in organisations for whom our research project is not their biggest problem. Our contributors provide seven vignettes for this section; the first of these (vignette 13) comes from Polly Black, who reveals why, when she was developing qualitative interviews, a pilot study was really necessary. Wojciech Kwiatkowski provides a story in vignette 14 that many researchers will appreciate, a tale of feeling strung along with the endless promises of physical access to collect data 'soon' that never comes to fruition. What do you do? When you do get access, can you be sure that it will be maintained? Not according to Ashlea Kellner who, in vignette 15, relays her experience of finding agreement with gatekeepers in seven organisations only to find her options shrinking and disappearing before her eyes.

Vignette 16 comes from Keith Townsend, who found himself in an interview with a recalcitrant employee, unwilling to offer anything to the research project. Given the project had reached the theoretically important point of saturation, the researcher decided that there was little point in persevering with the interview. Perhaps a different decision would have been made at a different point of the project, but that's why context is so important in the social sciences. In vignette 17 Catheryn Khoo-Lattimore wasn't going to take any chances with not having enough data collected, so she worked very hard in offering incentives to garner participation. Great idea until her examiner questioned whether the incentives were 'too lucrative': read her vignette to find out how she responded! Following this, we have Colin Hughes's vignette (18), which provides some hard lessons learnt during his doctoral research when being a researcher can often feel like being in sales. His vignette offers five valuable steps for the researcher to keep in mind when undertaking projects with practitioners. Before we move to the next section of the book, Qian Lee describes in vignette 19 being placed in the unenviable position of a senior manager continually rescheduling interview times before inviting a second interviewee in to the meeting. Sometimes split-second decisions must be made in data collection!

In our simple progression of the perfect project, we've managed to get started, got the data, now it's time for 'getting it together'. Our first chapter (20) in this section, '. . . Just one goat', brings an old joke in to modern academia. People interpret things differently, so this is something to be mindful of when you are interpreting your qualitative data, according to Keith Townsend and Rebecca Loudoun. What seems like a sensible idea at the start of data collection proved much more complicated for this project as the researchers found many people interpreted, and therefore responded to, the interview questions differently.

Sameer Qaiyum and Catherine Wang have contributed a conversation-style chapter (21) exploring issues of quantitative data analysis and issues associated with learning new statistical techniques. Sameer tells of times 'in the dark' and at least one 'wild goose chase' on their research project and the importance of thinking 'outside the box' when you are faced with problems of analysis. He also highlights how quantitative data analysis can be a messy business and that the associated learning is ongoing. And just when you think you have the analysis all covered: the writing – what if it doesn't just flow from the fingertips? We've all had those days in front of a white screen or written and deleted a sentence 17 times. In Chapter 22 Dawn Duke offers some insights for getting the writing part of your research project back on track 'when the words just won't come'. Emphasising that we all struggle with writing at some time [editors' note: we certainly both do!], she shares stories of researchers struggling with writer's block and, importantly, what helped them overcome this. Dawn also offers a series of excellent quotes, including fiction writer C.J. Cherryh musing: 'It is perfectly okay to write garbage – as long as you edit brilliantly'. Good advice for anyone struggling with a blinking cursor!

Our four vignettes in this section tell cautionary tales. Ilenia Bregoli reveals her affinity with feelings in a Led Zeppelin song about betrayal as she transitioned from paper to computer software for analysis (vignette 23), highlighting the need to really understand the analysis method used. In contrast, Rohit Talwar's story in vignette 24 emphasises the importance of making regular and frequent back-up copies. His cautionary tale of coffee and electronic devices tells of how a poorly designed coffee mug destroyed over three weeks of data analysis and associated writing. When you have your work written, sometimes it needs to be presented to humans and, according to Kenneth Cafferkey, that doesn't always go smoothly, particularly if one of your audience isn't really a 'people person' (vignette 25). Jennifer Kilroy, in Chapter 26, reminds us that sometimes the space for our research comes in the most peculiar places; nevertheless, we can often find these spaces when we plan well.

Well, the project seems to have gone well until now; we've got started, got the data, we've got our analysis completed and we've even got some writing done. Time for 'getting finished'. Getting finished sometimes requires wonderfully difficult conversations about authorship; just ask Kate Daunt and Aoife McDermott. Or better still, read Chapter 27, where these authors explore the complicated politics of authorship within academia, considering questions such as on what basis to award authorship and in what order and, crucially, what to do when things go wrong. These interpersonal tribulations are nothing compared to the internal struggle many of us feel when we pass our work to others for feedback (and that's before those pesky editors and reviewers!)

In Chapter 28 Amanda Lee provides us with an account of coming to terms with detailed feedback. More specifically, Amanda was convinced that one of her supervisors thought she was incapable of writing (which, when you read the chapter, you can see she is not) and struggled with managing her feelings, reactions to the feedback she was receiving, and her supervisor! Amanda embarked on a useful process of keeping a reflective research journal to help work through the difficulties that, as many of us can appreciate, affect motivation and confidence. Most of us develop 'thicker skins' as we progress through our career, but it is important to remember that the feedback we receive is rarely about us as people, but about the work that we've presented – an important distinction to make.

All the world is a stage, Shakespeare tells us, and academia is certainly verging on a pantomime sometimes. In Chapter 29, presented in three scenes, Kiran Trehan, Alex Kevill and Jane Glover explore issues associated with securing and maintaining research projects for researchers at different stages in their academic careers. For each career stage they reveal the messiness and complexities of keeping research projects on track and how, despite things going 'wrong', you just have to keep moving forward.

There's no question that the world has changed with the advent of 'smart' devices, phones, laptops and tablets. Billy Bragg has a lyric in a song voicing concern about 'smart bombs in the hands of dumb people'. Let's be more optimistic about the smart devices in the hands of educated people and, as Angelique Gatsinzi shows in Chapter 30, embrace what the 21st century has to offer. Here she offers tales of her use of social media as both a means of support and to enhance the development of her research projects. This is followed by Marian Baird, with a feminist tale of success in Chapter 31. Here she reflects on the lessons she has learned as a researcher, starting from her 'naive beginnings' and exploring her subsequent development when relating to clients and undertaking organisation-based research, revealing how the success really only came more than a decade after the initial research began.

As we head towards the end of this volume, Mark Saunders gives us some thoughts about rewriting. Drawing from Bruce Springsteen's autobiography, in vignette 32 Mark reveals how, like song writers with their lyrics, we write and rewrite each publication. Mark presents the process of development of a journal article that lived through 22 drafts before even being presented to a journal editor and which was finally published after 41 drafts. It may surprise readers to know that this introduction has also gone through a fair number of drafts . . .

Finally, in vignette 33 Peter Jordan reflects on his experience with research students who claim to be 'over it'. Over what, Peter contemplates ... the writing, the process, the research, the idea of research as a career perhaps? After reading the trials and tribulations of our fellow researchers (and ourselves) in this introduction you may have started to wonder why on earth we even do this job and question whether we should be 'over it'. You may be thinking, surely it's too difficult. But the enthusiasm we had as we developed the idea for this volume was matched by the enthusiasm of the contributors who were not only excited about the project and their chapters but also wanted to tell what they considered to be the interesting tales of when things went wrong and offer insights from their real research experiences. That's why we do research, because although it rarely goes smoothly, it is almost always exciting and interesting. The reality of doing research is that 'shit happens'. Things will never go perfectly. But we have a job to do, so we draw on the dozens of researchers who've found out that when things go wrong, you will learn, and you will be able to get your research project back on track!

NOTE

1. There is a photograph of the pub on the back cover.

REFERENCES

Saunders, M.N.K. and Lewis, P. (1997), 'Great ideas and blind alleys? A review of the literature on starting research', *Management Learning*, **28**(3), 283–99.
Townsend, K. and Burgess, J. (2009), *Method in the Madness: Research Stories You Won't Read in Textbooks*, Oxford: Chandos Publishing.

PART I

Getting Started

2. Developing research ideas

Bill Lee

INTRODUCTION

This chapter is about the development of ideas by academics in the course of a project. It focuses on the ways in which ideas do not necessarily comply with those that were expected at the outset of a research project. In the spirit of this book, these occurrences may be considered as something 'going wrong' as I generated findings that were not simple extensions of existing knowledge and one unit that I studied defied easy interpretation, even by the new framework that I developed. Yet viewing the events as ones where the research went wrong is only appropriate if one adopts particular viewpoints on the way in which academic knowledge progresses. If, instead, one views any event as possible, such findings offer challenges for interpretation and explanation. In order to understand this, it is necessary first to consider different ways in which academics have categorised the development of ideas.

The historian of science, Thomas Kuhn (1962), in his account of mature disciplines distinguished between normal science which involved the everyday resolution of simple problems as knowledge was applied and extended to new situations and revolutionary science in which one prevailing paradigm – that is, the mixture of knowledge and the beliefs on which that knowledge was based – was replaced by a superior one because the preceding paradigm was no longer able to explain the situations that were being encountered. Colquitt and Zapata-Phelan (2007) conducted an empirical analysis of 667 articles that appeared in 75 issues of the highly ranked *Academy of Management Journal* between 1963 and 2007. They found that although new theories stopped being developed in management disciplines after the 1980s, there were additions to theories in various ways. They group the authors of these additions into five categories. First, there were 'builders', who generated new additional concepts, using inductive logic. Secondly, there were 'expanders', who often used deductive logic to propose a new formulation of an existent theory. Thirdly, there were 'qualifiers', who introduced a new mediator or moderator of an existing formulation. Fourthly, there were 'testers', who generated new tests for existing theories and finally there were 'reporters', who tested a theory in a different setting. Both Kuhn and Colquitt and Zapata-Phelan – who may be seen as offering ideas derivative of Kuhn's – tend to assume management knowledge should be seen as at least potentially nomothetic in generating scientific types of laws similar to those found in the natural sciences.

This chapter starts from a different position that is not inconsistent with Alvesson and Sandberg's (2011) suggestions of starting by questioning the underlying assumptions of prominent theories, although I was only to question such assumptions once I had gathered the evidence that did not support the predominant theories. I started from a simple understanding that in disciplines where humans are involved, there is the capacity for humans to think in a variety of ways, many of which are not predictable, in any situation. In the social sciences this is manifest at two points. First, the academic studying a research question or problem is able to think about a range of possible explanations and theories as to why a problem is manifest and the potential solution to that. Secondly, the focus of social sciences is people who can themselves behave in a range of different ways according to their interpretation of the same situation. Thus, even though social sciences are mature, there is the potential for a range of different phenomena to appear within a broad category that leads to them being represented as the same, while it is also possible for different explanations to be offered of the same situation. It was this understanding that was to steer my development of ideas in the course of my own PhD research on the relationship between accounting and a particular engineering configuration, namely flexible manufacturing systems. I will explain the development of those ideas next.

MY STUDY OF ACCOUNTING FOR FLEXIBLE MANUFACTURING SYSTEMS

Two sets of ideas informed my research. I will return to the second below but for now it is sufficient to state the first, which related to the different logics in accounting and flexible manufacturing systems. Accounting practices were seen as derivative of high volume production organization and logic. For example, the logic of seeking increased efficiency in production meant that the main purpose of new technology was to displace or limit the input of workers to make each remaining worker more productive, which meant that investment appraisal techniques assumed that investment in a new system was only worthwhile if it was offset by the labour savings attained. Similarly, for cost monitoring and cost control purposes, the concept of standard cost had been a derivative of the notion of standard time in Frederick Taylor's (1911) book on scientific management and assumed that people would perform exactly the same operations in production of each unit in the course of their working day. By contrast, flexible manufacturing systems (FMS) – which were composed of a number of reprogrammable machine tools, linked together by a transport system that carried parts between the different machine tools, all under the direction of a host computer – were very expensive. Although the UK government had provided grants to the companies that first introduced FMS to help them purchase the new systems, subsequent installations could not be justified by labour savings alone. Instead, more attention had to be given in financial appraisals to the very many other benefits offered by FMS. These benefits included reduced inventory savings because parts were processed more quickly; enhanced quality of parts because of the extent of computer control over the process; the ability to machine a broad range of parts more quickly because of the way in which changeovers could be programmed to take place with maximum efficiency; rapid introduction of a new range of parts because of the ease with which synergies could be transferred from learning about how to machine one part to machining another; and reduced need for investment in new systems in the future because of the capacity to redeploy FMS for new purposes. Moreover, employment of standard cost types of monitoring would encourage companies to use FMS to manufacture large batches of parts over and over again to attain the lowest standard cost, even though it was more beneficial to continually re-programme FMS to produce new types of parts when they were demanded. The proponents of these arguments had failed to provide empirical evidence to support their claims, or their studies had been conducted in the USA, so there was no UK evidence.

Although I adopted a realist ontology that meant I saw flexible manufacturing systems, accounting mechanisms and practices and organizational hierarchies as real, my understanding was that – as indicated above – all of those aspects could be interpreted differently by the actors involved in any situation, both within a particular organization and across different organizations. The first stage of the project entailed familiarising myself with literature on:

- Forms of investment appraisal and cost monitoring mechanisms and the (in)compatibility of each with flexible manufacturing systems and different forms of their usage.
- Forms of flexible manufacturing systems, the different ways in which flexibility could be defined, the extent to which the different types of flexibility were compatible with each other, the types of tools and

facilities that were required to attain those forms of flexibility, the relative cost of adding those tools and facilities to attain the desired levels of flexibility and the types of advantages that flexible manufacturing systems offered over other forms of production system.

- The role of accountants and engineers in an organization, their relative positions vis-à-vis one another in organizational hierarchies and the influence that each had on investment in – and deployment of – production systems.

As indicated above, the ideas that prevailed in the wider literature were that accounting was either discouraging the introduction of FMS, or leading to them being misused if they were introduced. If these ideas were accurate, the patterns that I would expect to find were that most investment appraisals only addressed the labour savings attained, that FMS were being monitored using standard cost measures and, although they were highly flexible, they were being used to machine a limited range of engineering parts in large volumes.

THE MAIN STUDY

Fieldwork had to be conducted to examine the prevailing ideas. The population of organizations that had FMS were identified through the trade press. I visited 19 organizations that had introduced a total of 21 flexible manufacturing systems when I held interviews with accountants and engineers about the qualities of the FMS that had been introduced, the purposes for which the systems had been introduced, the financial benefits that were realised from the use of the respective systems and the way in which performance of the system was monitored. At the time of the visits, I also collected documents in the form of the financial appraisal that was conducted and any accompanying narrative to justify the introduction of FMS along with examples of the documents used to monitor the performance of the system and any details about audits of the systems that had been conducted. Opportunities were also taken to observe the FMS in operation, to talk with the operators and to collect any documents describing the operation of FMS.

Once the fieldwork had been completed, I analysed the evidence, first by writing a summary of each FMS installation around themes that I had identified both in the initial literature review and from recurring issues in the fieldwork. I wrote up details of each installation as a separate case in a standard pro forma that included details of the FMS, accounting methods, organizational hierarchies and the role of accountants and engineers in the

change process. This allowed initial exploration of the pattern of accounting and FMS use at individual companies. What became very clear was
that the pattern that the literature suggested that I would find varied from
the pattern that existed in reality. Although there were a majority of FMS
that had been introduced after labour savings had been given priority in
the investment appraisal and it was anticipated that they would machine a
limited range of parts in large batch sizes at high levels of system utilisa-
tion, there were other FMS that had been introduced after the investment
appraisal had emphasised reduced sub-contracting costs because of a
capacity to machine a broader range of parts in-house in small batch sizes
at a more limited level of system utilization. There were still others that
had been introduced after high levels of inventory and work-in-progress
savings had been built into the investment appraisal of a system that was
intended to machine a very limited range of high-value parts in batch sizes
of one, often at quite low levels of machine utilization.

What was also clear was that organizations were using standard cost
techniques to monitor the performance of FMS. However, the vast majority of FMS were being used as intended by the investment appraisal. That
is, a majority were being used to machine parts in large batch sizes to
attain high levels of system utilization; some were being used to machine
a wider range of parts in small batch sizes at intermediate levels of system
utilization; and others were being used to machine a very small number of
high value parts – such as the metal casings of heavy industrial goods – in
batch sizes of one or two, often at quite low levels of system utilization.
Accounting staff were using the notions of standard cost to define an
operational budget for the individual FMS based on the volume and
variety of outputs, the number of changeovers entailed and so on, as
specified by production managers. The evidence that I collected indicated
that the theories articulated by others were not applicable. However, that
evidence did not constitute a thesis. In this regard, it was problematic. I
had to find a way to explain my own pattern of results.

I decided to extend my analysis by creating a matrix with the names of
the cases down one axis and dimensions of performance – such as volume
of output, batch sizes, levels of system operation, range, levels of inventory
reduction sought – of the systems along the other axis. This confirmed that
there were three clusters of flexible manufacturing systems: namely those
that were being used to machine a limited range of parts in high volumes
at high levels of system utilization, those that were being deployed to
machine a much wider range of parts in smaller batches at lower levels of
system utilization, and those that were used to machine a limited range of
high-value parts, generally at low levels of system utilization. I then looked
in detail at the configurations of FMS that were used by each cluster.

It became clear that while the FMS systems that had been purchased to machine a wide range of parts in small batch sizes had a range of flexibilities in terms of the routes through which parts could proceed, the range of operations that could be performed at any one machine tool in the configuration and the envelope size in which parts could be fitted, FMS introduced for other purposes were more limited in their capabilities, even though they were all FMS. This highlighted that concepts such as flexibility were context-bound and the importance of an ethnographic form of content analysis (see Lee, 2012).

From this point, it was possible to start generating a new theory of the relationship between FMS systems and accounting practices. The idea that I developed was that production strategies were an important, but previously ignored, influence on the design and use of flexible manufacturing systems. I managed to write this idea up in two subsequent publications (Lee, 1996; Jones and Lee, 1998) where I argued that both the design and use of FMS had been influenced by one or another of the following three production strategies:

- *volume production* where FMS were designed and used to machine a limited range of parts in high volumes at high levels of system utilization;
- *flexible manufacturing* where FMS were designed and deployed to machine a much wider range of parts in smaller batches at intermediate levels of machine utilization; and
- *just-in-time manufacturing* where FMS had been designed and used to machine a limited range of high value parts at low levels of machine utilization.

Part of the argument of my PhD thesis was that although 'traditional' forms of accounting techniques were often used to justify and monitor the performance of FMS, they were being adapted to reflect the production strategy and concomitant design of a specific FMS.

THE ROGUE COMPANY

The assumption that accounting could divert the deployment of systems away from the best use for them if defined by their engineering merits also implied a second set of ideas: that accountants and accounting were more powerful than engineers in organizations. This idea also appeared in a number of different theories on the role of professional groups in organizations. Yet although there was evidence that accountants held positions close to the apex of the organizations that I studied, my findings on the relationship between FMS and accounting did not support the idea that accountants were necessarily always more powerful. This inference could also be considered as problematic and something going wrong in my research and so I sought an explanation of why, when accountants were deemed to be more powerful, they had not been in a position to impose their methods on FMS in an inappropriate way. The solution to this issue was suggested by one 'rogue' company. Its FMS system was achieving low levels of flexibility in terms of the range of parts and its design placed it in the category of FMS introduced to pursue a *volume production* strategy. However, it was also not achieving the levels of system utilization required, despite machining an even more limited range of parts than intended.

My interviews revealed that the reason why it had been introduced successfully in the first instance was because the engineer had knowingly provided false information about the capability of the system as his line manager had told him to prepare a financial justification that would lead to the system being introduced because that was the path of development that the line manager wished to pursue. The accountant had no prior knowledge of FMS and no way of refuting the claims in the financial justification. Interviews at the other organizations also indicated that it was engineers who initiated the introduction of new systems. They then provided the data on which a financial justification was prepared, which also influenced how a system was monitored. This led to the general argument in my thesis that power in a process should not be confused with position in an organizational hierarchy. Knowledge does give power and as accountants and engineers have different forms of knowledge, engineers have considerable power in influencing decisions about the introduction of new systems, especially when those systems are novel and accountants and other organizations have no previous experience of the systems. The 'rogue' company provided a subsequent opportunity to illustrate this argument in more depth in an additional journal article (Lee, 2000).

CONCLUDING REMARKS

This chapter has sought to address the question of what to do when things go wrong in developing your ideas. The focus for this discussion has been when analysis is being carried out. Central to the events reported in this chapter is an acknowledgement of humans as autonomous individuals – be they academics or research participants – who have the capability to interpret a particular situation in a given way and choose different ways of acting according to the event that they have just witnessed and to then shape their world in line with that understanding. It is inevitable that some findings in a research project will not confirm prevailing ideas and, even if they do, that may not be sufficient to publish the work. It will be necessary to think about an explanation of those findings. In this regard, I found it useful to organize my evidence using different configurative tools of analysis. So common themes were used to write up the cases to see patterns within each case and a matrix was used to compile and compare clusters across the population of cases. I also found it useful to have an understanding of ideas from a range of disciplines including accounting, engineering, operations management and organizational sociology so that I could combine different ideas to theorise the pattern of my findings in an appropriate context.

In closing this chapter, I think that an additional quality is necessary to complete a research project successfully and to overcome problems in the development of ideas. Here, I am reminded of a maxim that has been attributed to a number of people but without any reliable source. That is: 'A pessimist sees a difficulty in every opportunity. An optimist sees the opportunity in every difficulty.' My final remark is, thus, do not let a particular way of viewing the world constrain you so that when you are faced with a difficulty, you ignore the opportunity that it contains; be an optimist and look for the opportunity that any difficulty offers. Doing this should enable you to complete your research project successfully and provide opportunities to write up interesting findings for publication in journal articles.

REFERENCES

Alvesson, M. and Sandberg, J. (2011). 'Generating research questions through problematization', *Academy of Management Review*, **36**(2), 247–71.

Colquitt, J. and Zapata-Phelan, C. (2007). 'Trends in theory building and theory testing: a five-decade study of the Academy of Management Journal', in *Academy of Management Journal*, **50**(6), 1281–303.

Jones, T.C. and Lee, B. (1998). 'Accounting, strategy and AMT investment', in *Omega – The International Journal of Management Science*, **26**(6), 769–83.

Kuhn, T. (1962). *The Structure of Scientific Revolutions*, Chicago: University of Chicago Press.

Lee, B. (1996). 'The justification and monitoring of AMT: an empirical study of 21 installations of FMS', *Management Accounting Research*, **7**(1), 95–118.

Lee, B. (2000). 'Separating the wheat from the chaff: FMS; flexibility; and socio-organisational constraints', *Technology Analysis and Strategic Management*, **12**(2), 213–28.

Lee, B. (2012). 'Using documents in organizational research', in G. Symon and
C. Cassell (eds), *The Practice of Qualitative Organizational Research: Core
Methods and Current Challenges*, London: Sage, pp. 389–407.

Taylor, F.W. (1911). *The Principles of Scientific Management*, New York: Harper &
Brothers Publishers.

3. On the path to enlightenment? Reviewing the literature systematically – or not

Céline Rojon

As researchers, we all have to do literature reviews all the time for our research projects. Whenever we start out on a new study, or we write an article, we try to make sure that we know what others before us have found and we need to demonstrate that we are aware of the main issues discussed by the scholarly community. Having that knowledge also means we will be in a better position to articulate the contribution we hope our own research will make. So, in sum, as researchers we should all have (plenty of) experience with doing literature reviews. Well, I too thought I had experience with doing literature reviews, from having studied for a BSc and an MSc, when I started out on my PhD, some years ago now. Was I wrong? Perhaps not, but I did find that undertaking a literature review for a PhD, and subsequently doing literature reviews for other projects that I was working on, was quite a different ballgame from what I had been used to. In this chapter, I reflect on my experience with conducting literature reviews. As much of my experience comes from doing systematic reviews, this is what I will be drawing on mostly, with particular reference to my very first systematic review, which I did for the said PhD, but I will also give some insights into 'traditional' narrative literature reviews.

DECISIONS, DECISIONS, DECISIONS: WHICH TYPE OF LITERATURE REVIEW TO USE

When I started my PhD I did not fully realise there were different types of literature review. I was, of course, aware of the need to review the literature critically, but not of the various different types of literature reviews to choose from. Indeed, although it may seem that knowing about more types might make the decision harder (much like in those restaurants that have lengthy menus!), it is actually helpful as the different literature review

20

choices enable different research aims to be addressed or they can appeal to different populations. Like many researchers I was aware of what I now know as the narrative literature review. This is the traditional way of reviewing literature on a given topic and is still very widely found, typically summarising the current state of knowledge about a particular topic and making reasoned arguments (being critical) regarding what is known and not known. Whilst this is a pretty flexible approach that can be undertaken in various different ways to suit the researcher's needs, allowing them to explore their own ideas, I found there are also several disadvantages. It is often seen as being subjective and non-transparent, with no clear methodology – or at least not one that is made public to the reader – and the potential for the researcher to focus on their 'preferred' pieces of literature (or journals, or databases . . .).

Before I now say a bit more about the systematic review, which is the type of literature review I personally know best now, I think it is worth highlighting that aside from narrative and systematic reviews, there are also other types of review that merit consideration. The ones that I have encountered most in our subject area are realist reviews (also known as realist syntheses), (psychometric) meta-analyses, and rapid evidence assessments (otherwise known as rapid evidence appraisals). I found Jesson and colleagues' book (2011) to give a good overview of these and other types of review.

Over to the systematic review then. This type of literature review made its debut in Business and Management about ten years ago and is starting to gain popularity, having been successfully used in other subject areas, most notably in medicine/health-related sciences and education, for decades. Those who like systematic review methodology, including myself, claim that it can address some of the disadvantages encountered with traditional reviews. As much of this chapter is about systematic review, I will leave the discussion of my experiences – and why I found the process frustrating at times, but generally very useful – until a bit later. At this point, I will just give one of the most frequently cited definitions of systematic review methodology in our subject area, so as you have an idea of what it is: 'Systematic review is a specific methodology that locates existing studies, selects and evaluates contributions, analyses and synthesizes data, and reports the evidence in such a way that allows reasonably clear conclusions to be reached about what is and is not known' (Denyer and Tranfield, 2009, p. 671).

SYSTEMATIC REVIEW: WHAT IS THE BIG DEAL?

If, like some of my colleagues, you are wondering why to bother with doing a systematic review when you could 'just' be doing a regular narrative review, let me talk you through the advantages and disadvantages of systematic reviews compared to narrative reviews as I see them. It may help to provide some context of how I first came to learn about systematic review methodology. In the first month of starting my PhD (no rest for the wicked!), my supervisors suggested that I consider carrying out a systematic review as a first phase in my research, which was on individual workplace performance. At the time, now about seven years ago, I had not heard about systematic review and decided first of all to familiarise myself with the methodology by consulting what I still consider one of the most useful resources on the matter (i.e., Denyer and Tranfield, 2009). Back then, systematic review methodology was still very new in the field of Business and Management and Denyer and Tranfield (2009) in particular were interested in finding a way of adapting the methodology, from its more traditional usage within the medical sciences, to our domain. Systematic review methodology immediately appealed to me when reading up on it. Why, you ask? Because it is a very structured approach to reviewing the literature, which follows a series of more or less standardised steps; this sounded good to the organised person in me. Other advantages of systematic review methodology that I perhaps came to appreciate only later on include that it is a very thorough, comprehensive way of reviewing existing literature as one aims to look at all literature – that is, different types of publication (including, ideally, grey literature; Adams et al., 2017) in different subject areas – that is relevant to one's review topic. As a result of this comprehensive approach, I always feel more confident that my findings actually represent the current body of knowledge relating to my topic. I also found systematic reviewing to be really helpful at drawing together fragmented literature that is dispersed in different subject areas; in my experience, our discipline is prone to such fragmentation, seeing that it draws from areas such as sociology, psychology, economics, anthropology and so on. So, for me, the structured reviewing framework underlying systematic review methodology helps deal with the issue of the dispersed body of evidence.

Further, the systematic review approach is not only comprehensive and thorough, but many systematic reviews also build a 'critical appraisal' component into their review process, through which any potentially relevant papers are reviewed in light of not just their relevance for addressing the review question(s), but also in terms of the quality of the evidence that they provide. By critical appraisal, I mean a way of judging the quality of every single piece of literature that is being considered for inclusion in the review, for example in terms of how thorough the conducted literature review was, how robust the methodology used was, how well findings were explained, discussed and linked back to relevant evidence, how logical conclusions drawn were and so forth. I found this critical appraisal process can contribute to producing a high quality piece of review that reports on the most effective research in the area; this may positively distinguish systematic reviews from other types of review in which no obvious systematic critical appraisal takes place.

Moreover, I appreciated that it was possible to address quite specific review questions (in a similar way to how you would address research questions in an empirical study) rather than just to see what is out there in regard to a specific topic; for me, it made the whole process more defined and more tangible. For example, one of the questions I asked in the systematic review I did for my PhD was: 'How is individual workplace performance measured and why; what are the reasons for using certain methods of measurement and how solid are the arguments presented for different approaches?' Admittedly, this question turned out to be broader than I had imagined, leading to a large number of potentially relevant references (an aspect that I will talk more about a bit later), but it did mean that when screening papers for their relevance to my review, I could interrogate them with this question in mind. This makes it relatively easy to decide whether or not to include a paper in a systematic review on the basis of it speaking to your review question(s) – or not.

Also, often within systematic review methodology, insights gained are organised under three headings: 'what we know already', 'what we do not yet know' and 'how future research can take up from here'. This is something I personally found very helpful and that I think is useful in publishing one's findings, too.

Since that initial systematic review I conducted for my PhD, and which I have recently updated, I have returned to this methodology no less than four times, which, I guess, shows how useful I have found it. That is not to say that I think it is always the right approach for reviewing the literature nor that there are no challenges associated with using it; indeed, there can be quite a few and I will introduce you to the ones I encountered and/or that I am aware of through colleagues shortly.

One of the advantages of being amongst the first to use a 'new' technique in your field is that you can reflect on your experiences and share these with others, whether that is informally in chatting to colleagues, or more formally at conferences or in journals. This is what I did (e.g. Rojon et al., 2011) and I found that it gave me even greater insight into when and why systematic review methodology might be useful (and when it might not be).

SYSTEMATIC REVIEW: WHAT IS THE TURN OFF?

There are always two sides of the coin and that is also the case for systematic review methodology. Let me therefore fill you in on what I found to be its disadvantages or challenges.

A well thought out, comprehensive systematic review may very well draw on the guidance of an advisory panel, which researchers might consult to bounce off methodological ideas and validate own decisions for the systematic review. This panel can consist of fellow academics with similar research focuses, practitioners working in relevant areas, policy-makers with a vested interest in one's topic, subject librarians, systematic review methodology experts and so forth. I tend to use such an advisory panel mostly during the scoping study of a systematic review, which is a preliminary stage concerned with determining the specific focus of the review alongside the review questions that will be used to interrogate the literature. In my experience, depending on how queries to the advisory panel members have been phrased, and also depending on the composition of the panel, you may end up with very many and potentially very different suggestions as to what they see as useful points for examination for your systematic review. Certainly this is what happened in my first systematic review, where the questions I asked my advisory panel were quite possibly too wide-ranging and not focused enough, and as a result I found reconciling people's different perspectives a tricky undertaking. For this reason the answers I got were rather different depending on whom I had asked . . . and of course practitioners felt differently to academics; for example one advisory panel member, a specialist in psychometrics, was very keen to learn more about specific questioning techniques for use within performance appraisal, whilst one of the practitioners on the panel was interested in querying how performance management could be made more effective, a rather broad question. Arriving at a (common) point of focus to inform my systematic review was not easy! How did I get around the issue? Well, ultimately, I reminded myself that this was *my* systematic review project and I therefore should not let myself be led down too many different paths that did not correspond to what I had in mind. Whilst I most definitely wanted to take account of my advisory panel members' suggestions, I was also keen to interpret what they said in light of other information I had gained from an initial reading of relevant literature. As I had not thought clearly enough about how to make use of my advisory panel and the information they would provide me with, I had to spend more time 'negotiating' between what people had told me and what I had learnt already from relevant literature than I would have liked. Generally speaking, I have come to realise that it is useful to consider carefully, prior to embarking on a systematic review in earnest, how to make use of the advisory panel, when and how often to consult them and how to weigh different members' suggestions at different stages of the review.

Having determined my review's focus by consulting my advisory panel as well as through initial readings of relevant literature, I needed to formulate one or more review questions. This is where my second challenge awaited: if I phrased a review question too broadly, it would be likely to yield a very large number of references in my literature research and not offer as much specific, useful insight as I was hoping for. On the other hand, a very narrow review question that would only apply in very specific circumstances, to very specific populations and so forth was not going to be very helpful either. I therefore needed a good balance between too broad and too narrow for my questions. To get there, I found it useful to again consult my advisory panel members, at this stage especially those researchers that had expertise in my area of research. They were helpful in bouncing off and refining different versions of my review questions. Other individuals that could help with phrasing a 'not too broad, not too narrow' review question are researchers that have done systematic reviews themselves before and so therefore are aware of the issue and might be able to advise on how to get around it. For the systematic review I did for my PhD, however, I was not sufficiently aware of these issues and how to resolve them, so I learnt the hard way that having broad review questions can result in a lot of work . . . in this particular case, the three review questions I had formulated resulted in my having to sift through more than 65 000 literature references initially and my findings being perhaps not quite as focused as would have been useful!

The subsequent literature search was less challenging, though I was really pleased I had talked my search strings through with some members of my advisory board and with colleagues who had done systematic reviews before; this ensured that my searches would capture as much as possible of the relevant evidence base. Once I had searched various literature outlets, I came to the point where, having sifted through the publications retrieved – first by title, then by abstract and finally by reading the full text – I was ready to start making sense of relevant pieces of literature. I recommend the use of a data extraction form, which should capture not only data needed to answer the review question(s), but also some descriptive statistics (e.g. publication year and country), alongside further relevant paper information, such as the publication's methodology. All of this information helps contextualise the body of evidence that one is dealing with, when explaining the findings in relation to the review's question(s).

Having collated relevant details of publications that can be considered both of sufficient relevance and of high enough quality to justify their inclusion in the systematic review, a further challenge awaits in the form of the data analysis. Amazingly, I have found that only very little guidance is available on how to analyse data within systematic review methodology. One paper I came across though is by Popay and colleagues (2006), which explains how to analyse data narratively in systematic reviews. In my experience of conducting and reading systematic reviews, narrative analysis is what most authors in our field will choose to do, even though in many cases they do not explicitly explain that this is what they did and how exactly they did it. What is more, for the systematic review I did for my PhD, I was in the fortunate (or maybe not so fortunate?) position where I had not only qualitative data for analysis and synthesis (in that particular case in relation to how and why to measure performance in particular ways), but also quantitative data. This quantitative data consisted of correlation coefficients examining the relationship between personality and ability questionnaires on the one hand and performance assessments on the other hand. Given I had this quantitative data, I decided to embed a (psychometric) meta-analysis, that is, a 'summary' of correlations found across all those studies that examined the relationships between personality/ability questionnaires and performance assessments, within my systematic review. Although I would not go as far as saying that I regretted having done a meta-analysis as part of my very first systematic review, I got the impression afterwards that journals in Business and Management had not quite caught up yet with the idea of using systematic review methodology for selecting studies for inclusion within a meta-analysis. Even though I feel that such an approach is slowly becoming more accepted, trying to get a paper on the meta-analysis component of my PhD's systematic review published was rather difficult at the time – it just was not how meta-analyses had previously been done and reported on! The good news is that I did get the paper published in the end (Rojon et al., 2015), so there is clearly hope, but I do think it is a matter of thinking carefully how you 'sell' a meta-analysis within the framework of systematic review methodology.

LESSONS FOR KEEPING ON TRACK

- If at first you do not succeed . . . do not give up. There is a misconception that reviewing the literature – prior to starting out with a study 'in earnest' – is the easy bit that just 'has to be done' . . . it is not!
- Think of your literature review in the context of your research more widely. How does it fit in with any other research activities you are undertaking or planning to undertake? Where can it add value and

how will its findings contribute to your research and to the extant body of evidence? Having clear ideas of this upfront will help you to stay on track and motivated with your review.

- Time management can be an issue with literature reviews (and generally with research activities), whatever approach you choose to go for. Be aware of this from the start and give yourself enough time for each step on the way. Whilst most tasks will probably take longer than anticipated, happily some may actually take less time than expected.
- Talk to people! Fellow researchers or methods experts can be useful both in terms of exchanging experience and advice, as well as when it comes to venting your literature review-related sorrows (the voice of experience is speaking)!
- Go for it! If you have never undertaken a systematic review, but believe that it could be suitable for your next piece of research, think no more and just do it – hopefully the lessons in this chapter will help!

REFERENCES

Adams, R.J., Smart, P. and Huff, A.S. (2017). 'Shades of grey: guidelines for working with the grey literature in systematic reviews for management and organizational studies', *International Journal of Management Reviews*, **19**, 432–54.

Denyer, D. and Tranfield, D. (2009). 'Producing a systematic review', in D. Buchanan and A. Bryman (eds), *The SAGE Handbook of Organizational Research Methods*, London: SAGE, pp. 671–89.

Jesson, J.K., Matheson, L. and Lacey, F.M. (2011). *Doing Your Literature Review: Traditional and Systematic Techniques*, London: SAGE.

Popay, J., Roberts, H., Sowden, A., Petticrew, M., Arai, L., Rogers, M., Britten, N. et al. (2006). 'Guidance on the conduct of narrative synthesis in systematic reviews', Lancaster: Lancaster University. Available at: http://www.lancaster. ac.uk/shm/research/nssr/research/dissemination/publications.php.

Rojon, C., McDowall, A. and Saunders, M.N.K. (2011). 'On the experience of conducting a systematic review in industrial, work and organizational psychology: yes, it is worthwhile', *Journal of Personnel Psychology*, **10**, 133–8.

Rojon, C., McDowall, A. and Saunders, M.N.K. (2015). 'The relationships between traditional selection assessments and workplace performance criteria specificity: a comparative meta-analysis', *Human Performance*, **28**, 1–25.

4. The master and apprentice: lessons from two PhD supervisors and a recent PhD graduate

Jillian Cavanagh, Hannah Meacham and Timothy Bartram

The academic relationship between the supervisor and higher degree research student can be described as a 'master and apprentice'. Here we present reflections from the authors that offer understandings of the pitfalls and challenges and strategies associated with successful PhD supervision and candidature. If we develop our understandings of the potential pitfalls in the early stages of candidature we have a better chance of supporting our students to successful completion. We provide a focused and rich context for insights into some areas of concern for students, including our reflections around the key issues and challenges of both PhD supervision and PhD candidature, the commencing point for a student, academic writing, the differences between a literature review and a theoretical framework, commencing the research and we summarise with key lessons for both students and academics.

WHAT ARE THE KEY ISSUES AND CHALLENGES IN THE SUPERVISION OF PHD STUDENTS?

Supervisors and Students Need to Do Their Homework

One of the key issues for PhD supervisors is the selection of high quality students. Supervisors need to be very selective and do their homework on the student. The PhD process is often a long and emotional one. Supervisors need to be careful that they can work with the student and that the student has the foundational skills to be able to undertake the degree successfully. It is vital that the supervisor ensures that the student meets the basic entry requirements and has the necessary core skills and background studies in the discipline of study, has a strong work ethic, and the time and resources to be successful. PhD students also need to do their homework on the supervisor. Do they have a track record of publication in your area of study? Do they have a track record of successful supervision of PhD students? Are they supportive and do they have sufficient time and energy to supervise your studies? Do you get along well with them? These are basic questions for PhD students but the answers are very important for the successful and timely completion of PhD study. In short, the supervisors and PhD students need to be selective.

Often one of the key issues is getting students to write in a scholarly way. Academics can find it difficult to write in a less formal manner; in fact, writing this chapter was challenging because we have a tendency to formalise our language. The key point of the conversation is that if the student is a management practitioner or clinician, for instance, a big challenge for them is that they often think, write and communicate like practitioners. Many of them *do not have the skillset to think and write like an academic.* Not only are the skills important but so is the mindset. The way around it is obviously to use journal articles as templates and look at syntax, referencing and the structure of a completed PhD. Supervisors may have to 'baby step' students through the writing process in the beginning; too much too soon will often overload the student leaving them feeling overwhelmed; think tortoise . . . not hare.

Universities often have writing groups to practise academic writing or seminars on how to critique a journal article; students should go to these and practise these skills (tip: encourage the student to go more than once; it is difficult to pick up the skills in one two-hour seminar). PhD students: you need to realise that a PhD is often an apprenticeship in becoming an academic, so your writing has to conform to scholarly standards. You should have read hundreds of articles for your thesis. Reading these articles will help you to notice structures and patterns that you can use to model your future studies and articles on. When writing for journals we will often model the structure of our manuscript on published articles within the target journal. Remember you are writing for an academic audience, that is, depending on the PhD system, two or three examiners who are academics and who are judging your thesis on the basis of whether it makes a scholarly and significant contribution to knowledge.

English as a Second Language

It is increasingly common that PhD students will come from non-English-speaking backgrounds. What needs to be done in the early phase is to develop a team-based approach. Going forward, academics have an expectation that international students will need additional help. This level of competency and help required is going to differ from student to student so it is important that supervisors are clear on the levels of English proficiency of their PhD students. Setting goals to improve language skills and keeping students accountable for the quality of their writing is important. Patience from both sides is needed here; students should not expect supervisors to 'fix' their English comprehension and supervisors should not expect the same English proficiency they would find from a native speaker. Students need to be honest and upfront about their level of English proficiency; if the student is struggling, then they need to seek help as soon as possible because not seeking help is only damaging one person: the student.

Foundation Skills

In our experience it is important to learn EndNote and complete a course in how to work with a large document. Also, understand what a thesis looks like – understand the process. It is important to have a look at some theses in your area so you get an understanding of the structure and organisation of PhD theses, the major sections, standard and style of writing, how to organize the table of contents and, most importantly, how to develop a narrative between chapters. PhD students: do this before you start anything else. You may think you have good computer skills and can manage by 'clicking random buttons' but in reality some programs, such as EndNote, do require more than a basic understanding to be operated effectively, which will help you in the long run. University libraries often hold courses on various computer programs. Take advantage of these courses, even if they may not seem relevant at the time; when you are struggling to edit the contents page of your 300-page document you will wish you had gone!

Learning to Take Notes and Paraphrase

Academics often hear from students that the way in which an author writes an article is so articulate that they are not able to find a better way of expressing the message. Paraphrasing not only expresses the message in the student's own words, but at the beginning of the candidature can actually help in understanding the key concepts of the article. Get the student to create summaries of literature related to their topic; not only does this make a start on the literature review but also enables the student to understand the key theoretical frameworks and gets them into thinking about research questions. PhD students: make sure you write notes and summarise articles as these will form the basis of your literature review. Remember it is not enough to summarise articles; this is only a starting point. It is important that you read critically as you are trying to establish the gap in the literature so that your work will be able to make a scholarly and significant contribution to knowledge.

Good Study Habits

Students need to set goals in terms of what they need to do every day – developing a plan of attack. This can be done in partnership with the supervisor but at the end of the day it is the student's responsibility. It is important for the student to achieve something every day even if it is one paragraph – students: read and write every day! It is very easy at the beginning to think 'I have three plus years to finish this PhD, that's plenty of time', then all of a sudden four years have gone by and all you have is a first draft of a literature review. Supervisors and students should plan meeting times, for example, once a week/fortnight/month; this then gives the student easy landmarks for when work should be completed. If completion dates are being missed, it is important to address this as soon as possible, the reason often being that students are unsure of what they are doing or if they are doing it correctly. Supervisors and students: don't be shy if there is a problem; speak up quickly and sort the issue out. Time is the enemy of all PhD students.

Work–Life Balance

The best piece of advice is to encourage students to take time to relax, reflect and re-charge. Many students experience life-changing events throughout their candidature; this can be the birth of a child, the death of a loved one or a serious illness. However, finding work–life balance is not an excuse to only do a few hours a week of work towards a thesis. It is important to come up with a plan, when to work and when to relax, that fits in with when the student is most productive. This may be late at night, early in the morning or during a Monday–Friday 9 am–5 pm working week. Full-time PhD students need to treat their studies like a full-time job. Students should give themselves regular time off, such as weekends, as this will make the process seem much more manageable. Students need to note that during the last 2–3 months of their candidature there is often little to no work–life balance; that's just the way it is. They need to put their head down and power through; it will be over soon.

WHERE DOES A PHD STUDENT START?

Finding a Topic

Students: start with what topic areas you are interested in and passionate about. Writing 80 000 words on a topic you are passionate about and enjoy is going to be easier than writing about a topic you are not interested in. What areas do you see lots of opportunity to publish? What areas does your supervisor publish in? Where do you work? What/who are your contacts? Having contacts within industry and organisations will give you an advantage when searching for research sites. It is often easier to gain access to research sites if you have a personal contact; the old adage of 'it's who you know not what you know' is good to remember here. The topic must keep your attention for three years, if not longer, so being 'bored' of the topic is only going to slow you down. Integrating two ends of the spectrum is a skill each student will need to develop. By this we mean bringing the practical and the academic together.

Making a Contribution

Every thesis must make an original and substantial contribution to knowledge. At the outset, each student must have an idea of their intended contribution. This is often difficult for students to grasp. A previous student once accounted:

> At the start of my PhD I was trying to think of my elusive 'contribution' to knowledge. During a conversation with my mum I found out a family friend, who had recently completed their PhD in Dentistry, had discovered a new enzyme in the mouth as part of her research and had had the enzyme named after her. All I kept thinking was how was my research going to make such a contribution to research?

Think about what you would like to achieve; is there a gap in theory that nobody has examined before? Are there problems in the industry that your research could begin to address or at least shed new light on potential solutions?

Principal Research Question

The questions need to be built from the gap in the literature. PhD students have to read quite a lot of quality research to understand the gap. The research questions should be developed around finding answers to the identified gap/s. Yes, reading literature is boring; yes, you will find very inventive ways of not reading literature, but at the end of the day it has to be done. So do it. Rule of thumb, if you have not found any gaps in the literature, you have not read enough literature or reviewed it critically enough. It is also important to read through journal editors' notes and future research suggestions in leading articles as academics will often discuss the current research gaps, controversies and challenges. PhD students need to read critically and for purpose.

DIFFERENT GENRES OF ACADEMIC WRITING

The starting point here is to engage in conversation about the different genres of writing that a student will encounter when writing a PhD. One of the supervisors gave an account of a thesis in crisis that was passed onto him. 'The thesis was in crisis and one of the analysis chapters was almost 50 000 words. The supervisors worked with the student to take the thesis and reduce it by 30 000 words'. The main challenge for the student was that English was not her first language and she had serious challenges with English grammar. The supervisor sought to develop a team (e.g. language expert and co-supervisor) around the student to ensure that she had effective English grammar support.

Academics take the craft of academic writing seriously and explaining the different genres to a PhD student can be quite challenging. The introduction sets the scene and at the end of this section a reader should know the context of the research project, the purpose, the contribution, key question and structure of the thesis. The literature review is used to frame the study through critical examination of literature so as to unpack the research gap and research questions. The theoretical framework is the analytical tool or lens through which your study is framed as it provides the researcher with a structured and rigorous way of answering the research question. As a PhD student, it is important to read the best journals in your discipline – speak to your supervisor about academic rankings and which journals are best. It is best to read the best journals in your discipline to get a sense of which key theoretical frameworks are out there and why and how they are used as analytical tools to solve research problems. The methodological approach is important as it provides the researcher with a systematic, valid and reliable way of empirically testing or examining the research question; students can use either qualitative or quantitative methods and often mixed methods approaches are becoming common in PhD theses. The data collection procedures are critical to a high quality thesis and are often very challenging as the student is reliant on the goodwill of partner organisations and their staff. The results and analysis section of the thesis is a very exciting step, whether you are running regressions, doing structural equation modelling or using NVivo to analyse focus group and interview data. The discussion and concluding sections are very important to examine the extent that you were able to answer the questions and develop key discussion points that contribute to building theory, the empirical body of research, and implications for organisational or management practice (depending on the topic of your thesis), as well as documenting limitations and future research and providing some nuggets in the concluding section.

Publishing from a Thesis

In our experience it is important to publish during and immediately after your PhD candidature. Writing a journal article is important in terms of skill building but also to enhance your employability within academia. Our advice is to publish from your thesis as soon as practicable by focusing largely on empirical papers that use your data. A PhD student will usually start publishing with their supervisor – so have the conversation. The big question for many students is: do I go for high-level or low-level journals? Our answer is to think strategically and develop a publishing strategy and short-, medium- and long-term publishing goals. Get some runs on the board. There is nothing wrong with publishing a paper in a B ranked journal, but also think about aiming for A and A* ranked journals. Our advice would be to start with B and A ranked journals. The job market is very competitive, so get publishing!

COMMENCING THE RESEARCH

There needs to be a systematic approach to reading literature; do not rely on an internet search to begin with. Again, this is where the university library can help. Book a time with a librarian to help you undertake an in-depth search of journal databases. Librarians know the databases better than anyone, so take advantage of their unique skills and knowledge. They are generally very helpful and approachable. Know the leading journals and authors in your field. Take notes, and it would be a good idea to produce a plan and a spreadsheet of the key articles and the name of the journal. PhD students: take your time; reading, categorising and summarising literature is not a quick process, and that's even before you start to analyse and critique it. A detailed Excel spreadsheet is a must here. Note the journal article title and journal name, its academic ranking, the key concepts and methods used and its key findings. Parts of this spreadsheet can then be transferred straight into your annotated bibliography, which will be the base for your first draft literature review.

KEY LESSONS FOR PHD STUDENTS AND SUPERVISORS

In this chapter we have discussed some of the key challenges and lessons that we have learned, both as PhD students and supervisors. In summary here are key lessons that should help supervisors and PhD students stay focused and work effectively:

1. Keep a research project simple and achievable within three years' full-time study. Try not to be overly ambitious and narrow your topic.
2. A student's research project must be marketable. By that we mean students need to be able to use their theses to build future careers in academia or within the broader private/public sectors. Try to pick a topic that can solve or identify a progression to solving an issue within industry or society. This will then not only appeal to industry leaders but also to academics wishing to continue the research.
3. A student must be able to publish from their thesis and in most cases this will be done in collaboration with their supervisors. There should be at least two to three papers in any PhD thesis. The genre of journal writing will be different, but the concepts and data will be the same. Students need to be aware that writing a PhD and writing a journal article are very different. The processes and style of writing for a journal article can be difficult to adjust to. The 'master and apprentice' relationship does not often end at the completion of a PhD thesis. Students (with the support of their supervisor) should try to develop an article from the thesis during their candidature.
4. A PhD is only a means to an end. A PhD is a marathon and there are many highs, pitfalls and turns that will challenge both supervisors and students but the end point is really the beginning. It is not a student's life's work. A student's real academic writing starts from the point when they are writing refereed journal articles.
5. If students are struggling with any material or process during their studies it is important that these issues or challenges are dealt with quickly and effectively. Students need to work closely with their supervisors, so if there is a problem, speak up.

5. 'Finders, keepers, losers, weepers!' A doctoral candidate's reality of changing thesis advisors

Polly Black

Many people, maybe most people, have the luxury of pursuing their doctoral studies full time. Some of us, on the other hand, have full-time jobs or careers that we need to keep and these are often not near the university at which we wish to study. So this puts us in the group of those who jealously guard every moment of our intermittent free time to devote to our studies and who need a university that can support part-time and distance students. Such a one was I. More than just a little, since the university I was studying at was in the UK, but I was on the faculty of an American university, 3000 miles away.

FINDING A DIRECTOR OF STUDIES

The saga begins with my search for a good director of studies under whom to study. The topic I wanted to research for my PhD was about consumer trust and therefore spanned the trust and marketing fields. I looked at professors in both fields and decided that, since I already had considerable expertise in marketing as a practitioner who had risen through the ranks to the chief marketing officer level, I should find a director who was on the trust side. I identified a professor who was more of a generalist in trust theory, not focused on just one small dimension of trust and who had founded a centre focused on the study of trust at his university. The university in question was well set up to support part-time distance students and was near where I lived in the UK, so it seemed perfect. I rang him up.

'Well, I don't know. I'm very busy. But perhaps, perhaps. Your topic is interesting. Send me your proposal and I'll take a look.' So I sent him my proposal. He agreed to take me on, saying I was 'different' from other applicants. He never explained that, but it did not matter. What mattered was that I had a good director of studies and a place at a good university. Life was good!

Shortly thereafter my director found a second advisor for me. A second advisor who complements your director's skill sets can be a great help and a valuable asset on the team. This was not the case here. This academic was also on the business faculty with a speciality in trust, but was at a junior level, having only recently completed his own PhD. When I contacted him, he told me that he had not been asked if he would take me on. He was just signed up for it by my director of studies. Therefore he felt no particular obligation towards supporting me. He and I only had two other conversations and he never gave me any feedback on anything I wrote.

The literature review was the first challenge. During the first 18 months, I read and wrote. Periodically I sent drafts to my director. His advice and feedback, always by email or Skype, not annotation, was vague but encouraging. His comments and his reports on my progress led me to believe I was on track and making good progress towards my confirmation. In the UK, a third of the way through a PhD students are required to pass an examination, which confirms their standing and allows them to continue towards completion of the PhD. Frequently referred to as confirmation, transfer or upgrade, at the university where I was studying this comprised writing the first three to four chapters of the thesis covering a review of the literature, the contribution the research was likely to make, and the methodology and method to be used to collect and analyse the data. On this students are also examined in a comprehensive oral exam. Upon passing their exam, and providing their written work is satisfactory, students are allowed to proceed with their fieldwork and their thesis. Eighteen months in I had written the first full draft of my confirmation report, which my director told me was good and just needed a few adjustments to be ready. Then I got the phone call that derailed everything.

LOSING A DIRECTOR OF STUDIES

Out of the blue, my director of studies rang me up and in his usual cryptic fashion he said, 'Good afternoon. I am leaving this university and going to another. Do you want to come with me or stay here?' I was speechless. I stammered a confused response. He gave me a little more information and told me to ring him back when I had thought about it, and hung up. Now what? I was not at all sure how to proceed.

The decision was not an easy one. On the plus side, the university where he was going was a much better university and equally convenient for me in terms of location. Moreover, I would get to keep the continuity of working with this director of studies who seemed to have confidence in me and who thought I was doing well. On the minus side, the new university which my director was joining specialised in a particular area that was not relevant to my research at all, and the university did not have a strong tradition in trust research. This concerned me. I decided to consult my second advisor. My second advisor told me that I had 'struck gold' in my choice of director, since he was outstanding at getting students through the PhD process and choosing good examiners. Since the new university was also a much better known and more prestigious university, he recommended that I follow. Two days later I got an email from my second advisor saying he too was leaving and would no longer be my second advisor. I had no further contact with him.

I was adrift with no oars. I felt abandoned and my emotional reaction was to cling to the one person who seemed to have faith in me. This meant changing universities in order to keep the continuity with my director of studies. My rational side, however, told me I needed to do some careful research on what both options would entail and make a more educated decision.

I initiated the process with the new university to transfer with my director. I found out that it is very complicated to transfer if you have not yet passed your confirmation. The university where I would be going had different requirements on research methods, training modules and other first year taught modules, which did not align very well with those of my current university. Therefore, I would need to take modules at the new university and these were taught modules that were only offered on site. An extra complication in my case was that the new university did not have any provisions in place for distance students, though they did allow part-time study. This was a major roadblock for me. However, they bent over backwards to find solutions. In the end the head of the PhD programme there said the faculty had recently approved a pilot programme to accept distance students. This had not yet been activated, but he had got special permission from the faculty to have me as a test case. This put me in a very awkward situation because I did not feel that being a guinea pig was a good thing and yet he had gone out of his way on my behalf.

Meanwhile, I was also holding conversations with the head of the PhD programme for business students at the university where I was enrolled to see what the alternatives would be if I stayed. He had no idea. He had no clue who would take me on and no suggestions on what to do. (I later found out that this was because the university was going through a major restructuring, which included asking for expressions of interest in taking redundancy, and there were therefore many changes afoot in the faculty ranks, but I did not know this at the time.) When he asked me if I had any suggestions, I had no answer either. Because I was a distance student – and very far distant – I was rarely on campus and knew none of the other students or faculty. So I did not know anyone to talk to about this or any of the other faculty to ask to be my new director of studies. The head of the PhD programme thought that since I was proposing using a qualitative method, maybe someone in the Sociology Department might be good because they did a lot of qualitative research. Sociology? Really? Was there no one in the Business School who could take me? He said he would look into it. I left his office feeling discouraged, frustrated and not a little annoyed.

I asked my director of studies for a meeting and we met at a pub in town. We discussed the transfer and, to his credit, he did not try to push me one way or the other, but did give me some of the pros and cons as he saw it. I then asked him for a critique of the new draft of my work that I had sent him. He said it was almost there and with a little more work it would be ready, but when I pressed him on the specifics of that, he had nothing to say. I stared at the text. In that moment I realised that he was not giving me nearly enough critical assessment and without it I was not sure how to improve my work. He had been encouraging in making general comments and in suggesting additional texts to look at, but detailed critique on what was and was not working was not his style. That moment the penny dropped and when I looked back on it I recognised that I really had not been getting enough critical input all along. I needed more from him.

I walked back up the hill utterly disconsolate. As I saw it there was little reason to follow this director of studies and no one to be my director of studies if I stayed.

I chose to stay. I had no idea who my new director of studies might turn out to be, or even if they would be in the business school, but I turned down the offer of a place at the new university. There were several reasons. First, there was the bad fit between what I was studying and that university's focus. I felt a degree from that university would not have meaning in the context of my research topic. Close to that was the fact that the university was really not set up yet to handle distance students, and the university where I was enrolled was very well set up for that. But the final and most important reason, I had reluctantly come to see, was that I was not getting enough critical assessment of my work and really, if truth were told, I was floundering. I didn't even know whether my work was any good or not. I was not sure what to do next.

A short while later I received an email from the head of the PhD programme at the business school saying that he had found me someone who would act as an interim director of studies and proposed that I meet with this professor. I came into that meeting full of hope and expecting to have a positive and encouraging conversation. Instead, the first words out of the professor's mouth, after introducing himself, were, 'Don't take this meeting to mean that I will agree to be your director of studies ongoing. I have a lot of students already and I am going on sabbatical. So I will give you some advice today, but don't assume that this relationship will continue.' Disconcerting, to say the least, but as I knew he was only acting in an interim role, I mentally resolved to take full advantage of all the advice I could get while it was available to me. I found I liked him. He was straightforward and specific, which suited me well and was a refreshing change from my previous director of studies. So it was a great relief to me when I subsequently received another email from the head of the PhD programme saying that this professor had (reluctantly) agreed to be my director ongoing, since there was no one else! My new director asked me for a copy of the most recent draft of my confirmation report and then promptly left for Australia for six weeks. I sent him the report.

When the report came back to me I could barely read it for the amount of black notations in the margins. As I read through his notes, I could see his frustration growing as he shredded my work. Virtually nothing was salvageable. His comment was that the section on my research philosophy was passable and that I could write clearly. Other than that I had nothing. Devastating! Especially after having understood from my former director that this was good work and I was nearly ready to submit it for confirmation. However, I was heartened by the fact that he had actually read it all and commented on everything. Here was someone willing to invest his time and effort in helping me turn things around.

This is so important. I learned from what had happened that a director of studies who just encourages and does not offer much critique is not as valuable to the student as one who is more critical of the work, painful as the critiques can be at times. The encouragement is reassuring and feels good, but the critique strengthens and teaches you. Your work cannot improve without it. I clung to that consolation and started over. I rewrote just the review chapter on the trust literature, taking into account his comments. Upon reading the new draft, my new director expressed that he was impressed with the difference and was now ready to help find me a second advisor. That comment I interpreted at the time to mean he had been holding back his judgment and had not been ready to commit fully until he knew if I was worth his time. Reassuring to find that I was, but disconcerting to realise he had been less than committed. He later explained to me that the real reason for not picking a second advisor right away was because he wanted to be really clear about who would be a good fit in terms of skills and knowledge for my particular topic. This is a really important consideration.

My new director of studies found me a great second advisor who could bring experience both in qualitative methods (my director's natural affinity was more towards mixed methods and he had been trained in quantitative methods) and in consumer marketing (his expertise was more in trust). This balance is important. It is helpful to have a balanced team whose strengths complement each other because they can each offer advice on different aspects of your work. The only downside in this case was that my new second advisor was not experienced in supervising PhD students, though she was a good tutor and advisor.

Life was good again! A lot of work still lay ahead to get ready for confirmation, but my new supervising team was very supportive and gave good, constructive, critical feedback. I made great progress that year and caught up fast from the setback. And then it happened again!

KEEPING A DIRECTOR OF STUDIES

The next summer when I was back in the UK, my new director told me he too was leaving and going to another university! This was just before my confirmation. I couldn't imagine starting over *again*! I have to say that this time it didn't come as a surprise. He had given up his office when he went on sabbatical, and in my view professors usually don't give up their offices if they are planning on coming back. I had challenged him on it one day and he had given me an evasive answer. However, I didn't want to move. I was comfortable with the routine of this university and knew I could finish up on time within the deadline I had set myself. I didn't want to go through moving to another university. So I was cross about it when it happened. I was cross with him and I was cross that I was again faced with a choice that was unsatisfactory whichever way I jumped.

My director of studies said he would take me with him if I wanted to transfer, and reassured me that regardless he would continue to supervise me wherever I was. This time there was a better fit with the new university and the new university was set up to handle distance students to a manageable degree, though not as well as the university I was leaving. If I wanted to stay he recommended flipping the advising team and my current second would officially become my director and he would remain on the team as second advisor, although he assured me that in practice his input would continue as before. I didn't trust that assurance. I trusted his direction and his reputation for choosing good examiners and preparing students for the final exam, and I was concerned that if the roles were reversed, he would have less influence. I had a good director of studies and I was determined to keep him and to keep him as my primary advisor.

There were actually several considerations that governed my decision to transfer. First, I just did not want to start over with yet another advising team. I felt that if the advising roles were flipped, it would be like having another team because the primary director of my research would change. Since, as is common and not unhealthy, my advisors did not always see eye to eye on the direction they gave me, I feared that this would inevitably lead to reworking my approach and set me back further. Secondly, I felt my second advisor was perhaps not experienced enough to get me through. She was thoughtful and good and very smart, but I had been given to understand that she had not taken a PhD student all the way through to getting their degree before. I didn't know how good she would be at choosing examiners or preparing me for the final exam. On the other hand, I had every confidence in my current director who was very experienced, well known and well respected. I considered that his capability, and not least my confidence in that capability, counted for a lot. Lastly, as before, the new university was a much higher ranked university, though not as convenient in terms of location this time.

I applied to the new university. They said I needed to complete the confirmation first before transferring, which I did. The transfer process was slow. There were a lot of documents that needed to be produced, showing proof of my progress and that I had completed my confirmation. It dragged out and went back and forth several times. The primary concerns were making sure that the training modules I had taken were commensurate with their own, and also that I could complete this PhD part-time and long distance while holding down a full-time job. In the end they accepted my assurances and those of my director on this, but they were not happy with that. 'Distance' in their lexicon meant based somewhere else in England, not the other side of the Atlantic!

I learned two things from the experience of transferring. First, requirements, expectations, procedure and even terminology can vary widely from university to university. It pays to ask for clarification and specifics. Don't assume you know! Secondly, document everything you do for your PhD as you go along. I had a hard time tracking down some of the certificates of completion after the fact to prove my progress and performance. The requirements for documentation expected of PhD students at my new university were much more rigorous than at my previous university, so I did not have nearly the level of documentation they needed. But at last all was in order. I pulled the trigger and made the transfer.

Life was good again!

LESSONS FOR KEEPING ON TRACK

- When looking for a director of studies, try to find someone who complements your strengths. Read their work and know what their specialty is as well as their preferred research method, if any.
- Balance your advising team with academics who bring different strengths and areas of expertise to the table.
- If your director of studies does not give you much critical assessment, ask for more! Or, find someone who will critique your work.
- Do your homework before you make your decision on whether to transfer or not – don't make it on emotion.
- Keep calm and carry on! Even during the transition, keep working on your research. This will help to steady you and keep you on track.
- Make sure to build a network at your university so that you have resources in times of crisis – and for that matter ongoing.
- Challenge yourself to rise above the fray and clear the bar.

6. Reply all, tweets and social media: technological friends for developing a professional identity that need to be treated with care

Hugh T.J. Bainbridge

If is often stated that the most important asset an academic possesses is their reputation.

A reputation can be sullied in many ways, sometimes by bad luck or unfortunate circumstances beyond one's control. And, I suppose, sometimes by others. But most often, the damage that is done is self-inflicted.

For me, a formative experience in thinking about this occurred early. Flushed with the excitement of an acceptance letter for my first prestigious conference I had speed read through the letter to find that the paper had been scheduled as 'Poster session'.

I had already been informed of the status of this session format by other PhD students. I remembered the pearls of wisdom they had passed on. Poster sessions are 'the worst', they said. 'No one comes to them. You will go all the way to the conference for nothing.' And, devastatingly, 'They only give them to students. The real sessions are reserved for the important research.'

Aghhh! I thought and promptly fired off an email to my more experienced co-authors. '*Why did we get a POSTER SESSION?*'

But in my haste, I had overlooked one important detail. My indignant email to my co-authors was a 'Reply all' and was now also flying across the globe to the Conference Stream Chair . . .

***

Seeing my future career pass in an instant before my eyes, I did the only logical thing. I sought professional, expert, assistance. Not the medical kind. Real, expert, IT assistance.

A few minutes later a representative from the university IT group looked at me with bored indifference. I rapidly explained the seriousness of the situation with accompanying hand movements that helpfully indicated the direction taken by outbound and inbound emails. Finally, he tired of my explanation. 'No', the IT expert said. 'I can't delete your email before the recipient reads it.'

So, resigned to whatever fate awaited me, I trudged back to my desk to await a scolding email from the big name in the field, which I thought would probably foreshadow a cascading set of consequences that would forever blight my career.

And true to my fears, there at the top of my inbox sat an email from the Stream Chair . . .

***

It turns out that the Conference Stream Chair had the tact and presence of mind (as opposed to me) to write a generous reply that outlined the merits of the session format.

I've often reflected on this 30-minute period. In an age where social media facilitates instant responses to a broad audience, and technology makes bad decisions forever accessible, it helps me often to think about this formative experience and to consider the merits of a 'pause' before pressing the button 'SEND'.

7. Coming up with a research question: opinions, feedback and networking

Deisi Yunga

At the beginning of my doctoral programme, I had very ambitious plans for my thesis. My goal was to come up with an all-encompassing research question that, after being answered, would solve one, if not more of the problems within my research field. It was a little naive, to be sure.

The first months of my programme were, to say the least, full of concern and self-inflicted stress. I wanted to absorb every piece of information available in my research field. This approach got me lost in the literature and I did not know which path to follow. It seemed that in each article I read, there was a new piece of information or idea that could enrich my research question – Eureka! – or at least, I thought so every time I would finish reading a paper. In the end, I realised that although these ideas were often good on their own, they would eventually lead me in different directions.

Some months later, when I thought I had my ideas clear, I nervously presented my initial research question to some of my colleagues. I received mostly very valuable feedback. However, the most frequent advice was 'it's too big, narrow it down' and each of my colleagues gave me ideas on how to do this and what literature to read. However, each colleague recommended very diverse literature that started with Plato and ended with last month's publication of the most popular indexed journals in my field – only 2400 years' worth of material to review! I was going to get lost – yet again!

I wasn't expecting this: why? Well, at the time I thought that because my colleagues belonged to the same specific subfield, they would naturally recommend to me the same, or at least similar, literature. I would just have to read it to clarify and narrow my research question down.

My initial naivety became panic. At this point, I was pretty aware of my limits. I knew that trying to integrate dozens of different articles and my colleagues' opinions was, without doubt, impossible and I would inevitably broaden my research question again.

So my first learning was: just don't do it . . .

Every time somebody gave me advice about my research, she or he did so (probably with the best intentions) from the narrow perspective of her or his own specific research and experience. However, rather than getting completely lost in the initial excitement of a new paper or book that appears relevant, I now evaluate the methodology, findings and theories deeply before deciding whether or not to make them part of my research.

I've also learned to scan literature people recommend. To my surprise, I can make an unexpectedly fast selection of the papers that truly interest me and appear relevant and discard the ones that don't. I am finally on track and defining the characteristics of my own research study.

This experience of massive feedback also heightened my awareness of the world outside my supervisory team, a world full of experts, some of whom could help me. I decided to be more proactive, contacting researchers in conferences and through email. The worst they could tell me was 'I have no time for you', assuming that they would answer me at all.

When looking for experts in my field and seeking advice, I didn't find the 'bow tie-wearing martinets' I always pictured the H-index 20+ university professors would be. Instead, I found a dynamic network of knowledgeable people who have advised me, not just about my research question but also about methodological design, possible outcomes, and what to do if things go wrong. Of course, not all answers have been positive. Sometimes, I've been told to contact them later upon reaching a more advanced stage in my research and others simply have not replied. Yet, at the end of the day, I gained much more than I expected.

Not surprisingly my second learning and advice is: *do not* be afraid of contacting seemingly unreachable experts in the field. I write emails, join research networks, approach people in conferences, and so on. I've expanded my network and hopefully begun to enrich my research and my future work. Realistically you never know if the person who answers you will become your greatest advisor, next collaborator, best friend – or all of the above.

In retrospect, I'm glad of my initial naivety because it made me discover what was out there. My panic made me aware of my own abilities as a researcher and the need to develop. I'm thankful for the network in my field whose collective experiences and opinions have helped me begin to develop my own experience, shape my research question, and start to find my own angle on one aspect of one of my initial research questions.

PART II

Getting Data

8. Finding epistemology

Neve Isaeva

Could we imagine a researcher without an epistemology? Absolutely not. Although to my utter surprise many researchers have argued differently, as I discovered throughout my investigation into the epistemologies of leading trust researchers. There was maybe a time in the past when I was one of them. I did not think about epistemology. However, this was not due to my ignorance. I was brought up in an environment where it was thought that there is only one 'right way' of conducting research and I was unaware of alternatives.

When I first had to reveal my own epistemology, I realised that I did not have an answer. Although unconsciously I would have considered myself a positivist, I had quickly realised that this did not fully reflect my beliefs and assumptions. Suddenly, I discovered myself in no one's land without an epistemology but in a desperate need to find one. This is my story where I took a long journey from a place of clueless despair to a point of confident revelation. It is a story of self-discovery as well as one of having the right people supporting me throughout the ups and downs of my journey.

I have found my doctoral studies to be a very long and sometimes overwhelming journey, requiring tremendous motivation, determination and dedication. Although the path leading to a doctoral degree appears to be an individual process, it is in fact one of the greatest examples of dedicated teamwork combined with an extended support network. I consider myself to be extremely lucky in that sense. I had people helping me to shoulder all the difficulties and supporting me in every process. Nothing I wrote could have been accomplished without them – my supervisors.

I started my doctoral studies with an especially high level of enthusiasm. I was ready, dedicated, and determined to be a very successful academic. As a part of my programme, I was enrolled in some research methods modules, one of which was 'Foundations of Management Research'. That was the first time that my confidence had been shattered. We were talking about so many alien terminologies such as 'ontology', 'epistemology', 'axiology', and so on. I was quick to realise that I needed more than a basic book definition of the terms to be able to grasp the true meaning. It did not matter how many times I checked the definitions of those terms, I was quick to forget what they really meant as they were so abstract in my mind.

It has taken a while to gain a deep understanding of such topics but now I have reached a point where I feel confident, even love, discussing them. Since increased confidence brings heightened impatience, I want to start telling my story and explain one of my favourite topics: epistemology. Epistemology concerns the beliefs and assumptions we make about knowledge and what constitutes acceptable, valid and legitimate knowledge (Burrell and Morgan, 1979). Epistemology along with ontology (nature of reality) and axiology (researcher's role in the research process) form research philosophy. A researcher's philosophy has fundamental implications for the whole research design and consequently for the knowledge that researchers contribute to their field (Burrell and Morgan, 1979; Tsoukas and Chia, 2011). It took me a while to grasp the depth of the meanings of these terms but it has been an incredible journey to do so.

My biggest challenge had been to discover my own epistemology, a roller coaster journey with its ups and downs. There have been times when I was drifting between a feeling where I wished I had never learned about epistemology and a belief that knowing my own epistemology was the best possible thing that could happen to any researcher. Now, three years later, I have become a strong advocate for researchers explicitly reflecting on and understanding their own epistemologies. I believe that engaging in reflection on one's own epistemology, as well as the alternatives, will establish a better awareness towards contributions made to knowledge. I understood the importance of epistemological reflection from very early on; however, I did not know where my assumptions belonged. This is why I charged into a full search for my epistemology, and this is my story of finding epistemology.

I guess 'confusion' is the feeling that best describes my initial reaction when I first learned about research philosophies. It was the same confusion I saw in the students whom recently I had the pleasure of helping with the discussion groups for a module where they have to learn and reflect on their own research philosophies. I could see that they were trying really hard to clarify those concepts in their minds. I could really sympathise with their situation and tried to help them as much as I could by talking about my experience in which I started with no knowledge on the subject matter and progressed to where research philosophy has become one of my favourite research topics. I tried to emphasise that confusion is actually a normal reaction. The leader of the module I took three years ago often emphasised that it was okay to be confused in the beginning, as being confused was often the first step in the process of understanding one's own epistemology. In her words, she explained:

sometimes you need to get thoroughly lost before you can find your way – you need to question everything you were certain about previously; you need to get confused so that you can look at things differently and then decide where you want to go from there. Otherwise, you will be continuing along the same path you've always trodden unthinkingly.

I was so relieved to hear that and to realise that nothing was wrong with me.

Things got a little better when I started learning about the actual epistemologies. The first epistemological position, positivism, I realised later on, was actually what I had adhered to until that time, albeit unconsciously. Quite often, I questioned whether my lack of knowledge on the issue was due to my ignorance. But is it possible to be ignorant on an issue that you are not aware of? I was trained in a certain way regarding conducting research and it never occurred to me to question that. Only one thing was clear at that moment, which was that I was not really a positivist. The assumptions I made or the choices I took did not coincide wholly with a positivist epistemology.

My rebellion against positivism complicated everything and left me more confused than before. I knew that I was no longer a positivist because I believed, and still do believe, that it is impossible in social sciences to be wholly objective. I do not think research can be totally divorced from the researcher's ideas, beliefs and assumptions, neither do I advocate that they should try to achieve this. Although there may be instances calling for absolute objectivity, especially in natural sciences, in social sciences I believe that the researcher is the instrument whose participation provides a valuable contribution to the research process. I was back at square one. I realised that I certainly was not a positivist, but what was my epistemology?

I really wanted to say that I did not have an epistemology. However, despite my lack of knowledge, I was not so naive as to make such a claim as I knew in my heart that every researcher, aware or not, makes epistemological assumptions, which in turn influence the decisions they make about the research design, and consequently impact the contributions they make to the current knowledge. The issue was that I did not know how my assumptions aligned with specific epistemologies. Rather, with every new epistemological view I learned, I found an aspect with which I agreed; yet none of them fully reflected my own assumptions. Consequently, I did not have a label to give when I was asked about my epistemology. In a way, I was adamantly against labelling myself as something, or in the module leader's own words, I was 'raging against it'. I believed that I did not have enough knowledge regarding different epistemologies to be able to draw solid conclusions and determine correctly 'the one' epistemology for me.

In order to be sure that I chose the epistemology that reflected my beliefs and assumptions, I needed to undertake far more reading and to process and synthesise the information I gained.

My immediate problem with not having an epistemology was that I had to write an essay outlining my own epistemology and reflecting on the epistemological approaches in my doctoral field of studies. I was far from finding my own epistemology, so how was I to comment on others'? Besides, how do you determine others' epistemologies if they are not explicit about it? I knew there was (and is) a pattern of language pointing towards specific epistemologies but this does not guarantee a correct inference. For instance, how do you know what the outlined epistemology is of a research piece which utilised questionnaires and thereby quantitative methods? Possibly, the first thing that comes to mind might be a positivist epistemology. On the other hand, the authors may be critical realists or even pragmatists who believe that the best way of addressing the research question is through quantitative methods. Alternatively, authors may have been recommended to make changes in line with the directives of the editors or a particular journal's requirements, which in turn might result in the misinterpretation of the authors' epistemology. For example, a section of an article called 'implications for management' emphasises the intent of producing knowledge that can be applied to practice, thereby perhaps indicating a possible pragmatist epistemology. However, such a section is required by some journals and so can be considered as being imposed on the authors. I was feeling desolate.

I did not want to write about the authors in my field of study in case I misinterpreted them and was therefore unfair to them. Then it occurred to me that no one is likely to know more than the authors themselves. I therefore decided to ask the authors directly. I was expected to write a reflective essay on the field of trust research, but I went beyond the requirements of the assignment and found myself conducting an empirical study. I emailed 35 leading trust researchers (LTRs) and inquired after their epistemology.

I was hoping these academics would be helpful but the response rate exceeded my expectations and I was pleasantly surprised to see the extent of the willingness to help. I felt I was part of the community throughout the process. Of the 35 people I emailed, 27 had responded. Although the request was only for a short answer, many sent long responses, showing interest in the subject matter and my research. Suddenly, I was supercharged with enthusiasm. I found myself exchanging emails in the middle of the night, at 3 am. I felt so much more motivated to continue with my PhD. My gratitude to those who responded was enormous and this was clearly conveyed in my responses.

On the other hand, I was still searching for my own epistemology, though feeling much closer to finding it. I was not feeling as desperate as I did before. I was feeling like a teenager who had the privilege of interacting with their favourite rock music idol. I was corresponding with some of the most influential trust researchers who I previously could only dream about talking to. This process made me realise that a researcher's epistemology is a mirror to their way of thinking, which I think serves as an invitation to enter into the hidden world of their work. Therefore, I was better able to assess their contributions to knowledge as I now knew what kind of assumptions they held as researchers.

It did not take too long to come back from this dream world to the harsh reality of my PhD where the clock was ticking and the deadline was fast approaching. Although I had managed to write a good section about the leading trust researchers' epistemological positions and the dominant epistemologies in trust literature, a very important part of the assignment was still missing: my own epistemology.

I continued spending time on reading relevant materials to gain more insightful knowledge. I found myself waking up in the middle of the night with some questions in my mind and spending the rest of the night reading instead of sleeping. I became almost obsessed with finding my epistemology. I was chasing every academic at the university, inquiring after their epistemology and the reasons behind adhering to it. I still could not fully associate with any of the epistemologies and had a constant feeling that I did not have enough information to make my decision.

I felt as if I had been forced into writing about something that I did not wholeheartedly believe in. Yet, although extremely reluctantly, I decided to go with what was expected from me for the assignment and chose a position that was relatively close to my assumptions. I promised myself that later I could freely discover more about the epistemological positions and find one that better represented me. To choose one, I decided to use the process of elimination. I already knew that I was not a positivist. In addition, I thought the epistemological positions such as postmodernism and poststructuralism were totally out of my comfort zone as they did not align with my beliefs. I knew that I was also not an interpretivist, as I was still deeply rooted in positivist feelings. This dilemma left me with two choices: critical realism and pragmatism, both of which sounded plausible options.

As I read more, I began to feel that pragmatism was closer to describing my approach to knowledge. It would allow me to embrace the methodological pluralism that I was so insistent on having. For a pragmatist, answering the research question is the most important aspect; I was free to choose whatever method I thought would best work in addressing the research question. I believed then, and still do, that both quantitative and qualitative methods have their own strengths and weaknesses. Therefore they both may play a crucial role in different instances. This is why I have always questioned the obsession of using a single type of method whatever the question is because the school of thought the researcher is in dictates it. However, I was not completely satisfied that pragmatism was me. The main reason for that would be the common depiction of pragmatism as its being about providing useful knowledge for practice, in which 'practice' almost always referred to the practitioner's community.

I did not have much of a choice as the deadline was approaching. I surrendered to writing about pragmatism as my epistemological view, which I was not happy about and was insistent on mentioning that at every possible opportunity. I was very careful to stick with the aspects of pragmatism that I agreed with and I had sufficient knowledge to argue convincingly. I do not think I can write satisfactorily about something if I do not wholeheartedly believe it. I therefore did a mediocre job with that aspect of the assignment. I was much happier with the part of the assignment where I reflected on the field of trust and underlying epistemologies. I wrote an empirical study going beyond what was asked or expected from me. The process provided me with much valuable information about researchers in my field. It filled me with hope as there are others, many of whom are the leading researchers in their areas, who share very similar beliefs, and possibly occasional confusions like me.

After long struggles and many sleepless nights, I was finally done with the assignment. Eventually, I got a relatively good grade. However, my quest of finding my epistemology continued, even more ardently. In line with my supervisor's suggestion of writing a journal article on the research, I extended my previous sample of 35 leading researchers to 265, of whom 167 leading researchers responded (see Isaeva et al. 2015 for details). Among those researchers there were many who did not know what epistemology is; who did not think about epistemological matters; who strictly adhered to one epistemology; or who accepted being influenced by more than one epistemology. Positivism emerged as the dominant epistemology in my field (trust), especially among the North American researchers. The number of researchers who did not know or did not follow an epistemology was the highest in North America. No wonder I had no clue on the issues of epistemology with my American training.

My obsession with, and strong desire for, better understanding of the field I study and with finding my own epistemology and not abandoning my quest in despair has paid off. At my supervisor's insistence, we presented a paper at a trust conference. Here the Chair of my stream, who was also an editor, asked us whether we would consider submitting this paper to the *Journal of Trust Research*. The paper was worked, submitted, reviewed, revised, and resubmitted, reviewed again, resubmitted, and finally accepted!

Our paper was published in August 2015 (Isaeva et al., 2015). Somewhere during this process, I was no longer confused about my epistemology. I enjoyed the epistemological discussions I had occasionally with the participants and with my co-authors and the reviewers during the publication process. From a person who was not sure about her own epistemology, I became a strong advocator for researchers to explicitly reflect on their own epistemologies. My engaging in epistemological reflection had resulted in an awareness of my own epistemology, as well as the alternatives, which in turn facilitated my interpretation of others' contributions in their writings.

I found 'the one' epistemology, which, as you have probably guessed, in my case was indeed pragmatism. However, while explaining my understanding of pragmatism, I was careful to point out the significant distinction between pragmatism as philosophical thinking, and the pragmatic decisions made during the research process as in the literature. Quite often I have seen pragmatism being confused with pragmatic choices or sometimes even with opportunism. Another distinction I made was on the understanding of what 'practice' means – the issue I mentioned previously. I always endeavour to make my position clear that the concept of practice goes beyond the common attributed understanding of producing useful knowledge for the practitioner community. It also includes research that involves any aspects of human conduct which are shaped by actors' choices based on their anticipation of the likely outcomes of the social actions that consequently shape their worlds. Now, a few years later, if I am allowed, I can go on and on explaining what pragmatism means to me. I have not only found my epistemology but I have also found my soulmate which will guide me through my research career!

KEY LEARNING POINTS

- Every researcher, aware or not, makes epistemological assumptions. Therefore, it is crucial to know what they are and actively reflect on them.
- Our epistemological beliefs drive our research design and methods used. It is not the other way around.
- It is normal to be confused at the beginning. The important thing is not to give up.
- We are never alone. Do not hesitate to reach out to more experienced researchers for help when you need it.
- Last but not least, know what your epistemology is, so that in the future if a young doctoral researcher inquires after your epistemology, you have an answer!

REFERENCES

Burrell, G. and Morgan, G. (1979). *Sociological Paradigms and Organizational Analysis: Elements of the Sociology of Corporate Life*, Burlington, VT: Ashgate.

Isaeva, N., Bachmann, R., Bristow, A. and Saunders, M.N.K. (2015). 'Why the epistemologies of trust researchers matter', *Journal of Trust Research*, **5**(2), 153–69.

Tsoukas, H. and Chia, R. (2011). 'Introduction: why philosophy matters to organization theory', in H. Tsoukas and R. Chia (eds), *Philosophy and Organization Theory*, Research in the Sociology of Organizations, vol. 32, Bradford: Emerald, pp. 1–21.

9. Bounce back, firewalls and legal threats: reaching respondents using Internet questionnaires

Mark N.K. Saunders and David E. Gray

INTRODUCTION

Over the years we must, between us, have undertaken a fair number of research projects where data have been collected using questionnaires. Through these projects we have gained some understanding of the realities of distributing questionnaires by hand, by mail and, more recently, using the Internet. Respondents to our questionnaires have included employees in a single organisation, customers of different organisations and people with specific roles, such as owner/managers or directors of services, working in a wide range of organisations. In other words, we would like to think that we are reasonably experienced in the process of designing and conducting survey research using questionnaires.

However, rather than write about our experiences of the entire process of conducting survey research using questionnaires, in this chapter we are focusing upon what we believe to be a crucial aspect: gaining access to potential questionnaire respondents. Although the issue of access is often considered in the methods literature, the focus is usually on gaining cognitive access. In particular it is concerned with leveraging the likelihood of respondents consenting to take part, answering the questions and returning the questionnaire, particularly through its design and that of the accompanying cover letter. In other words, the literature focuses in the main upon ways to enhance response rates once the potential respondent has been reached. Where difficulties associated with gaining physical access, that is, getting in to undertake research, are acknowledged, the focus is usually within the context of collecting data from a single rather than multiple organisations.

In this chapter we focus on difficulties associated with gaining physical access to respondents holding a particular role in a large number of organisations. In particular we are concerned with the considerable problems we

experienced when our initial plans to email a link to an Internet questionnaire online to over ten thousand Small and Medium-sized Enterprises'
(SMEs) owner managers failed. We outline how, despite a carefully prepared plan that we had discussed and debated with colleagues, we were
unable to gain physical access to a substantial proportion of previously
identified potential Internet questionnaire respondents. Within this we
begin by describing the context of the research, we then outline the practical difficulties we faced when trying to gain access by using a purchased
list. We then discuss the operationalisation of our back-up plans of collecting data through existing networks, directories and from contacts, before
concluding by outlining our learning from this experience.

THE RESEARCH CONTEXT

A few years ago we were approached by a large United Kingdom (UK)
firm, and asked to bid to undertake a fully funded research project focusing on the triggers that make SMEs successful. In our research proposal
we outlined a mixed methods research design comprising focus groups,
an Internet questionnaire, and interviews. A research contract was signed
with the client and a date was set four months hence for the public launch
of the report findings at a major venue in London. We would be presenting the findings with the firm's Chief Executive Officer (CEO) and the
Government Minister for Business and Enterprise. The firm's Public
Relations Officer had ensured us that the main quality UK newspapers
had been invited alongside an audience of over one hundred interested
business leaders.

The study had been commissioned because it is well known that one
element that differentiates SMEs from other sizes of firm is their prema-
ture mortality. Indeed, our reading of the literature and UK government
statistics had revealed that approximately only 60 per cent of SMEs were
still trading three years after start-up, with about 40 per cent surviving
after five years. However, the commissioners of our research were not
interested in discovering why SMEs failed. Rather, the research focus was
on those SMEs that had survived the financial downturn that followed the
2008 worldwide financial crisis, seeking to identify those factors that had
contributed to their longevity and robustness.

In designing this project, it had been made clear to us that the research
needed to incorporate a quantitative study. The funders wanted to be
able to make generalisations about the triggers for success of UK SMEs
from the data collected. This we knew would entail having a representative sample and a sufficiently large number of returns. In our bid for the

research project we made a commitment to attaining a return of at least 1000 questionnaires, these being distributed via the Internet using a hyperlink within an email. Given that the population of private sector SMEs in the UK was 4.5 million at the time of research (Department for Business, Innovation and Skills, 2012), we had calculated this should provide a margin of error of 3 per cent at 95 per cent confidence limits, providing our sample was representative (Saunders et al., 2016), thereby, we hoped, allowing for generalisation.

Following our proposal being accepted and the contract awarded, we now had to deliver; we had to undertake the research, write the report and prepare the presentation. Alongside the focus groups and interviews, our deliverables, outlined in the proposal, as indicated, included at least 1000 complete responses to the Internet questionnaire. It is this aspect of the research that provides the focus of the chapter. We approached the project with considerable enthusiasm, blissfully unaware of the true difficulties in ensuring our Internet questionnaires even reached our intended respondents.

Following acknowledged difficulties of accessing SMEs and the wide variations in web-based survey response rates reported in previous research (Shih and Fan, 2008), we decided to be cautious and assume a likely response rate of 10 per cent. This was the lowest percentage suggested by Baruch and Holtom's (2008) analysis of published research. It also meant we needed to deliver our questionnaire to at least 10 000 SMEs to achieve the 1000 responses. Using the UK Government's Department for Business, Innovation and Skills (2012) data we devised a quota sample of SMEs comprising six separate size bandings (based on number of employees) for each of the UK's 12 economic regions, a total of 72 different groupings. Through this we hoped to represent the variability in size and number of the population of private sector SMEs.

PRACTICAL DIFFICULTIES

List Errors: Bounce Back and Firewalls

Contact details and demographic data for 10 000 private sector SMEs matching our quota specifications were purchased from a reputable database company. Alongside demographic data for each SME, details included an email address, telephone number and named contact, allowing us to personalise each email accompanying the questionnaire. Acknowledging that some email addresses were likely to no longer be valid (termed 'hard bounce back'), the database company provided details for a further 1789

SMEs, giving a sample of 11789 SMEs. Within each of the regional quotas, each SME was checked by us to ensure it met the SME size criteria of fewer than 250 employees (as defined by European Union recommendation L124/36) and was in the private sector. This resulted in 913 SMEs being removed from the sample provided because they were large enterprises (for example a major snack food manufacturer), in the public sector (for example a National Health Service pharmacy) or in the not-for-profit sector (for example a registered charity). Using the contact details our questionnaire was then emailed to the remaining 10876 SMEs.

Within a week of distributing our Internet questionnaire we knew we had a problem with gaining physical access. Some 4892 emails containing the link to our questionnaire had been bounced back, having not reached the intended recipient. This meant that 4892 of our intended respondents were non-contactable. We spoke to the Information Technology (IT) services people at our university, who informed us it was impossible to work out the precise reason for bounce back and advised us to contact the database company. We did this, providing them with a sample of 91 of the email addresses that had 'bounced'. Following their checking, the company responded that, of these 91, only nine were invalid and that a bounce back of 10 per cent was 'well within the expected bounce back rate for emails that are invalid'. They informed us that the problem of bounce back was beyond their control and our emails were being blocked due to one or more of a number of reasons. These included the content of the email such as the hyperlink or particular words such as 'survey' or 'questionnaire', the recipient's email server settings, SPAM filters and/or anti-virus software, or for some other reason triggered by our email and hyperlink to the Internet questionnaire we had designed. In short, it was not the database company's problem to solve but ours.

This left a potential sampling of 6084, not only far fewer than we were anticipating, but also insufficient if our cautious response rate of 10 per cent was realised. One month after the launch of the survey, despite two follow-up emails to the sample, the scale of the problems became clear. Although 578 questionnaires had been returned, only 508 were complete and useable, a response rate of 8.5 per cent after excluding non-contacts. This was insufficient for our analysis purposes as we were hoping to disaggregate the data by sector and region, and commercially unacceptable given the commitment of a minimum of 1000 returns we had made to the client.

Very Few Will Answer the Telephone Questionnaire

The database we had purchased contained telephone contact details for the majority of SMEs. We therefore decided to advertise for temporary research assistants to telephone these enterprises and invite them to complete the questionnaire via the telephone. We advertised the job vacancies, interviewed and recruited four recent graduates, and set them to work within a week.

Unfortunately by the end of their first day of employment we were facing further problems. Our temporary research assistants were dispirited as the potential SME respondents were, with a few exceptions, refusing to take part in our research. We decided to incentivise our employees, offering them a bonus in addition to their hourly pay rate for each questionnaire that was completed. The incentivisation of completed telephone questionnaires resulted in a small improvement in the numbers being completed. However, all of our temporary research assistants had resigned by the end of the first week, and we had only an additional 70 completed questionnaires. As our problems mounted we decided to send out another follow-up email to the sample, thanking SME owner managers who had already responded and inviting those who had not yet responded to take part.

Threatened Legal Action

But then a crisis arose. We were attending a conference in Portugal when one of our mobile telephones rang. It was someone in the IT services team at our university saying that she had just received a very irate email from the director of an SME regarding our repeated emails to his company requesting he complete the questionnaire. Within this email he threatened legal action, stating: 'the matter has now been escalated to a formal legal issue against the university'. One of us immediately telephoned the company's director and discovered that the email address provided by the database company was incorrect. Rather than it being the address for general communications, it was the company's 24-hour emergency email address, only to be used by the company's clients if there was a business-threatening problem requiring immediate attention. Inadvertently we had called staff away from other work three times by our email request to participate in our research. Fortunately, our sincere telephone apology to the SME and follow-up email later to the correct address that day was accepted. Not surprisingly we deleted the 24-hour emergency email address from our database. The database company also apologised to the company director and admitted liability.

BACK-UP PLANS

Existing Networks

The questionnaire delivery seemed to be turning into a strategic disaster. We needed an alternative plan and quickly, and it turned out to be this: as gaining physical access using a purchased database of contacts had not provided sufficient questionnaire respondents, we would try using our networks and contacts. We knew that Chambers of Commerce and other employer groups nationally had large numbers of SMEs as members. One of us had collaborated with a local Chamber of Commerce on a previous research project, so contacted their Chief Executive, asking for help with contacting her network of members. Here, our own research and experiences came to the fore. We knew that, as commercial organisations, Chambers of Commerce rely on membership fees and other sources of income to continue to provide their services. Hence, offering a financial incentive to persuade them to email the survey directly to their members was not just prudent but vital. We decided to offer £10 for each questionnaire returned. Fortunately for us, we could afford this from our project budget.

The Chief Executive of our local Chamber of Commerce agreed to email all their SME members using an introductory letter we drafted. This explained the purpose of our research and invited the SME member to participate, providing the hyperlink to our questionnaire. Whilst outside our circles of influence and networks of contacts, these SMEs were clearly within the Chief Executive's circle of influence, operating from the centre of her network. However, one Chamber of Commerce was unlikely to be sufficient either in terms of number of responses or geographical coverage. Using contact details for the Chief Executive Officers of other Chambers of Commerce provided by our local Chamber of Commerce Chief Executive, we adopted snowball sampling to involve other Chambers of Commerce Chief Executives and their equivalent networks.

Three further Chambers of Commerce gave significant support to the Internet questionnaire delivery. In addition we gained support from a range of employer groups with whom we had already made contact, who in combination with the Chambers of Commerce eventually provided 589 responses. As before, we made comprehensive efforts to explain the purpose of the survey to each Chamber of Commerce and employer group and how the data provided by their members would be handled with rigorous attention to confidentiality. Fortunately the emails sent on our behalf by the Chambers of Commerce and employer groups received negligible bounce back. A week after these first emails had been sent, one follow-up reminder was sent. This thanked those who had responded, and encouraged those who had not to do so.

Directories and Contacts

We were keeping a daily running total of the number of respondents completing our questionnaire and, although the number of responses was increasing, it did not look as if our back-up plan would provide sufficient complete responses. We therefore decided to incentivise direct mailings by selected directories of small businesses, resulting in 349 additional responses. A further 84 responses were generated by emailing our existing SME contacts and asking if they would also be willing to help.

Success . . . Eventually

Six weeks later, having followed the daily tantalising rise in the total number of respondents, we had received 1600 useable responses that met our research funder's criterion of being private sector SMEs. Of these, 1004 we deemed complete, using the American Association for Public Opinion Research (2011) criterion of 80 per cent or more of the essential questions being answered. We had met the number required by our funder, although when compared with our initial quota we had over-representation of SMEs from certain UK regions (notably London and the South-East). Whilst we would need to establish the extent to which these differences between our sample and the population impacted significantly on our findings, we were now ready to continue with our interviews.

SO WHAT DID WE LEARN?

In reading our account, we are sure that you will have thought of a number of learning points that may be applicable to your own research. Despite this, we feel it may be helpful for us to list those we feel comprise our key learning:

1. Always have a contingency plan that can be put into operation if response rates are lower than expected.
2. Carefully check externally produced databases for accuracy, whatever the reputation of the source from which they are obtained.
3. Recognise the importance of contacts and networks in gaining physical access and, where appropriate, incorporate this in the research design.

4. Ensure the sample selected is sufficiently large to overcome very low response rates.
5. Think carefully about incentivising completion of questionnaires and, if possible, allocate funds to do this.
6. Monitor questionnaire returns on a daily basis so that potential problems are ascertained as early as possible and the contingency plan can be activated.

REFERENCES

American Association for Public Opinion Research (2011). *Standard Definitions: Final Dispositions of Case Codes and Outcome Rates for Surveys*, 7th edn, Lenexa, KA: AAPOR. Accessed 12 February 2017 at: https://www.esomar.org/uploads/public/knowledge-and-standards/codes-and-guidelines/ESOMAR_Standard-Definitions-Final-Dispositions-of-Case-Codes-and-Outcome-Rates-for-Surveys.pdf.

Baruch, Y. and Holtom, B.C. (2008). 'Survey response rate levels and trends in organizational research', *Human Relations*, **61**, 1139–60.

Department for Business, Innovation and Skills (2012). *Business Population Estimates for the UK and Regions 2011*. Accessed 21 October 2012 at: http://stats.bis.gov.uk/ed/bpe.

Saunders, M., Lewis, P. and Thornhill, A. (2016). *Research Methods for Business Students*, 7th edn, Harlow: Pearson.

Shih, T.H. and Fan, X. (2008). 'Comparing response rates from web and mail surveys: a meta-analysis', *Field Methods*, **20**(3), 249–71.

10. Finding the truth amongst conflicting evidence

Heather Short

INTRODUCTION

As a researcher, I frequently worry about whether my research is unearthing the truth, but what is truth? As my research perspective is subjectivist, I believe that meaning is created through social interaction, changing according to context and so leading to new realities. Consequently I believe that there is more than one reality, each of which is constructed from how people perceive things and how they act: everyone sees the world differently and has her/his own interpretations of how she/he and others act. This can really complicate finding the truth in research – but does make it very interesting! An obvious problem is: whose truth am I looking for? Mine – or the research participants'? Bearing in mind that each person is likely to have a view of the truth that is not only different from me, but also from each other, this becomes very complicated. I could get completely stuck in 'analysis-paralysis' regarding this and so I accept that people are 'truthful' if they seem to be reflecting reality as they see it, so, on a very simple level, if what they say aligns with what I see them doing.

At the start of my research career, the more academic literature I read, the more convinced I became that some researchers were paranoid; while some were content to believe everything that their research subjects told them, others seemed reluctant to believe anything and went to extraordinary lengths to prove the wisdom of this approach. On reflection, I realised that these extremes aren't confined to academia, as such views are common in all aspects of life. The more I thought about it, the more I recognised that, although my own inclination to believe others varies between these two extremes depending on the circumstances, I needed to use a more sceptical approach in my research if it was to be credible and widely accepted. Also, as I read more and more academic research literature, I appreciated that I should consider whether I was always willing – or able – to hear the truth; to quote George Bernard Shaw, admittedly out of context, might I and my research participants be 'separated by a common language'?

Therefore, in this chapter, I will first look at possible reasons for research participants appearing to be less than truthful, including my own short-comings. I'll then explore specific instances of this in my research, which will lead to my Lessons for Keeping on Track in the search for finding the truth amongst conflicting evidence.

WHY DON'T PARTICIPANTS TELL ME THE TRUTH?

My early research was predicated on the premise that everyone who took part in it wanted to tell me 'the truth, the whole truth and nothing but the truth'. However, the more research I have done, the more I have discovered that this is seldom the case. That is not to imply that I am unlucky enough always to choose research participants who are outright liars, more that they are a mixture of normal people who may not appear to be wholly truthful for various reasons.

Some people are just too nice and give me answers that they think I want to hear, even if they know these don't reflect reality (Yin, 2014). Once, I asked participants in a group interview (who knew I was researching the importance of trust in workplace settings) 'Do you think that trust is important at work?' They answered 'Yes', which I accepted unquestion-ingly, not realising that they had automatically given me the response they thought I wanted. I am still blushing at the naivety of my questioning. Now I would ask several more probing, open-ended questions which would be more likely to build up a picture of the role of trust in the workplace.

Other research subjects appear to hope that their answers will make them look more impressive than they actually are by exaggerating their role in situations or their position in their organisation's hierarchy. The latter is exacerbated if people see themselves as representatives of their organisation and so give corporate answers (Watson, 2011). Participants appear to be 'puffing themselves up'; they seem to grow in size, their chest is often thrust out and their gestures become more expansive. Now I always emphasise that I am interested in the individual's opinion, rather than the official company line, which I can obtain from its annual report. I also use my first name – certainly not my title (Doctor)! – and try to put her/him at ease and to make the situation uncompetitive and non-threatening. I adopt a relaxed approach with straightforward language and welcoming gestures, such as smiling and nodding while the participant is speaking.

Sometimes research subjects seem to want to finish an interview as quickly as possible and so give monosyllabic responses which do not invite further exploration of the topic. They also look at the clock and may even be reluctant to take their coat off or to sit comfortably. I was surprised the first time this happened because I try to conduct interviews at a time of the interviewee's choosing and I make it clear how long the interview will last – and ensure that the time isn't exceeded. However, when I looked at this objectively, I realised that the interview had been arranged several weeks beforehand and that it was taking place in what was now a very busy time for the interviewee. Consequently, however interesting I thought my questions were, all this person could think about was how soon he could get back to his day job. I now rarely arrange interviews more than a couple of weeks ahead and always check before the interview begins that the time is still convenient – potentially this saves both of us time and effort.

WHY DON'T I HEAR THE TRUTH?

With experience (and maturity) I have realised that research subjects aren't always responsible for (apparent) lack of truth in their responses: *I* may be at fault . . .

Although I try very hard to be a neutral researcher, I am aware that my personal biases, preconceived ideas, experiences and relationship to the research and with participants will inevitably colour my memory and interpretation of our conversations. Therefore, provided interviewees agree, I always record interviews to avoid poor recall and inaccurate/ biased memories.

Sometimes I realise – typically when transcribing a recorded interview so it is too late to do anything – that I have not grasped what an interviewee is trying to tell me and so I have not explored a potentially important area. This may be because the participant used technical language and/or acronyms and abbreviations that I didn't understand, perhaps deliberately to try and impress me with her/his expertise. Again, the tape has helped me recall 'puffed up' body language with the interviewee probably speaking quickly, to deter interruptions. I used to be too frightened to interrupt when this happened – I didn't want to look silly – so I didn't seek clarification and consequently my data was of less use than it could have been.

Occasionally, again as interview recordings show, some interviewees appeared to have perceived that I was not understanding, even if I hadn't realised this myself, and consequently they have dumbed down their answers so that the interviews have been less useful than they might have been.

Nowadays I try to admit how little I know and ask for explanations. Although this usually gives me more useful information, a couple of interviewees have become impatient at, for example, my inability to grasp what they see as simple concepts and the interview has effectively ended. In both instances, I appreciate that I should have been sensitive to the interviewee's mood, but I'm uncertain of how I could have gained value from an interview where I understood very little of what was being said (even when I listened to the recording several times).

Just as demands on interviewees' time can change between planning the interview and it taking place, sometimes I have been pressed for time or preoccupied by other matters when conducting interviews and so have failed to take opportunities to clarify what interviewees are trying to tell me. This has been painfully obvious when listening to the recording of such interviews. Now I would ask the interviewee whether we could rearrange the interview at a mutually acceptable time.

However, these were not the only problems encountered during my PhD research . . .

WHAT HAPPENED IN MY PHD RESEARCH

By the time I started my PhD research I knew, at least in principle, much of what I have already discussed concerning potential lack of truth in research participants' responses and so I decided to undertake ethnographic research which would include observations, interviews, both semi-structured and informal ones, and photographs. I felt that this would give me a better opportunity to find out about e-learning in Small and Medium Enterprises (SMEs) than visiting organisations occasionally to conduct interviews or sending questionnaires to participants.

In exchange for researching within an organisation, I offered to work there unpaid. As an SME owner-manager with considerable business experience in areas such as project management, general management, IT and finance, I thought this would be an attractive proposition. It would also be very advantageous for me; I felt that by working in an organisation alongside its employees, I would be able to see and hear what was actually happening, as opposed to what people chose to tell me, so that I could then explore specific issues further through interviews. I thought that this would help me discover the truth – even possibly revealing instinctive behaviours of which the participants themselves were unaware!

I was confident that I knew many of the problems I was likely to encounter and how to deal with them. However, I was not prepared for the extent to which research participants, potential and actual, would give me misleading and exaggerated or understated responses. Although these distortions of the truth were seldom deliberate, they led me down many blind alleys and ultimately changed my intended research substantially.

DESPERATELY SEEKING RESEARCH SITES

I wanted to undertake my ethnographic research in three SMEs which employed at least ten people who undertook some e-learning. I expected to work in each place for about three months, which I hoped would be long enough for the research participants and me to get to know each other so that they would be more likely to be honest with me than they might have been with an interviewer they met only fleetingly.

Although I expected that finding suitable research organisations would need time, hard work, much planning and some luck, I was surprised that it took more than eighteen months. Initially I allowed self-selection by making friends, colleagues and acquaintances aware of my quest, interrogating an online business directory and undertaking extensive networking, both online (LinkedIn and Twitter) and face-to-face, including business networking breakfasts, meetings and exhibitions. Some organisations appeared suspicious of my offer to work unpaid or were reluctant to give a stranger access to their inner workings. Apart from these few exceptions, there was much enthusiasm for my unpaid labour.

Some responses ignored my requisite organisational size; one-(wo)man-bands blithely glossed over having no employees, which I only discovered after concentrated probing. People from other – larger – concerns, seemingly keen to benefit from my unpaid work, actually lied about the size of their organisation, later justifying this by saying something like 'We function like an SME'. In retrospect, I remember that few of them would meet my eye, some fiddled nervously with their tea-cup/pen and most of them spoke very quickly, talking over my questions.

However, the biggest 'untruths' concerned use of e-learning, perhaps through genuine ignorance /confusion about what I meant by e-learning. Although I read my e-learning definition to participants, my assumption that we were 'singing from the same hymn sheet' was mistaken. Contrary to what I thought, we weren't: as I eventually realised, we each had a different understanding of the term. This was more difficult to detect than other 'untruths', perhaps because these were genuinely held opinions; participants were using their own understanding of e-learning, with both of us unaware of the chasm between our definitions.

I realised – in retrospect – that many people thought that e-learning referred to formal learning methods, typically online courses, which few had experienced or indeed which few organisations could afford. They ignored my definition's inclusion of informal methods such as use of social media and forums.

Consequently, in my initial discussions with gatekeepers, many SMEs who were using informal e-learning excluded themselves from my study and I missed the opportunity to research in some potentially relevant organisations. Longer, more probing conversations might have rectified this, although discussions at networking meetings are, through necessity, constrained by time and fairly superficial. Although it took me a while to realise the gulf between our definitions, it was better late than never. Had I continued with this fundamental misunderstanding, it may have invalidated my research. From then on, I discussed the term 'e-learning' more fully with my research participants; I no longer assumed any common understanding of it and it became the crux of our conversations and interviews.

IS IT TRUE . . . ?

More worrying were the people who seemed deliberately to mislead me regarding their organisation's suitability in the hope that, by investigating e-learning within it, I would actually introduce and implement such learning. This level of deception was very difficult to ascertain in initial conversations as some people spoke very plausibly about the e-learning which occurred in their SME; indeed, I nearly selected one such organisation as a research site!

The CEO of this organisation convinced me that the company was an ideal research site, speaking with authority, giving me little opportunity to ask questions and, when I did, sweeping on, ignoring my question. Needless to say, I wanted to see how this 'ideal organisation' functioned. My visit started badly when I discovered that the address they used was for mail only; the work happened, not in the impressive historic building at which I arrived, but in a tatty, temporary-looking 'hut' around the corner. My suspicions increased as I saw piles of paper on every desk and available surface (even the floor!), but little computer equipment. Seemingly oblivious to the incongruity of this, the CEO ushered me into a meeting room, introduced me to the Managing Director and proceeded to talk enthusiastically and assertively about their huge e-learning opportunities, which included selling it to organisations and running courses for a local college. He brushed aside all my questions; he was a very large man and literally waved his arms as if to push my questions away and he acted as if my questions were not worthy of his time – I would see how it worked when I joined them for my research.

It was so surreal that when I emerged into the fresh air – I had felt stifled throughout the meeting – I could hardly believe it had happened. Had they really expected me to introduce e-learning to their organisation and to spearhead its move into selling e-learning, with complete disregard for the fact that this would afford me no opportunities to undertake my planned research activities? Apparently so: I moved on . . .

Whenever a suitable organisation was suggested, I telephoned the gatekeeper, typically the Managing Director or a senior manager. During this conversation I checked the organisation's suitability by ascertaining its size and turnover/balance sheet total, and questioning the amount of e-learning undertaken. This removed several businesses from my rapidly diminishing shortlist.

Next I arranged face-to-face meetings at seemingly suitable organisations which allowed me to ask more probing questions to give me a more holistic view of the company, particularly regarding e-learning. I also tried to meet as many employees as I could and to see them working (Savin-Baden and Major, 2013). This left me with three seemingly suitable SMEs so my research could begin. However, more 'untruths' emerged during the research itself . . .

'THEY TOLD YOU WHAT?!'

Management at my first research site ('MakingCo') had said that staff undertook some e-learning and that this should grow, so I was surprised when initial conversations with employees suggested that little, if any, occurred. This became more confusing when I saw them using lots of informal e-learning, such as watching YouTube videos and using online help facilities.

Further discussions with managers clarified that *their* concept of e-learning only considered formal online courses. However, informal conversations and semi-structured interviews with workers revealed that none of *them* undertook any online courses and they were surprised that management thought they did. Furthermore, many of them hadn't considered that e-learning could include some of the very informal methods they used, which they thought didn't seem like 'real learning', and so they had told me that they did very little e-learning. They were too busy to read the two-page explanation of my research and it became obvious that they hadn't listened to my brief explanation of the research, much less to my definition of e-learning.

MakingCo's employees were so busy that they could pay limited attention to me; they all seemed totally consumed by their jobs. When they could spare me time, I needed to use terms they could relate to, while trying to check their understanding of the term 'e-learning'.

However, on reflection – and listening to interview recordings – it is clear that, although participants and I were confident that we were talking the same language, we definitely were not. Despite my having several conversations with MakingCo management before starting there, assertions about e-learning usage were based on misunderstandings and miscommunications between management and workers. Although I had chosen MakingCo as a research site because of inaccurate information, my research there was useful as it alerted me to potential gulfs of understanding about e-learning, both between me and the research participants and between management and workers.

Armed with everything I had learned at MakingCo, I was confident that my time at the next SME, 'LearningCo', would be even more useful. I had been particularly impressed by its Managing Director's claim that all employees had access to extensive e-learning: LearningCo seemed to use lots of e-learning.

LearningCo's online learning system appeared to be very comprehensive so I was surprised to see few employees using it. One claimed that it took too long to find information so she used Google instead, while another appeared to have no idea how to use the system. The Managing Director assured me that she regularly accessed it to brush up on particular subjects before visiting clients and also said that several clients had chosen LearningCo specifically because of its e-learning system.

Part of my work involved ascertaining how many people in each client company used the e-learning system so I was astonished to discover that not only did few customers use it, but that no-one at LearningCo had accessed it for at least six months. Again my choice of research organisation seemed to be based on an untruth or, at best, a misconception. However, discovering why LearningCo employees didn't use their own e-learning system ('too time-consuming'; 'too complicated'; 'not user-friendly') added an interesting dimension to my research. Also observing them using simple, free, informal e-learning methods/media instead was invaluable. Nevertheless I continued to question whether I could have chosen my research sites more carefully.

Having learned so much about how to deal with 'untruths' at MakingCo and LearningCo, I was confident all would go smoothly at HelpingCo, my third SME. I had already met the CEO and the manager for whom I would be working and it appeared to be an ideal research site. Employees' use of LearningCo's e-learning system was apparently so successful that it was being sold across its industry and I was promised access not only to employees who used it, but also to customers.

I put into practice everything I had learned at MakingCo and LearningCo. For example, I discussed the concept of e-learning I was using for my research at length with all research participants. Again I found disparities between the e-learning that management told me employees undertook and what employees did. It was immediately evident that HelpingCo employees did not like using the in-house e-learning system; they appeared to use it only to the extent necessary to successfully 'pass' their annual performance review. The rest of the time they used a wide array of e-learning, ranging from Wikipedia to technical forums.

It was becoming increasingly obvious that I should change the title of my PhD. Originally I had planned to explore the role of trust in e-learning in SMEs, but it had become more and more evident during my research that, although this was an interesting area which had not yet been explored, there was a more fundamental yawning gap in research, namely: how is e-learning understood and undertaken in SMEs? This new thesis title sat more comfortably with the realisation that most people were not deliberately lying to me; we each had a different understanding of e-learning.

HelpingCo was the only research site where I felt I had been deliberately misled. It became apparent during my time there that the manager, who had assured me that I would be able to discuss usage of HelpingCo's e-learning system with customers, was deliberately obstructing any possibilities for this. For example, dates and times of visits to clients were changed at short notice to occasions when I had other commitments. I am still uncertain whether this was to ensure that I was not distracted from the substantial amount of work allocated to me or for some other reason.

WHAT DID IT ALL MEAN?

Looking back at this research experience, I wonder whether I was unlucky or gullible. On balance, I think it may have been a mixture of both, but I am certain that such situations are not uncommon in research. I learnt so much during my ethnographic research; I gathered huge amounts of useful data, but I also picked up valuable experience in how to deal with seemingly less-than-truthful research participants. I now observe body language much more carefully to try and gauge how truthful someone is being; for example, people who avoid my eye, mumble, fidget, play with jewellery/gadgets or talk over my questions, are seldom telling the truth, or at least not answering everything I'm asking about. I have also learnt that it is not the end of the world if I have believed an 'untruth', provided I recognise it at some point; indeed, it can add interesting additional dimensions to my research findings, perhaps even changing the focus of my research.

Below I have summarised some lessons I've learnt about keeping my research on track in the face of misunderstandings, exaggerations, understatements, omissions, 'untruths' and downright lies.

LESSONS FOR KEEPING ON TRACK

1. Spend time understanding potential research sites before committing to collecting data there, recognising that they may not be what they seem.
2. Look for hidden agendas in both gatekeepers and participants.
3. Ensure common understandings of the research focus and terms – and of each side's expectations; for example, ask for the same information in different ways and compare results.
4. Observe body language carefully.
5. Expect the unexpected – keep calm, remain positive and you will probably still obtain useful data (even if it is not what you were originally looking for).
6. Reflect on and review interviews/observations carefully, immediately after they have taken place.

REFERENCES

Savin-Baden, M. and C.H. Major (2013), *Qualitative Research: The Essential Guide to Theory and Practice*, London: Routledge.

Watson, T.J. (2011), 'Ethnography, reality and truth: the vital need for studies of "how things work" in organisations and management', *Journal of Management Studies*, **48**(1), 202–17.

Yin, R.K. (2014), *Case Study Research: Design and Methods*, 5th edn, London: Sage.

11. Rolling with the punches

Sharyn Rundle-Thiele, Julia Carins and Christiane Stock

Much of our professional practice is underpinned by the cycle of planning. Most research projects require a plan to be set during the funding application process, which establishes expectations for colleagues working on the project that reports on milestones and deliverables at particular stages are clearly communicated to all research stakeholders. We all know that planning has many benefits. The process of planning helps us to set objectives, which for many of us increases the likelihood that things will be completed, making a final outcome (a published paper, a presentation, thesis or report) more likely. Another key benefit delivered by the process of planning is that it compels us to set a course of action to achieve the objectives that we set. Ideally, from time to time during the process, we should make sure that we are on track to deliver.

In academia we are encouraged to network, which allows us to share our knowledge and learn the languages needed to clearly communicate our work to others. Universities across the globe encourage partnerships with other universities, industry, the non-profit sector and the governments who fund our work. To deliver the large-scale and long-term projects needed to deliver cutting-edge science, researchers work within the networks that they have established. To deliver the largest projects we must form and maintain working relationships with other academics and practitioners. In this way we can deliver results in a way that provides cutting-edge science while meeting the needs of project stakeholders. For example, the research work that we do can help our research partners to solve a problem, improve their processes, or through discovery can uncover new technologies and ways of practising.

As a Masters or PhD student, an early- or mid-career researcher, or even an established or senior researcher, the start of a research project generally involves the creation of a supervisory or advisory team. The rationale for creating an advisory team for a research project is to have support to progress and complete the research agenda delivering a contribution that advances knowledge in your field of science. When the particular research project forms the basis of your PhD candidature, or when you are an early- or mid-career researcher working within a team for the first time, you will be confronted with some challenges. Your performance within the team will be carefully considered by your senior colleagues and your work will be evaluated and judged. Your performance will be directly compared to the performance of your peers, which naturally creates competition. If you can perform as a valued member of a team, it is likely you will be retained within the team beyond that project, or recommended to colleagues in your advisory team's networks. If your performance exceeds your peer(s), your ongoing employment prospects are further enhanced. At a team level a reputation for delivering on time, every time, and within budget, will ensure that you are competitively placed to win future projects, which also helps to build research capacity at the organisational level by creating jobs and keeping junior members of the team employed.

Regardless of your role in the research project – as a project leader, senior team member, junior team member, assistant or research student – working within a network to deliver your project on time, and for some within budget, is a challenge given that your project is reliant on others. You need to learn to work effectively with others and create a network that helps you all to deliver more – synergistically, and in a way that strengthens the efforts of each member – without being seduced into trying to win at all costs.

So what happens when plans fail? We all know that the very best plans can and do fail, and this is why we wanted to share our stories with you. If you are a high achieving individual (if you are reading this, it is likely that you are) you are used to being in control and are probably very capable of delivering on time all of the time (or at least most of the time). By sharing our stories with you we want to help you to understand that it is really important to learn to roll with the punches. If you can overcome the obstacles blocking your path with a smile and positive attitude, you will be viewed more positively than colleagues whose behaviours are negative and counterproductive. There is no point yelling at people, having a tantrum and engaging in any form of negative behaviour. Simply approach your project *as though things will go wrong*. Being prepared for this possibility makes you better equipped if things do go wrong. This means that you need to plan extra time or larger research designs for the things you can't see, don't yet know and for the others you are working with (bearing in mind the composition of the team may well change by the end of a multi-year project). The contingency of extra time will ease the pressure when something inevitably goes wrong.

STEPPING OUT OF A CONTROLLED ENVIRONMENT INTO THE FIELD: DEALING WITH UNPREDICTABILITY

Field research provides a number of opportunities to gain valuable insights into phenomena of interest, or to empirically determine whether any strategies devised through research can be successfully transitioned into practice. For these reasons we consider that research conducted 'at the coal face' as an indispensable part of the research process – the litmus test of whether a theorised occurrence plays out as intended, or whether a recommendation results in the intended benefit. Whether you are a novice or an experienced researcher, conducting field research, or collecting data beyond the laboratory or controlled environment, can evoke feelings of both excitement and terror.

Field research can be incredibly motivating and inspiring, providing the opportunity to observe complex behaviours playing out in dynamic environments in order to advance our understanding. At the same time field research can also scare the hell out of us. We often head out into the field with fears both imagined and real. The real fears come from the experience or awareness of what has gone wrong in earlier field trips, while the irrational fears can be even more daunting. Consider some of the many things that can and do go wrong – a flat battery in a research device, forgetting to hit 'record' on an audio recorder, server breakdowns, power outages – right through to an aberration in the space–time continuum which produces a weird alternative universe, and in turn produces data that is meaningless or completely contradicts everything that is already known in the field (we did say irrational!).

Julia Carins's research adopts a social marketing lens to understand eating behaviour. The aim of her PhD research was to devise strategies that result in healthier eating practices in order to increase health, performance and well-being, within a workplace setting. Her work was sponsored directly by her employer, and was client-partnered research. Over the course of her PhD, Julia applied a mixed method approach to capture what individuals choose to eat, and to understand what influences people to make those choices, whether they be individually motivated or driven by the surrounding environment.

One of the methods that Julia employed in her mixed method study was observations. Observations provide the opportunity to objectively capture what individuals do rather than relying on self-reports of their actions, which are subject to both memory and social desirability biases. Julia's work has used both manual observations (structured observations with accompanying field notes) as well as photographic techniques. Using a structured observational technique requires preparation to ensure that the aspects of the behaviour of interest can be observed and quantified in a reliable and meaningful manner. This involves starting with sessions in the chosen context, to understand what elements are important and relevant, as well as what feasibly can be captured in the data collection instrument (structured observation sheet). These early sessions provided Julia with practice, allowing her to get a sense of what was occurring, to determine where the best vantage points were, how fast the 'action' was, what discrete actions should be recorded . . . and so on. In many ways, Julia used these early sessions to troubleshoot, and to feel confident that once she started the structured observations sessions, nothing could possibly go wrong . . .

Until it did.

Julia's PhD project involved observing diners making food selection choices in a workplace buffet-style cafeteria. She planned to use photographic techniques to capture individual food choices, and then to pair these data with manual observation techniques to examine patterns within the dining room. The photographic technique essentially meant approaching diners at the point where they finish making choices from the buffet counters, and asking to photograph their plate of food. Equipped with the caterer's menu and some leading nutritional analysis software, the photographs would provide a dataset for later examination, allowing Julia to quantify the types of foods being chosen on an individual basis; she could then determine the healthfulness of the choices made at lunch and dinner. Of course as this was a busy cafeteria, she was not able to photograph the plates of every diner, so this set of photographs would provide information about the food choices of a subset of diners at each meal. The manual observation involved a team of observers stationed at various points in the dining room (near each of the buffet counters) to record each time a diner made a selection from the dishes available. This provided a dataset of all of the selections being made in the dining room – 100 per cent coverage – but at a dish level rather than an individual level. This allowed Julia to correlate the two datasets – to ensure patterns observed in the smaller photographic subset were representative of the patterns in the cafeteria as a whole, and also to examine 'popularity' of particular dish types.

Preparation for data collection progressed according to plan; Julia had visited the cafeteria a number of times to see the 'lay of the land'. She had noted the fast paced, but predictable traffic flow – where people enter, how they progress past the counters, where they exit the food area to find a seat to consume the meal. She had noted approximately how many diners attended for lunch and dinner, and started to map in her head where observers would need to stand to record data. It was quite a large space, only ever about half full, and there were spare food counters that the caterers said they only used when they had extra groups in for training. An observation template was prepared to structure observations of food selections, and a team of observers organised to observe four meals (two lunches and two dinners on different days) to test the data collection methods devised for the project. This test aimed to make sure that it was possible to record everything needed to capture data for the project. Everything ran smoothly. Julia followed this dataset through to analysis to ensure that the data collection and analytical approach was sound, and that it actually produced the kind of insights she expected. It did! She believed the data collection approach was ready to be used during field experiments, to measure the effect of the healthy eating strategies she and the research team had planned to deploy in this setting.

Julia planned her data collection days, taking care to avoid training weeks, and started pre-measures ahead of strategy implementation. The first meal observed by Julia and the team ran like clockwork. Just like during the other meals they had observed during preparation, the first ten minutes were the busiest, as those who had been waiting in a queue filed through. The rest of the meal was a steady stream of diners. It was the second meal where things started to unravel. The busy rush persisted during this particular evening meal; diners were almost running into each other . . . serving themselves as if at a table of discount kitchen utensils during a Boxing Day sale – tongs and spoons going everywhere! Fortunately Julia's data collectors were well caffeinated, and with some very intense focus were still able to capture the selections. Until – unannounced – the caterers opened a second serving point. It took Julia a few minutes to notice, as she was busy photographing plates (what the . . . ?!). Half of the queue migrated to the new servery, but there were no spare observers to cover the new servery! Julia and her team were no longer able to monitor the entire dining room, meaning that the dataset would no longer be complete. This also had implications for her photographic dataset, as she could no longer compare the two to give the required confidence that the subset was representative of the larger dataset. Julia finished observation of the meal with a sense of dread that the entire session had been a waste.

The most predictable thing about field work is that it is totally unpredictable. Things change very quickly, and even with a carefully prepared and pre-tested data collection strategy you can be caught off guard. Although Julia had liaised with the caterers beforehand and they understood what she was trying to achieve, they were focused on delivering a good service, and research requirements were possibly the last thing on their minds during the meal itself. Julia was fortunate: she had planned to collect data from a number of observation sessions, so she could afford to ditch one incomplete dataset. Our institute was also able to bring another research assistant on board for future sessions in case it happened again (it didn't).

TAKING THE GOOD WITH THE BAD: NAVIGATING AND NEGOTIATING WITH CLIENTS AND PARTNERS

Imagine this scenario. You have been working together for months. Over the months, you have agreed on a research plan, and designed and executed your first study in this new partnership. During the project you have collected and analysed data to meet the research objectives set for the project. All of this work has been compiled into a report which is tabled to the research partner and your next course of action becomes apparent. By successfully delivering the first agreed project on time and within budget the people you work with in your partner organisation are highly supportive of your work and they would like to progress to a new phase of work. They are so happy with your work they have now introduced you to colleagues and your reach within the organisation has grown. This is evidence that your work practice is sound, and that you have delivered scientific and rigorous research while also being able to meet your project partners' goals. The future is looking rosy. Work commences on the next project phase and everyone is really looking forward to seeing the outcome with some testing in the field locked in.

And then it all goes wrong.

The Director doesn't approve the field work plan, the research partner won't allow you to publish the findings due to reputational concerns, or the project is put on hold due to extenuating circumstances. These are all examples that we have been faced with and on far more occasions than you would imagine.

The largest projects are funded by one or more organisations, and in these large projects work is delivered in collaboration with academic colleagues within your own university, across universities, and by practitioners or specialists in partner organisations. Working in funded projects with research partner organisations definitely has its benefits, which include (but are not limited to) access to respondents, data, and the financial and human resourcing to deliver work at a level you just simply can't achieve on your own. Perhaps most importantly in our line of work, which is social marketing and public health, the opportunity to deliver funded projects allows us to be personally involved in the delivery of behavioural change. While testing messaging we can simultaneously be changing attitudes (e.g. towards violence); while conducting research we can be raising awareness for very important causes (e.g. organ donation); and importantly, when we are testing programs and interventions in the field we can also be delivering behavioural change (e.g. increases in healthy eating or decreases in alcohol drinking). Working in the field, in partnership, allows first-hand experience of the impact of the research work that you are undertaking, which is motivating, helping you to stay focused on your research goals. Large funded projects delivered in partnership with organisations and collaborating academics offer many benefits, but there can be downsides: goals can differ, and some people simply don't deliver on their promises. Together, these can create a host of unforeseeable problems.

Quite often we are asked for advice on how to navigate this highly competitive world we work in. Our advice is simple. Try to network and through your networks build a team of people that you can trust to reliably deliver on time, every time. Don't be seduced by a big name in the field, instead take your time and understand their work practice. You want to know you are about to work with someone who will give as much as they get from you in return, ensuring that you both benefit from working together over time. We recommend you start with a small, tightly defined piece of work to see if working together is mutually beneficial and that you increase project size and scope as you gain confidence that you have found a mutually beneficial working relationship. That early test can save a lot of long-term pain by revealing the people that work well with and for you, and giving you the opportunity to say 'thanks, but no thanks' to future projects with those people with whom it didn't work so well.

When it comes to working in large teams there are ways to avoid problems over the course of the project. For example, on project commencement we recommend, as a team, you develop a clear plan to guide the programme of work, assigning defined tasks to team members to meet project milestones. You should also think about publications that will eventually arise from the project. Once again, within large projects we recommend you develop a publication plan with the team on project commencement, assigning authorship and responsibilities for the publications that are expected to arise from the project. Make sure you are familiar with rules governing authorship and intellectual property rights and, when you are in doubt, seek advice. Too often we see senior academics claiming authorship on papers citing old rules of thumb which have been passed down over academic generations. When negotiating authorship and developing publication plans, be clear about the activities constituting authorship for each individual piece of work. To be an author on a paper clear evidence needs to be demonstrated on one or more of planning the research design; undertaking data analysis and interpretation; and drafting or critiquing the manuscript so as to make a substantial contribution to that piece. Too often, academics claim involvement when no evidence of contribution exists. Establishing expectations from the outset and carefully managing progress during the course of the project can help to keep teams working functionally, which is better for everyone in the long run.

Establishing plans is always recommended, because collaboration within larger teams or partnerships has many benefits, including scientific gains (e.g. through the acquisition of larger datasets, acquisition and development of new knowledge) and the ability to develop synergies allowing more work to be delivered. Working in partnership is indeed required in the cases of grant applications to major funding bodies, but it is important to acknowledge that the best plans can and will fail. Extenuating circumstances will arise outside of the project that can have an impact, and it is in the face of the biggest challenges that clear communication, and your own willingness to compromise, is needed. Projects can be derailed within a funding organisation for reasons beyond the control of the direct project team you are working with (e.g. change of government with a new government no longer backing the project). It is at these most challenging times that your response matters the most. While getting the original short-term outcome may seem to be the most important, we know that an ability to be flexible and find 'work arounds' could offer a much greater gain in the longer term. When the worst happens to you, our advice is: do not pick up the phone, type an email or speak until at least 24–48 hours after notification. It is important you give yourself the time needed to rationally (and not emotionally) think of solutions to overcome the challenge that has emerged.

BE PREPARED AND BE FLEXIBLE: WHAT DOESN'T KILL YOU MAKES YOU STRONGER!

Research is a wonderful life. There are few jobs that provide the flexibility and freedom to pursue a topic that you are passionate about. Any project that you are responsible for (especially your PhD project as your first independent research endeavour) requires you to apply project management skills to deliver the project on time and within budget. Those who are attracted to research as a career understand it is a very competitive landscape. From Day One you are competing with your PhD peers or with other more senior research staff. We are all different, and it is important that you stay true to yourself. To navigate the complex social setting that is research, you need to consider carefully what is important to you, knowing that each and every decision that you take can and will have repercussions. We urge you to roll with the punches, knowing this is not easy at all. If you love research as much as we do, you are here for the long term. You have one reputation and what you do and say will be judged, remembered and, unfortunately, in some cases it may be held against you.

So do all the things we do: be prepared, be flexible where you can, and then expect the unexpected. Working outside a controlled environment is exactly that: uncontrolled. But it is real, and it is exactly where you want to apply (at least some of) your research skills – to demonstrate that your research delivers an impact in a dynamic world.

We recommend that you build research partnerships, and think long term. The best research comes from a body of work undertaken over time and this can only occur if you can establish strong, long-lasting relationships where the people you choose to work with deliver work for you as much as you deliver work for them. Do your homework and seek people who deliver work for you – preferably on time, every time. There is certainly no formula to guide you clearly. Don't be fooled by gossip and other people's opinions. We encourage you to interview the people who have worked with someone you think you want to work with. Learn from their experience. It is always important to know their experience won't be yours but the same feedback from many people is a clear warning sign: while a person may seem to be someone you want to work with based on the public profile that you can see, their work practices may be highly questionable and not in your personal development interests. We are all different and this means that a person you work well with may not work well with another person that you work with. We advise you to search for people with a mixture of academic and personal qualities that match (or complement) your own qualities. Search for those who work similarly to you, where you each provide strong skills in areas where the other may not be as strong, and even seek out those who challenge or inspire you. And if you happen to be working with others not of your choosing – look for these things in those people. By finding such people (or those qualities within people) you will unfold your full potential.

LESSONS FOR ROLLING WITH THE PUNCHES

- Always be one step ahead: don't plan to fail, but recognise that it will happen, and plan to be able to respond or make changes if it does.
- Outline and communicate (or be aware of) the responsibilities each person has within a project: this can help keep the team on track and save unnecessary conflicts arising.
- When calamity strikes, don't act immediately: give yourself time to take a step back and consider the entire situation – to see the full

picture and to think rationally. You will win in the longer term by being kind and seeing it through someone else's eyes.

- Stay positive and smile: people are in this game for a long time and once burnt, some bridges can't be rebuilt.
- Know that what happened was meant to be: today's obstacle may be tomorrow's blessing, and even if it isn't, you will be better equipped to avoid that obstacle next time.
- Try before you buy: start building your networks by testing people out on small projects; keep the winners and politely ditch the others.
- Remember there is no 'I' in team: large projects require many people and team players will be stronger academics in the long run.
- Find the people who work for you and with you; not only will you create a smoother ride, but synergies that benefit all.
- Recognise that support goes both ways and all ways, from the mentor to the mentee, from the assistant to the leader, and between peers within projects and across networks. Give as much as you get.
- Know the rules of the game – and play within the rules of the game. Also know that the rules change over time. Just because it once was, doesn't mean it always should be. This applies to publishing, IP (intellectual property), research agreements, roles and responsibilities.
- Finally, take a moment once in a while to reflect on the path you have chosen. Following your passion for research can be very rewarding – even when things do go wrong!

12. Access, involvement and interference: encounters and experiences of case studies

Kenneth Cafferkey

While it is easy to acknowledge that researchers are infinitely more interested in and excited by empirical work than the research subjects themselves, this usually masks a sense of being stuck between a rock and a hard place on behalf of the researcher. Unfortunately there has always being an empirical gulf between what researchers would like to do and what they are permitted to do in terms of access. Having a well-crafted research question is simply not enough; having the right access for the right question has become equally important.

Research access is a complicated part of our business. Just ask any PhD or Masters student what they are researching and you are more likely to get the name of a company than a research question. The 'who' of research is increasingly becoming as important as the 'what' of research. Anyone who has endeavoured to gather original data understands that access to case organisations or subjects to research is a game of trade-offs, compromises and sacrifices (Leonard-Barton, 1990). Getting in, staying in, and getting out with something valuable is akin to walking a tightrope. No longer can academic research be seen as a novelty from an organisational perspective; it would potentially be more realistic to view it as a hindrance due to the deluge of research requests contemporary organisations receive.

With ever-increasing numbers taking up Masters and PhD programmes, alongside the changing pressure within the academic landscape to produce, it is easy to see why organisations are under heavy bombardment in terms of access requests (Flyvbjerg, 2006). The tide has well and truly turned and a power shift is clearly evident: while a generic, almost sterile report on the overall findings was once considered the acceptable acknowledgement for access, this is no longer the case. Organisations are increasingly aware of the costs (their costs) of allowing research participation and are increasingly looking for something more tangible and useable from the research. To illustrate this point I draw on a conversation with an HR director of a multinational company. The plan was an entire workplace survey of almost 1000 people. I arrived at our meeting armed with the research instrument, pleasantries were exchanged, and the HR director asked, 'How much will this all cost?' I replied, 'Nothing, I will incur all the costs.' I was then asked how long the research would take per person to fill in the survey, to which I responded, 'Circa 15 minutes.' The HR director then proceeded to explain that it cost on average around $40 per hour per employee and that if I wanted to survey approximately 1000 employees that would cost the organisation $10 000 in wages alone, not to mention the lost revenue as a result of loss of production. I was speechless and left that meeting under no illusion that access is not only a complicated part of our business, but it is 'big business'. What is more, the HR director politely and generously informed me that sponsoring the local tiddlywinks' team for $10 000 would generate more goodwill in public relations terms and was infinitely less risky than allowing the research.

While access can be viewed almost as the Holy Grail in the research process, the reality is that it is not as simple as first assumed. Organisations increasingly want something tangible for the time, effort and costs associated with granting research access. This is where academic credibility and organisational reality face off in what can be a very uncomfortable series of exchanges for the prospective researcher. Organisations don't really care for academic integrity, methodological requirements and absolute independence on the part of the researcher nor, to a certain extent, should they. Previously validated scales mean little or nothing to an organisation, psychological properties even less. From an organisational perspective if you want to know if someone is happy: 'Are you happy? Yes/ No' is probably the most legitimate way of answering such a question. For researchers, however, it's understandably a little more complicated. Organisations couldn't care less about desirability bias or leading questions and in all honesty you really can't blame them for that; where academics answer to anonymous reviewers, organisations answer to shareholders and stakeholders. It is a classic chalk and cheese relationship and here the story begins. While the case method is possibly the most exciting and rewarding form of research in the social sciences, it is none the less a very fine balancing act in which multiple considerations have to be taken into account simultaneously (Stake, 1995).

In this chapter I explore access, involvement and interference to illustrate five points that relate to my experiences with research projects.

1. issues of finding suitable research site/location to answer problems/ research questions posed;
2. negotiating access;

3. gaining respondent participation and involvement;
4. when involvement becomes interference;
5. readjusting research instruments while also keeping research criteria on track.

ISSUES OF FINDING SUITABLE RESEARCH SITE/ LOCATION TO ANSWER PROBLEMS/RESEARCH QUESTIONS POSED

As previously stated, research access is possibly the top concern of any prospective case researcher as, let's face it, sending out a largely anonymous postal survey to a few hundred managerial respondents is infinitely easier and less time consuming. However, finding the right research site to study a specific question is altogether a more difficult, if not daunting matter (Baxter and Jack, 2008). There almost always seems to be a divide over the right access versus the right opportunity (i.e. any access). While acknowledging the purposefulness of the trajectory from research question to method/ instruments to securing the right research subjects or case, in reality it is not as simple as that (Saunders et al., 2011). In an ideal world we would all study innovation at Apple, human resource management at Google, and marketing at Facebook. Unfortunately we don't live in such an ideal world and therefore academics essentially study what they can. Take, for example, an area of interest the author has in High Performance Work Systems (HPWS). One would assume that a prerequisite to researching HPWS would be that any participant organisation would be 'high performing' on some easily recognisable dimension, whereas in actual fact nothing could be further from the truth. It appears that academics essentially study whoever will grant them access, whether in terms of a cross-sectional multi-organisation survey or an in-depth case study, irrespective of suitability. As a case researcher one has to become accustomed to hearing the word 'No' or worse still, being completely ignored, so much so that any semblance of hope in access can be viewed as Nirvana.

The process of locating and cold-calling suitable case participants can be an arduous task; it's hard not to feel as if you are posting out something similar to the dreaded stationery catalogue we all receive every month in the mail. After repeated failure from the cold-calling method one cannot simply give up and abandon the case method, which would be the easy option. Some years ago I used a survey to find prospective case study participants. A cross-sectional, multi-industry study was used to find participants for case studies. The survey research consisted of creating an index of the 'best of the best', so to speak, and contacting the companies in question to inform them of their exemplary managerial success while simultaneously pitching the possibility of an in-depth follow-up to extol the virtues of their accomplishments. Surely this would work? Reporting high instances of relative success over competitors, hailing unparalleled levels of innovativeness, and acknowledging excellent strategy configurations would undoubtedly awaken the deepest sense of desire for acknowledgement from even the most stiff-upper-lipped of management. Well . . . kind of.

While flattery is always a useful starting point, in any event most of the organisations declined the opportunity. Flattery was naively viewed as the trump card whereby the managing director would run to the board with the acknowledgement of greatness and further avenues for the researcher to eulogise the inspirational company would undoubtedly be forthcoming. How wrong could I have been? After contacting the top ten companies, seven never even acknowledged receipt of the request, one respectfully declined, one agreed to meet and then declined, and one company after a mammoth series of negotiations finally agreed to participate. On reflection, those negotiations were possibly the most interesting aspect of the entire research – perhaps I should have kept a detailed research diary and tried to publish that experience in a methods journal! In any event a suitable case organisation for the research was sourced; in fact it was a perfect organisation to study on every parameter; however, the process of finding and securing access in that instance could have made for interesting research in and of itself. While extremely time consuming the process did have a few advantages. The survey gave a level of validity to the case selection, which in turn enhanced the credibility. While ultimately time consuming in the extreme, without going to such extremes a suitable company would have never been sourced. Would I recommend this approach? I would if you have the time and resources available after exhausting all other avenues.

Lessons Learned

On reflection, finding more common ground between the research question and the objectives of potential case organisations to research would possibly have proved more fruitful instead of merely looking for a host case organisation to conduct the research in. Again, this was possibly naivety on my part. From experiencing a series of failed research funding attempts this is now better understood; no matter how much the researcher believes they have an extremely interesting and well thought out proposal, it must serve some higher purpose. Unfortunately, interesting to the researcher may not be interesting enough! Alignment of interests is the best ploy, whether it is securing access to a case or acquiring research funding. This does not necessarily mean any compromise in the research or any bias of the results; it simply suggests a mutual gains approach whereby the researcher has to do extra or supplementary work that is outside the remit of the actual study for the organisation's or funding provider's benefit. Again, it's a balancing act.

NEGOTIATING ACCESS

As previously stated, negotiating access is an extremely delicate process (McDonald et al., 2009). There are two main approaches to finding a case organisation. The first is what I term the 'speed dating' method, whereby the prospective researcher sends out many requests for access and hopes to evoke a sense of interest from a prospective organisation. It's a one shot only method: the researcher has a single-page letter or phone call to stir enough interest or all is lost, similar to speed dating, whereby it all hinges on a three-minute impression. The problem with this method is that there are multiple researchers and limited case organisations, and how does one make a lasting impression? What do you talk about? What do you leave out? What commitment are you looking for? All the while trying not to come across as desperate. Unfortunately the success rate can be negligible, as it has been with my experiences of speed dating.

The second approach is the 'flirting' method, where you make eye contact, pay a compliment, ask a witty question, smile and hope to stir some level of interest. In research terms this approach is more strategic and can yield more success. The emphasis is on building rapport over a longer timeframe, establishing a sense of trust between the parties whereby mutual gains can result. In contrast to the speed dating method, the flirting approach allows the researcher preparation time and is also spanned out over a longer timeframe that allows the opportunity to build relationships. Within this method there is the opportunity to use multiple means to increase the credibility of both the research and the researcher. This leads to an interesting example of a previous case study.

Rapport with this company was already established, as a small project had been conducted there years before; however, a number of the core people had since moved on or retired. Nonetheless a letter of introduction was sent to the Managing Director and the Human Resources Director, from which a sterile and almost instant generic response emerged, declining participation. Completely dismayed with such a response there was a feeling that all was lost. Reminiscing about the excellent relationship that had been established with the previous managers and team leaders, surely that was worth something? Something drastic needed to be done so the research team proceeded to contact previous managers, some retired, some working for competitors, and asked if they would be prepared to give a 'nudge' to the present management to consider the research. Lo and behold, the previous managers agreed to assist and a letter was received from the company asking for a meeting to discuss access. A flat refusal was turned into an opportunity, and that was all that was needed.

The access negotiations began in earnest. Compromise, sacrifice and U-turns categorised the proceedings. Access negotiation is such a delicate process: the organisation can pull the plug at any time and the researcher is left with nothing. Both parties are all too aware of this power imbalance. The issue becomes one of preservation whereby maintaining at least some semblance of integrity over the initial research question becomes paramount while also making accommodations in the organisation's favour. This is an often overlooked aspect that few researchers tend to talk about; unfortunately in the 'real world' the integrity and credibility of the research in and of itself may not be enough to evoke the required interest from a case organisation. Balance becomes paramount; all too often an inexperienced researcher or research student goes into a negotiation meeting with a research question and comes out with a completely different one, such is the dominance the organisation has over proceedings. Again this is a topic that many are not too willing to talk about as perhaps they view it as a slight on their credibility. Knowing the line between efficacy and futility is a key consideration in this respect. In this instance, after an exhaustive process a balance was finally reached which consisted of addressing all of the initial research goals while also conducting supplementary research on behalf of the organisation. In reality it was about a 70–30 split (in my favour): time consuming, yes, but the research goals would be achieved.

Lessons Learned

There are a number of ways and means to gain research access: using personal contacts can assist greatly. Such is the problem with the flood of access requests that contemporary research takes on a 'needs must' approach. The caveat to remember is that it is not access at all costs, as sometimes those costs can be too great and the research suffers and, unbeknownst to the researcher, they have suddenly morphed into some sort of organisation consultant at the behest of management. Overall the key thing to remember is that flexibility is critical to ensure the negotiations are a success.

GAINING RESPONDENT PARTICIPATION AND INVOLVEMENT

Building a connection and getting interviewees and survey respondents to open up to organisational reality can be extremely difficult. We have all encountered a reluctant or downright uninterested interviewee and despite cajoling or encouragement they simply refuse to open up (Dundon and Ryan, 2010; see also Townsend, Chapter 16, this volume). The uninterested interviewee is perhaps a bridge that can never be crossed, and no common ground can be found, and it's important not to dwell on it. The reluctant interviewee is an altogether different issue, they toe the company line and never venture off script in almost a 'Big Brother is watching' sense. Thankfully most interviewees fall somewhere in between these two extremes. The same can be said for quantitative research in a case study, where some employees are all too aware that the employee attitude survey has a code number (overtly or covertly) and may answer with that in mind. Similarly reluctance can compromise research whereby a respondent almost uses a single continuous line to answer multiple Likert-style questions simultaneously, which leaves the researcher with an awkward moral dilemma.

Dilemmas can turn into absolute hazards when participation and involvement take a sinister twist, whereby the organisation or a particular manager 'plants' particular individuals in the research to ensure a particular predetermined outcome. Having encountered such incidents on a small number of occasions, this can really make the research futile in the extreme. In one instance a stratified sample of employees was requested for a particular focus group, which was to be determined by production requirements (a normal occurrence in case research in a manufacturing environment) (Kitzinger, 1994). What actually transpired was that a particular manager filled the focus group with his golfing buddies who were obviously prepped to portray the organisation, and the manager, in an overly positive light. It was only later that an employee exposed the situation and stated, 'They done you up like a kipper.' In another incident in a different organisation, a focus group on employee engagement from (supposedly) shop floor employees turned out to be a group on a graduate programme (a programme that was effectively a year-long job interview), who spoke as if their lives depended on projecting a positive light on the organisation. In this instance the research simply had to be aborted as it was futile because the organisation in question was merely using the research as some kind of public relations exercise. What this exposes is a situation in which participation perhaps needs to be better thought through, as in this instance research access was requested and negotiated with senior management. The vast majority of those involved as participants in the research did not have any say in these negotiations and, with that in mind, could one actively say that their participation was voluntary? This is a very muddy area in research; for example, take a hypothetical situation in which a middle manager meets the researcher and agrees to an interview and compare it with the same manager who receives an email from the HR Director or CEO directing them to participate. In both instances the starting point for participation is entirely different and therefore the potential for bias raises its head.

Lesson Learned

It is always best to check and double-check participants before and during interviews, ask for background information from HR etc. and confirm this in the interview and/or ask a third party to confirm who the participants are. It must be stated that suspicions were raised when at a managerial meeting it almost felt as if the answer was a starting point and the role of the researcher was to cheerlead all the way to the predetermined answer. Essentially the thing to understand is that people have different motives that can have a massive influence on what happens. The old adage applies: if it looks or sounds too good to be true, then it probably is.

WHEN INVOLVEMENT BECOMES INTERFERENCE

Projecting a positive slant can be a priority for an organisation; some-times, in extreme cases, the level of involvement can actually constitute interference. Similarly, certain topics can be off limits and the elephant may be in the room but we are not permitted to acknowledge its presence. This is extremely difficult as a researcher's natural instinct is not only to acknowledge the elephant, but also to question the elephant. Items such as industrial action, redundancies or scandals can be viewed as portraying an organisation in a less than favourable light and in a public relations sense organisations may not want these issues highlighted. However, sometimes what is off limits can extend beyond what is normally classified as front page news. There was one incident a number of years ago where despite agreeing to a Human Resources study, the HR manager wanted questions on work–life balance to be removed as the manager did not want to give the employees 'notions'. Maintaining the integrity of the research can be problematic in such instances. Interference can also take the form of the over-eager (or possibly sinister) manager who shadows the researcher. One's sense of awareness is always raised when a manager will not let the researcher out of their sight. Another occasion was when the researcher was briefed and debriefed before and after focus groups, which clearly showed a sense of paranoia of the manager in question who was anxious about what the employees were saying in a confidential interview. The same manager actually walked me into the office of each interviewee and then set about watering plants in an attempt to stay in the room, to the point at which it was bordering on comical in a Sir Humphrey, *Yes Minister*, fashion. In such instances there was a sense of wearing a cow bell, whereby everyone knows you are coming and acts accordingly. It actually turned out that the manager in question was paranoid and was of the opinion that the researcher was there to spy on *his* work. In the same organisation the simple act of requesting to sit in the staff room for no particular reason, bar interacting with employees, caused absolute consternation for the same manager.

Lessons Learned

What was learned in such instances was that the merits of what one is researching may not be the same as the reason why someone participates in the research. The researcher should always be cognisant of this fact. People naturally have their own agenda and generally will not do anything to compromise their own situation or reputation. It is when reservation turns to smoke and mirrors that issues can arise and the research can then become compromised.

READJUSTING RESEARCH INSTRUMENTS WHILE ALSO KEEPING RESEARCH CRITERIA ON TRACK

As previously stated, organisations usually have little regard for previously validated scales and possibly even less for reverse or negatively worded questions. It can become extremely problematic when management refuse to allow a reverse worded question in a survey, for example: 'I do not receive the necessary support to do my job properly.' In certain contexts, positivity takes priority over reality in terms of survey design and organisation, or at least some managers are more concerned about a sterile '85 per cent of our staff are happy', than about actually delving more deeply into reasoning and reality. This is not only confined to quantitative research; it also happens in qualitative research. In qualitative research, management too can veto certain questions; one instance highlighting this point is when a manager said, 'Don't ask that, we are not great at that, ask this . . . instead'. This bending approach happens frequently when signing off on qualitative research schedules. It becomes more serious in relation to tampering with previously validated survey questions.

Readjusting takes on a whole new meaning in certain contexts or high power distance cultures where everything is sanitised by the organisation, and above all else, management and leadership is required to be seen in a positive light, that is, 'our beloved leader' type research. In some senses it's almost as if everything ought to be seen through an organisational filter or lens, where academic research credibility is irrelevant and the researcher is almost viewed as a journalist with the sole purpose of 'happy clapping' or projecting the organisation or certain people in a positive light. In a qualitative sense, in certain cultures, interviews can become futile, and projecting oneself in a positive light in the hope that such information is then passed on to superiors can become commonplace.

Regardless of the adjustments required in some situations, it is always best to use multiple sources to answer a specific research question as this can sometimes provide interesting insights into what is actually happening. Drawing on one particular example, using a qualitative focus group to interpret results of a survey led to a realisation that the demarcations in the survey were seriously flawed and did not reflect organisational reality. Therefore what the survey addressed and what the participants interpreted were completely different. This meant having to change tack on the spot and returning to the research questions to find if there was any qualitative support for what the research was trying to achieve. In terms of keeping the research on track, such an approach led to completely different but more interesting findings. The actual findings and resultant conclusion to that particular research would have been completely different had only the quantitative approach been employed.

Lessons Learned

Readjusting instruments to reflect organisational reality or organisational pressure can be problematic on a number of levels. First, the integrity of the research can be compromised, and secondly the possibility of publishing the finished work can run into all sorts of difficulties. While organisations may care little for validation, journal editors certainly do. It is well worth the fight to retain as much previously validated work as possible as it is too easy to compromise in the heat of the moment in the quest for access. Sound reasoning at the start can alleviate many problems later on; unfortunately, most of us learn this the hard way. Overall in case research one has to balance a degree of rigidity with fluidity as situations change; too much of either can seriously compromise the research.

CONCLUSION

While case research can be very daunting and full of pitfalls it is also extremely rewarding in terms of the richness of what can be achieved. Case research is undoubtedly very time consuming and it takes a significant amount of practice to do it correctly; it is nonetheless possibly the most enjoyable form of social science research. Cross-sectional quantitative design prevails mainly because of its simplicity and convenience in what can now be termed a 'time to market' approach of academic research. Case research offers a counterbalance to the trend. As academic work becomes more and more publication and metric based, and where a race to empiricism by any means takes precedence above all else, the in-depth case study will become more elusive but will remain a thing of beauty that academic discourse craves. Once you walk the tightrope that is case study research you just want to do it over and over again, regardless of the dangers and pitfalls.

REFERENCES

Baxter, P. and Jack, S. (2008). 'Qualitative case study methodology: study design and implementation for novice researchers', *The Qualitative Report*, **13**(4), 544–59.

Dundon, T. and Ryan, P. (2010). 'Interviewing reluctant respondents: strikes, henchmen, and Gaelic games', *Organizational Research Methods*, **13**(3), 562–81.

Flyvbjerg, B. (2006). 'Five misunderstandings about case-study research', *Qualitative Inquiry*, **12**(2), 219–45.

Kitzinger, J. (1994). 'The methodology of focus groups: the importance of interaction between research participants', *Sociology of Health & Illness*, **16**(1), 103–21.

Leonard-Barton, D. (1990). 'A dual methodology for case studies: synergistic use of a longitudinal single site with replicated multiple sites', *Organization Science*, **1**(3), 248–66.

McDonald, P., Townsend, K. and Waterhouse, J. (2009). 'Gaining agreement does not mean gaining access: the complexities of supported research', in K. Townsend and J. Burgess (eds), *Method in the Madness: Research Stories You Won't Read in Textbooks*, Oxford: Chandos Publishing, pp. 119–33.

Saunders, M., Lewis, P. and Thornhill, A. (2011). *Research Methods for Business Students*, 5th edn, Pearson Education India.

Stake, R.E. (1995). *The Art of Case Study Research*, Thousand Oaks, CA, USA and London, UK: SAGE.

13. Is a pilot necessary?

Polly Black

Pilots are essential – that is the valuable lesson I learned. Why? Because there is always something you have not foreseen that will derail or weaken your research if you don't test the approach ahead of time. It is OK to have a derailed pilot – indeed it can be advantageous. It is not OK to have your main study derailed!

In my case, I was thinking of using qualitative interviews. I didn't want to bother with a pilot, but I'm very glad that I did. I learned three big lessons from doing the pilot study.

First, remain in listening mode; resist the temptation to engage in the conversation. I thought I knew how to conduct interviews, having done a number of them and having watched others doing them behind a one-way mirror more times than I could count. However, listening to the pilot interview transcripts I saw that often the key phrases were in my words as I checked for understanding. Thus what I had on the tape was the participant agreeing with me on the summary, not the key data summarised in the participant's own words. I addressed this in future interviews by asking the participants instead to summarise their thoughts to capture their main point(s) for me.

Second, use the findings and material from your pilot to strengthen your main study. I was doing exploratory interviews and therefore was using a relatively unstructured approach. However, I found that several of the participants had difficulty articulating their thoughts in such an unstructured format. This meant I needed to think of an alternative way to get to the information. I therefore used some of the data collected in the pilot to develop plausible examples as vignettes for participants to react to. This was very helpful in opening up the conversation. Participants said the vignettes were very realistic. This meant that the participants could easily relate and this allowed the conversation to flow naturally while ensuring discussion of the specific areas of interest to me.

Third, use the pilot to test for weaknesses in your overall research design. In my case, I had too narrow a target population. From the literature, I had decided on a target population that I thought would be an intense sample, but the pilot data made me realise that this target population was too narrow and I was not getting the full story. Without the pilot I would not have seen this weakness in the research until later, and that would have added both time and cost to the research.

I am converted! I now know first hand that pilots are invaluable. I will never undertake a piece of research without doing a pilot first.

14. The precarious nature of access

Wojciech Marek Kwiatkowski

My PhD research project, which examined the delivery of knowledge-intensive business services highlighting the subjective and social qualities of knowledge, utilised an interpretivist case study research strategy. Concerned with depth of understanding rather than theory-building, I sought to collect all data from a single organisation. I was fortunate to get in touch with an Operations Manager of a suitable organisation months before I was ready for fieldwork. Although my newly acquainted gatekeeper lacked the authority to grant access himself, he seemed convinced he should be able to persuade the Managing Director to let me in.

Intending to begin data collection in July 2016, I contacted the Operations Manager in June and was provided with the email address of the Managing Director. I reminded my gatekeeper I was waiting for a reply every fortnight. In August he told me he did not think there was anything he could do. I had no reason to question his intentions. It seemed that he had simply overestimated his influence. Perhaps I was somewhat naive in thinking I had access before actually getting my foot in the door of the organisation, before obtaining formal, virtually irrevocable approval and conducting the first interview.

Finding a replacement organisation was a laborious and debilitating process defined by repeating a script over the phone, generic mailboxes and false assurances that someone would get back to me. As time passed and pressure mounted I was increasingly frequently slipping in and out of a defeatist attitude. I do not think I would have persevered if it was not for the support and advice of my most-trusted colleagues. I finally secured access in December 2016, meaning I had my first interview and not simply assurances of future interviews.

My experience serves as a warning about the precarious nature of access. It is a caution that although it might easily appear as having been secured, it might eventually slip through the fingers of the qualitative researcher, putting his or her world in turmoil. Restoring balance can be difficult. Therefore, I would advise against locking other people out and making it a personal failure.

15. The diminishing dissertation: seven cases to three+

Ashlea Kellner

When I started my doctorate, my supervisors and I had grand plans to conduct a multi-industry study of human resource management systems in franchises. We were lucky, at first, and secured access to speak with at least one upper management contact in seven franchises: real estate, fast food, banking and four cafés. I had dreams of collecting over a hundred interviews within a few months, ready for analysis and write up of the thesis within the golden three-year window. It did not go to plan.

First I realised that the real estate franchise was structured very differently from the others and didn't fit the important specifications I had for my case studies. So I said goodbye and decided we could still work with six cases. Our gatekeeper from the banking franchise had been extremely helpful and engaged, so much so that we thought we might ask him if he was interested in some kind of research partnership arrangement, funded by the bank. After this conversation he stopped replying to all communication. Down to five cases.

Four of the remaining five cases were coffee-based café-style franchises, and the other was a large pizza chain. Discussions with my supervisors led us to decide that the pizza chain was a poor fit with the others, and we would have a 'neater' group of cases if we stuck to four more comparable coffee chains. They really loved the idea of a 'two-by-two' matrix, where I could compare the four cases along two different dimensions, so I said goodbye to the contact at the pizza franchise and got busy collecting data.

Arranging interviews took time, a lot longer than I had hoped and the fourth case – a comparably small and new franchise – was the most difficult. I had completed all interviews and transcribed and analysed the data for three cases by the end of my second year, but there were ongoing access issues with the fourth. By the time I was two and a half years through the thesis, I was getting desperate. The gatekeeper was very polite but there was always something preventing him from giving me access to franchisees: an upcoming conference, a new marketing promotion, lack of interested interviewees. The end date was looming. I had to cut them loose.

In the end I had conducted, transcribed and analysed 45 interviews, eight of which could not be included in the main study. Our matrix was put to rest, but it wasn't all bad news. The franchises I ended up with turned out to be small, medium and large in size, which made for a tidy little model. It was hard at the time, but I think there were some important lessons to be learned. Finding contacts can be the hardest part of the project, so don't stretch the relationship with your gatekeeper, and always remember to be flexible with your research design!

16. So, I guess we're probably finished then

Keith Townsend

The old adage that one should 'never give up' was clearly not thrust in to the popular lexicon by a qualitative researcher. Sometimes you have to know when it's time to give up.

This is relevant not only for the number of interviews you might complete, but also when you know you are just not going to get quality data from an interviewee.

Throughout 2011 I was involved in a research project that looked at a range of HRM topics in multiple workplaces. I had completed more than a hundred interviews across five different organisations when the next interviewee (let's name her Jenny) entered the room to meet with me.

I was as charming and welcoming as possible and I tried all the tricks of engendering rapport that I'd learnt through my life and research career.

For 11 minutes the conversation was one-sided. My side. Jenny's responses were mostly monosyllabic, occasionally grunts, and all delivered by a person whose body language made it very clear that she would rather be anywhere but in that room with me.

If this were in the first 10–20 interviews of the project then I probably would have persevered, worked harder to find middle ground and to develop rapport further, but Jenny was the most active 'non-participant' I'd met in over ten years and hundreds of interviews. So after 11 minutes I gave up and said, 'So I guess we're probably finished then.' To which Jenny replied, 'I guess so.' Please note that it was a statement, not a question!

Our project had reached the point of data saturation long ago, and we were looking at more organisations for some level of generalisation. But Jenny wasn't willing to contribute and I wasn't willing to waste any more time trying. It's only with experience though that one can recognise the point where different tacks, different strategies are better than giving up. Sometimes you just have to give up.

Thank you Jenny; you may have contributed little to our project, but you have contributed much more to my understanding of qualitative research methods.

17. Your incentives are too lucrative: caution in rewarding interview participants

Catheryn Khoo-Lattimore

As a new researcher, I had heard many stories in the lunch room and at research seminars about the difficulties of gaining access to participants. The stories included those of doctoral students whose theses could not be completed on time because they could not find people to interview, and stories like these worried me at a time when I was dependent on a time-bound scholarship. I was determined that I was not going to be held back by my participants, or lack thereof.

I started planning months prior to data collection. I had needed to follow homebuyers from when they first begin to look for a house to the point when they sign the final Sale and Purchase Agreement, so I knew I could be following some people for months or even, possibly, years. Debates on whether or not the promises of incentives will motivate research participants to be involved remain unresolved (see for example: Frick et al., 1999; Perez et al., 2013), hence my plan was to make it very attractive for people to want to participate in my project. Rapport development strategies discussed in qualitative research methods literature were put into practice as I attempted to convince local businesses to help with my access to participants. I persuaded a mortgage broker and a few real estate agents to help me recruit potential homebuyers. I convinced businesses to throw in vouchers for free carpet underlay for the participants' new home, a free colour consultation for any interior decorating work they might want to undertake, and access to two hours of electrical or plumbing work. I also had a law firm donate a $600 home transfer package as a prize draw that my participants would be eligible to win after their interviews with me. As it turned out, I had gone overboard.

My research project, as one can imagine, sailed through without any trouble with participant access. To make a long story short, I completed my PhD ahead of time, and was called into viva. I was somewhat confident, until one of the examiners asked me about the impact of the participants' incentives on the trustworthiness of my data. 'Excuse me', I had said, as a strategy to buy me two more seconds of thinking time, to which he replied, 'Did it ever cross your mind that your data might be biased because your respondents only participated in your research because of the incentives?' Of course it had not. And neither had it occurred to any of my three supervisors. In my reply, however, I explained to the panel that the winner of the home transfer package did not even claim her prize despite my repeated reminders through emails and phone messages. This implied that the respondents were genuinely motivated to share their stories for my research. The panel was appeased by my response.

I have learnt since then not to give my respondents anything more than $20 worth of vouchers – one of those things you will never pick up from a research methods book, except for this one of course.

REFERENCES

Frick, A., Bächtiger, M.T. and Reips, U.D. (1999). 'Financial incentives, personal information and drop-out rate in online studies', *Dimensions of Internet Science*, Lengerich: Pabst Science, pp. 209–19.
Perez, D.F., Nie, J.X., Ardern, C.I., Radhu, N. and Ritvo, P. (2013). 'Impact of participant incentives and direct and snowball sampling on survey response rate in an ethnically diverse community: results from a pilot study of physical activity and the built environment', *Journal of Immigrant and Minority Health*, **15**(1), 207–14.

18. Sales skills for researchers

Colin Hughes

In 2015 I set out to gain access to locally based ICT multinational firms to collect data using semi-structured interviews. I had good contacts in a lot of organisations so I assumed that access wouldn't be an issue. How wrong I was! I learnt five key lessons which, with my background in sales, I should already have known. These could be viewed as lessons relating to the sales skills researchers need to gain physical access – in other words the process of selling the benefits of their research to participant organisations.

LESSON 1: BE CLEAR ABOUT YOUR RESEARCH NEEDS WITH POTENTIAL PARTICIPATING COMPANIES

As I was hoping to finalise participant organisations I hit a major stumbling block. I had first-hand knowledge of many organisations who were utilising virtual sales teams (the focus of my study), with managers and employees located in different locations. I assumed, incorrectly, that most global organisations were operating the same model, given the oft-cited advantages of virtual working. However, I soon realised that many organisations had recently decided to co-locate all of their sales managers and employees. While they were willing to participate, they couldn't offer me the right kind of access. Once I was aware of this issue I saved a lot of time in subsequent dealings with companies, as rather than arranging meetings I arranged phone calls and asked a small number of qualifying questions up front.

LESSON 2: SEEK PERMISSION FOR ACCESS FROM THE 'REAL' DECISION-MAKERS

In another organisation I was assured that access would not be an issue. The person, who was quite senior, had no idea that their colleagues in other parts of the business would object so strongly. In this instance others in the organisation were afraid that the findings would not reflect positively on them. Maybe if I had spoken to the 'real' decision-makers earlier in the process I could have built relationships and gained access. It is always worth asking the question, 'Is there anyone else in the organisation that needs to approve this research and if so can we engage them as soon as possible?'

LESSON 3: COMMUNICATE THE VALUE OF YOUR RESEARCH

Customer Value Proposition (CVP) is a common term used by sales professionals. Researchers too must communicate the value of their research and link this to the organisations' challenges or needs. At first I was finding it a little difficult to connect the two so I developed a one-page explanation outlining the common issues faced by virtual teams (which were likely to be common to the organisations I spoke with) and highlighting how my research could help to resolve such issues.

LESSON 4: BUILD TRUST WITH DECISION-MAKERS

As there are certain risks associated with granting access, organisations need to be able to trust researchers. Their decision to trust is based largely on perceptions of trustworthiness related to the researcher's ability, benevolence and integrity (Mayer et al., 1995). I needed to ensure I was coming across as trustworthy by highlighting my track record as a researcher and scholar and the fact that the research would be of a high standard (ability); by assuring the organisation that I would protect the organisation and participants throughout the research, e.g. confidentiality or anonymity (benevolence); and lastly by convincing the organisation of my honesty and character (integrity). As such I had to ensure that any information I provided to the organisation or which was discoverable online (e.g. on LinkedIn) communicated my trustworthiness.

LESSON 5: ALWAYS AGREE THE NEXT STEPS AT THE END OF EACH MEETING

My first request for access was with an organisation with which I had significant work dealings. While there was an open door and people were interested in the research, they were also very busy. I didn't set any firm dates for follow-up as I was busy at work and wasn't quite ready to conduct the research. However, after three months had elapsed my contact left the organisation before agreeing my access with colleagues, which meant I had to start again from the beginning. I learned that it is always useful to confirm the next steps (with agreed dates) at the end of each meeting. At least that way the contact person has a deadline to work towards and you can keep the research on track or find out early if there are problems with access.

REFERENCE

Mayer, R.C., Davis, J.H. and Schoorman, F.D. (1995). An integrative model of organizational trust. *Academy of Management Review*, **20**(3), 709–34.

19. Being flexible in interviews: make sure that you account for power imbalance

Qian Yi Lee

Like all PhD candidates going through the adventure of qualitative interviews, I struggled with a multitude of issues (yes, the consent forms need to be signed; yes, all information will be de-identified and anonymous). I was lucky enough to have been prepared by my supervisors and peers on almost everything that could go wrong but there was still one hiccup that might have turned out differently had I been ready to handle it.

I undertook a total of 56 interviews across two organisations; in the 56th and last interview with the most senior manager of the second organisation, a *unique opportunity* was presented to me. Before this, I had faced occasions where interviews with this manager had to be postponed due to work issues that had cropped up at the last minute. On one of those occasions, she offered me her deputy to be interviewed instead of her, and like all good PhD candidates I would never say no to extra interviewees, so I told her I would like to be able to speak to them both on separate occasions if possible. The manager said she would get back to me. A few days later, I was able to secure a slot for her interview but no word on her deputy so I thought that was an opportunity missed although I was confident with the volume and quality of data I had already collected.

On the day of the interview, I was ushered into the room with the manager inviting me to take a seat, when she said, 'Oh! If you don't mind, my deputy would be joining us'. I had a split second to make a decision and at that point in time I felt that saying yes was the only way to go. This was because I needed some data from the deputy and if I said no, I might have been unable to arrange another time to speak to the deputy, or worse, I might have even lost both participants. I was leaving the country in a couple days so it wasn't as if I could make another convenient time.

Throughout the interview process I tried to tweak the questions that I had prepared for one-to-one interviews to include both participants but it only took the first question for me to realise that the power was skewed towards the more senior participant. The deputy was extremely reserved and seemed to spend most of her time there taking notes or nodding silently. Thankfully, she did make contributions at certain junctures, even though the bulk of her responses were mainly backing up her boss's statements or filling in the gaps that her boss may have missed. I don't believe that she was scared of her boss per se, but it seemed that she was unlikely to contradict what her superior had to say. So the deputy would allow the manager to speak first and if she had anything to add she would do it after.

Had I been notified beforehand, I might have insisted on conducting the interviews separately or, alternatively, I would have prepared other questions that would allow participation from both parties. Alas, not everything in research can be planned for. You think you have it all planned out, but there is always something that happens that you are not fully equipped to handle. So, when collecting data in the workplace, be prepared and ready for whatever could be thrown at you to make the best out of what you have. And remember, in unusual situations it would be beneficial to make additional field notes to help you during the analysis stage.

PART III

Getting It Together

20. '. . . Just one goat': the importance of interpretation in qualitative data analysis

Keith Townsend and Rebecca Loudoun

INTRODUCTION

There is an old joke about a man who despairs about his tarnished reputation after 'just one' indiscretion with a goat – I'm sure each country has a version of such a joke and if you are unfamiliar and wish to acquaint yourself with such humour then a quick google will allay your curiosities. Without going too far into the premise of the joke, it is an anecdote that demonstrates that people can interpret the same activity in different ways. Transported to the qualitative data setting, this story is an important one about how one individual's perspective can be substantially different from others' in the interpretation of interview questions and how this might impact data analysis. While qualitative research is valuable for answering the 'how, rather than how many' questions and for understanding the perspective of those people being studied, deliberate strategies need to be used to evaluate the interpretation of meaning from the swathes of qualitative data that can be collected in a research project.

According to Miles, some four decades ago 'qualitative data tend to overload the research badly at almost every point: the sheer range of phenomena to be observed; the recorded volume of notes; the time required for write up, coding, and analysis can all be overwhelming' (1979: 590). Computer-based technology and data analysis software can be of great assistance; however, the qualitative researcher still has to be able to establish the validity and credibility of the data collected and interpretations and findings arising from these data. Researchers must also be cognisant of the reality that interviewees might have differing interpretations of the interviewer's or interviewers' research protocol.

This chapter reports on the experience of a baseline data collection designed to establish an 'anchor' to compare qualitative data over three time periods. We were well aware prior to any data collection that this project would face challenges eliciting information as the organisation was beset by low morale and low levels of trust in management. As a means to overcome these difficulties, we implemented a method of inquiry that is rarely used in workplace research. The interview schedule involved 'word association', a technique that has been used in psychology for a century and in market research for decades. This research method, however, while providing the authors with a means of placing a measurement on the 'Time 1' experience of the employees, was not without its problems. For example the participants' interpretation of the questions and instructions were varied, and furthermore, when it came to be time for the researchers to code the data, many responses proved complex and ambiguous. Aligning with the theme of this volume, this chapter does not have a research question as such; rather, it tells a story of an experiment in data collection that became more complicated than we had anticipated. We also describe and consider how successful our strategies were to get the project back on track.

The value of qualitative research has been questioned in some circles recently, however, the value of this research over time is undeniable (Cassell and Symon, 2007). Linking events and meanings during the construction of a social reality is a key goal of qualitative research (Van Maanen, 1998: xxi). Just as there are a variety of research analysis techniques, researchers must also be aware of the danger related to the various possible 'interpretations' of their data. Alvesson (2011) argues that the complexity and uncertainty of the research practice and meaning taken from interviews is contestable. It is unreasonable to expect then that all interviewees will interpret questions the same way.

The Word Association Technique

Psychologists have used word association tests for more than a hundred years; it is considered one type of 'projective technique' where participants are given a stimulus and asked for an immediate response (Lykke Nielsen and Ingwersen, 1999). The method emphasises immediacy and limits the participants' capacity to formulate what might be deemed an 'appropriate' response in their context. Although the technique can be quite time consuming, it can hold benefits as well, depending on the research questions under investigation. Industrial relations researchers tend to be less interested in the personalities of research participants, instead focusing more on their *experiences*. Hence, it seemed as if this approach might pay dividends when investigating matters in an organisation that was known to have problems with employee morale, trust and culture.

DATA COLLECTION APPROACH

The research project for which these data were collected is an ongoing project designed to measure change in one division of an Australian public sector organisation with approximately two thousand employees. Six executive-level, head-office managers were interviewed and 52 additional interviews with staff at all levels of the organisation were conducted across five of the 15 worksites. This number of interviews fits within the upper end of the zone presented by Saunders and Townsend (2016) as appropriate for single sector research projects. At each worksite a vertical (various levels of management and employees) and horizontal (across various departments) representation of the workforce were interviewed. While the employees were randomly selected from the roster and invited to participate in the interviews, the site managers of each workplace were not randomly invited as there was only one at each site.

Longitudinal qualitative studies are somewhat rare in Human Resource Management (HRM) research, so the researchers turned to different disciplines for ideas on data collection methods. This seemed a reasonable course of action as researchers regularly draw from different disciplines for theory – why not methodology?

The interviews began with a series of introductory questions aimed at rapport building where the interviewers would ask about the interviewees' background and share overlapping experiences. Given the low levels of trust in this organisation, the rapport-building stage was particularly important and was often longer than would typically be the case. Once this stage was completed an explanation of the remaining interview process was provided along the following lines:

> There will be a handful of questions and I will ask you for many of them to give the first three words that spring into your mind. Kind of like a word association thing; for example, if I was to say 'sky' you might say 'blue', 'cloud' and 'grey'. There's no right or wrong answers here, just throw out the first three words that come in to your head.

It was following this outline that the interview generally began. Three examples of interview questions within the protocol are as follows:

1. When you think about the relationship between the union and management at this workplace, what are the first three words that come to mind?
2. When you think about the future of your organisation, what do you think are the three key issues facing your organisation?

3.   When you think about the person who is your immediate line manager, what are the first three words that spring to mind?

After documenting these responses on a worksheet, the researchers then progressed to delve into the individuals' answers to gain a deeper understanding of the respondents' views on the matter. This initial stage of data analysis involved the researchers discussing their findings between interviews, and then again at the completion of the interviews each day. This process allowed developing themes to be further investigated at the next data collection point, which in this case was within a day or two.

Following the interviews, key words provided were transferred to an Excel spreadsheet and coded using a colour. For example, positive descriptive words were highlighted green; negative descriptors were highlighted red; neutral words were highlighted yellow; and words that did not seem to fit this initial allocation were highlighted grey.

As we had six word association questions with three response words to each and 52 participants ($6 \times 3 \times 52$), almost 1000 data points needed coding for each of the three time periods. We naively thought we would eventually transform our words to colour coding, and then to numerical data for quantitative analysis, which seemed to make a great deal of sense to us until we started the second stage of the data analysis.

DISCUSSION

One of the first identifiable problems with this approach was the diverse verbal communication skills of the workforce. Simply put, some employees could not generate three separate words to explain what they wanted to say. This meant that our optimistic expectation of having three responses from each participant was not met.

Other interviewees provided statements or monologues instead of three words as requested. They found it difficult, and sometimes impossible, to narrow this down to only three separate words. We drew on a number of 'plan B's' to deal with this problem. One strategy was to select keywords for the participant and check with them if they were a fair representation of what they were saying. This was successful most of the time but there was still the risk of the researcher adding their interpretation of the meaning of the interviewee's thoughts rather than the participant having their own spontaneous voice still.

An example of this potential for misinterpretation occurred when one participant was asked about the *relationship* between the union and the management at their workplace. We naively expected the employee to use words that described 'the relationship'. However, the participant responded: 'Well, I reckon that staff representatives are too cosy with the union here, but I'm not sure of a word that you could use for that.'

In this instance determining one word to represent this view was beyond the comprehension skills of the individual; we felt the word 'cosy' did not adequately represent the views of the employee and would lead to misinterpretation during the analysis phase. 'Cosy' can be interpreted as warm, gentle and positive, but just like the individuals in movies and jokes who faced different views over their various one-off indiscretions, there are multiple ways to interpret 'cosy' under these contextual circumstances. If we were to return to the dataset at Time 2 and just see the word 'cosy' without the context around it, that might conjure warm, positive thoughts, not the negative connotations that the employee was trying to convey.

Another strategy used was to record a short phrase rather than key words. This was the approach taken in the example of 'cosy' above. The downside of using this approach was that as researchers we would lose (to some extent), the single thing that the word association method was most revered for – the immediacy of thought as opposed to the formulation of a response that seemed appropriate in the context.

Interpretation of events and words is essential for those of us who perform qualitative research. We do not measure volume as such, nor do we measure numerical associations, we interpret meaning. Context is often an important part of understanding research – the context of a particular team working in an organisation, the context of a particular industry sector, the context of a particular organisation operating within multiple national regulatory regimes for example. However, the context of individual quotes becomes important for researchers and the end users of our research as well. This means that researchers should aim to avoid 'cherry picking' the quotes that best illuminate their research agenda, but use those quotes that illuminate their research agenda within the context of the quote provided. This reminds us of a research project where an inexperienced researcher came to our team meeting with enthusiasm about an idea for an article. The research team enquired and thought yes, indeed this was a good idea. So how much data did we have to support this? Well, our inexperienced enthusiast told us it was just really from one interview. Okay, but it was a key theme from this interview? 'Not really', explained the inexperienced enthusiast; 'it was one quote in one interview'. Running the risk of mixing metaphors, that 'cherry picking' was veering off towards the 'just one goat' territory.

Another example of this interpretation problem is a respondent who answered the same question about relationships between union and management with the word 'rabble'. The respondent was very quick with this word and said it with great enthusiasm; we presumed it was meant as a description of a poor relationship. 'Rabble', after all, means disorderly, easily interpreted as negative. When pressed on what he meant by rabble, the respondent went on to explain that in his view, the union was such a 'rabble' and he thought it was wonderful to see. He liked the fact that his union appeared slightly disorganised, but excitable on issues. For this employee, 'rabble' should not be coded red as a negative word, but green as something positive.

The question about management–union relationships illustrates the third problem we found with interpretation. Some participants did not focus on the 'relationship' between union and management at all. Where we were expecting words to describe the relationship along the lines of 'mistrustful', 'positive', 'adversarial' – all of which are easy to code – instead we were given words to describe one party in the relationship such as 'good union reps'.

We initially considered these responses unhelpful for the research and put our heads together to try and think of a way to better phrase the question to ensure that participants focused on the relationship rather than the parties. However, after some discussion we decided that this type of comment was useful after all. Although it was beyond the dichotomous 'positive/negative' coding, ultimately phrases like this were worthwhile because they could be coded as 'positive towards union' and hence, comparable with data collected at Time 2 and Time 3.

In combination, the strategies used to address these problems of interpretation meant that we had multiple categories for each question rather than the expected three (positive, negative, neutral), resulting in seven categories. In the example of the relationship question discussed here our coding ended up as follows:

- generally positive;
- generally negative;
- neutral;
- positive towards union;
- negative towards union;
- positive towards management;
- negative towards management.

REFLECTIONS

It is not unusual when using a new research method for the first time to face developmental problems. This was certainly the case for us with the word association technique. It was clear that we were unable to use our word association data as we had originally hoped. Virtually all of the problems encountered with the approach centred around interpretation: participants interpreting the questions differently from how they were intended; participants providing answers that didn't fit the format requested and thus required the researchers to convert their response to the one-word format; researchers trying to ensure ambiguous words provided by participants were coded in such a way they didn't lead to misinterpretation in the future.

However, there were many positive aspects of this data collection approach as well. For example the method resulted in a large bank of data from 52 interviews for each of the three time points coded in a relatively user-friendly format. This helped with the often time-consuming task with qualitative data of theme identification. We were able to identify a high level of consistency in themes quite quickly. Words could be transformed into numerical data and along with this came the corresponding strength of numerical values. The quotes garnered through interviews were more than enough to flesh out the data and provide the 'lived' example to the themes. Our capacity to provide the organisation with a report with some measureable level of satisfaction or dissatisfaction was difficult, but we were able to provide the organisation with some tangible points to compare their results following forthcoming interventions.

Despite these benefits we have not been able to use this data in any scholarly management journal articles, primarily because we have not been able to come up with a way to fit our 'three words' data with appropriate theories. Perhaps that's just our failing, but it may also suggest the approach is in need of further development before it can be useful to both an academic audience and an industry audience. By adapting our analysis to be more inclusive of context, we provided a more nuanced understanding of how employees feel about various aspects of their working experience. There is no doubt this was attractive for the partnering organisation as it allowed us to provide a more interesting and detailed report of the intervention under investigation. The strategies employed to overcome problems with interpretation mean that the possibility of developing this approach further for future studies could yield rewards for researchers and their partnering organisations. We came to the end of the project, looked at each other and said, 'Just one word association technique', but we do not hold out hope that this will become an often-used phrase of despair!

LESSONS

- By all means experiment with data collection techniques on projects that allow experimentation; on your PhD, you need either to stick to tried and true approaches or to back up your methods with a very convincing argument about why you've taken your particular approach and the specific benefits of that approach.
- Maintain the importance of context in qualitative research, but do not let context overtake your key role – understand the phenomena under investigation.
- Trying to quantify the qualitative can lead to the worst of both worlds, but sometimes it can be quite useful. Practitioners often want different things to academics, so don't be afraid to offer practitioners something that might not get past the conservative review process of top journals, but might offer the practitioners some interesting insights.

REFERENCES

Alvesson, M. (2011), *Interpreting Interviews*, London: SAGE.
Cassell, C. and Symon, G. (2007), *Essential Guide to Qualitative Methods in Organisational Research*, London: SAGE.
Lykke Nielsen, M. and Ingwersen, P. (1999), 'The word association methodology: a gateway to work-task based retrieval', MIRA'99 Conference, Glasgow, available at: http://bcs.org/upload/pdf/ewic_mi99_paper6.pdf.
Miles, M. (1979), 'Qualitative data as an attractive nuisance: the problem of analysis', *Administrative Science Quarterly*, **24**, 590–601.
Saunders, M.N.K. and Townsend, K. (2016), 'How many participants are sufficient? An analysis of research articles using qualitative interviews in highly regarded organization and workplace journals', *British Journal of Management*, **27**, 836–52.
Van Maanen, J. (1998), *Tales of the Field: On Writing Ethnography*, Chicago: University of Chicago Press.

21. Analysing quantitative data

Sameer Qaiyum and Catherine L. Wang

Catherine: Quantitative research has numbers, statistics, but also some element of art to it. People and organisations that we study are not just objects; they have feelings, emotions and characters. A good quantitative research design must capture the intricacies of people and organisations, in choosing samples, developing research instruments, putting in place measures to ensure robustness, and executing the research. A too simplistic research model (say, simply testing 'one variable just influences one other variable') cannot reveal true relationships between variables in a complex world or business system, as such relationships are often confounded by other intervening variables. I like to think that quantitative research is a balance between science and art, in order to seek truth as close to the reality as possible. In this chapter, Sameer (who was my doctoral student) and I discuss his experience of designing his doctoral research, screening data and analysing data.

Sameer: I agree with you, Catherine. When I designed my research, I followed your advice and included the most important mediating and moderating variables that may influence the relationships based on the literature review. My research focused on how firms can implement strategy processes to develop organisational capabilities that subsequently improve firm performance. I developed three research models to examine: (1) the influence of strategy processes on firm performance; (2) the mediating effects of different organisational capabilities in the relationships between strategy processes and firm performance; and (3) the moderating effects of environmental dynamism and other factors on the above relationships. I then used questionnaires to collect data from 260 Indian high-tech firms, plus another 26 second questionnaires from 10 per cent of these sample firms. The 26 second questionnaires were collected to test common method bias, as you advised. I took the issue of common method bias very seriously, and really benefited from thinking about it at the research design stage.

Catherine: That is right, Sameer. As I tell my students, a strong quantitative study requires a great deal of insights into theory, methods and reality. A robust quantitative study starts from the research design. To achieve this, when I design a study, I use certain techniques (what we call procedural methods) to optimise the validity, reliability and generalisability of the study. For example, I have often been asked by journal reviewers about the common method bias in my data (and indeed, as a reviewer, I have also asked many authors about it!). If a common method variance is high, the strength of a significant relationship (between two variables) could have been inflated by using a single method or a single respondent. This is why common method bias can be a concern. There are several ways to deal with this; for example, by gathering objective data (such as financial data) that have been audited and published in the public domain, and/or by collecting data from more than one respondent about the same issue or the same organisation, in order to corroborate data. In your case, Sameer, we discussed the different options. You mentioned that reliable objective data from Indian high-tech firms were rarely available, so you decided to collect the second responses. Now, let's talk about how you use statistical methods to screen data to ensure their validity and reliability.

Sameer: I have a mathematical background (as part of my first degree in engineering). I never felt intimidated by quantitative methods, but again I never thought that I would encounter so many challenges when I started data analysis. Although simple tests like non-response bias using ANOVA and common method bias using Harman's one-factor test (Podsakoff and Organ, 1986) were easy to grasp by just reading the SPSS Manual, the first hurdle arose when you suggested that I use Structural Equation Modeling (SEM), a more stringent test of common method bias (Podsakoff et al., 2003). This was a challenge to me, as there were only a few very technical articles that described the test, and no textbooks or Internet resources available at the time. Having gone through these articles, I reverse engineered how to do it by painstakingly dissecting the diagrams that described the test. After much trial and error, I was able to conduct the test. This boosted my confidence, and momentarily I thought I had conquered data analysis. Little did I know my roller coaster journey of data analysis had just started.

Catherine: I believe that using SEM to test common method bias was your first brush with SEM. You taught yourself and used it correctly. Regarding common method bias, there was a second issue that you faced: how to analyse whether the second respondent from each of the 26 firms (10 per cent of the sample) statistically corresponded in the same fashion as the first respondent in the same firm. Any statistical difference between the two respondents responding to the same question for the same firm can spell trouble, as it may raise concern about common method bias. What tests did you use?

Sameer: Once again, I was in the dark, as there were no textbooks on how to analyse the extent to which two respondents on the same issue within the same organisation converge, and even papers published in top journals only reported that they had conducted the analysis, with no elaboration! After much learning and reverse engineering, I worked out how to use Microsoft Excel to calculate the inter-rater agreement between the two respondents (LeBreton and Senter, 2008) and the intraclass correlations to confirm that the two responses converged. To do this, I had to understand the mathematics behind those techniques, something which most of us doing quantitative analysis are surprisingly not used to.

Catherine: That sounds great, Sameer. I always think that, once data are screened, the most exciting phase of data analysis happens. This is when I test research hypotheses, and I do this with anticipation and trepidation. It's all comforting if my hypotheses, or at least some of them, are supported, and I can move on to write up my findings, and of course, research papers. But, there is always a but, what if many or even all of my hypotheses (in the worst case scenario) are not supported? What if I need to use some unfamiliar analytical techniques to try and resolve some of the problems? What if new software packages have to be used? Such surprises can throw us into complete darkness – hopefully momentarily. My experience is that these surprises often lead to new ventures that often take me to new discovery and learning. Sometimes the rejected hypotheses tell us fascinating stories, if we can find out why. Sameer, you have these sorts of experiences in the ups and downs in your data analysis, don't you?

Sameer: Yes, I do. After data screening, I felt that half of the data analysis task had been done. However, I was wrong! Several impediments were waiting to reveal themselves as I moved to test the hypotheses in my first research model. The first of these impediments, or roadblocks as I like to call them, was how to test a mediation model (where an intervening variable acts as a mediator between two other variables). If I had followed Baron and Kenny's (1986) traditional approach to testing mediating effects, I could have calculated regression coefficients using SPSS. However, Catherine, you suggested a more stringent test using covariance-based SEM (Preacher and Hayes, 2008). There were a number of software packages for performing SEM which could do this, and I decided to use

AMOS for two reasons. First, my university had a licence for AMOS, as I did not want to pay for software from my limited funds. Second, there were plenty of textbooks and Internet resources on how to use AMOS. I taught myself AMOS and the theoretical underpinning of the covariance-based SEM. Learning the former was much easier than learning the latter. To learn AMOS, I read textbooks and articles, and also watched some great videos available on YouTube that succinctly described how to do analysis in AMOS. However, learning AMOS's theoretical underpinning, the maths behind it, was easier said than done. AMOS is like Windows, and its user-friendliness means that you do not necessarily need to learn the mathematics behind it. However, I wanted to. For me, it was important that I had at least a working knowledge of what I was doing and not just producing results by pushing a few buttons. I did learn some of the mathematics behind it, but by no means all of it. I did not have that much time during my doctoral study to indulge in such luxury as to master the mathematics of covariance-based SEM.

Catherine:　I remember very well how impressed I was at how quickly and accurately you grasped the covariance-based SEM. That also boosted my confidence in your ability to learn and use advanced statistical techniques, though your challenge did not stop there. Usually, mediation models have only one mediator variable, but your first research model had more than one mediator. How did you solve the problem?

Sameer:　Yes, mine was a multiple mediator mediation model that required even more advanced techniques. I kept on searching for an article that could put my misery to rest. In the end, I managed to find one (Macho and Ledermann, 2011), and after at least 30 readings of this article, I managed to decode this unique technique that is, for some strange reason, called phantom model technique. No wonder; I did feel like a phantom after learning the technique! To perform the technique, my working knowledge of the mathematics behind covariance-based SEM came in very handy. I never realised that a stand I had taken earlier to learn some of the mathematics of covariance-based SEM out of principle would come to help me later on in such a fashion. However, it did.

Catherine:　Excellent, Sameer. You completed the analysis for your first research model. Let's talk about your two other research models that required the construction of a second-order construct. A second-order construct is a latent construct that is statistically created out of the first-order variables that are directly measured using questionnaires. Thus, second-order constructs are measured indirectly through a statistical construction done at the data analysis stage. Moreover, your second-order constructs were formative constructs (as opposed to reflective constructs). Formative second-order constructs cannot be analysed by covariance-based SEM. How did you go about the analysis?

Sameer: This again sent me on a frantic search to find a suitable analytical technique. I then came to know about an alternative technique called PLS-SEM, which can handle second-order formative constructs. PLS-SEM and covariance-based SEM shared some of the theoretical underpinnings. That meant that I could learn PLS-SEM quickly. To perform PLS-SEM, I also learned two rival software applications, SmartPLS and WrapPLS, making use of their trial versions as the licences were not available at my university. However, these trial versions came with either severe restrictions or expiry dates. By this time, I did not have funds to buy an individual licence, but I noticed that SmartPLS offered a free licence of the previous version of the software to individual researchers. Smart marketing technique, I would say, to get researchers hooked onto the software! I immediately jumped on this opportunity and secured a three-month licence. Even better, they still automatically send me a three-month licence after three months, even now. I again followed the trusted path of reading and re-reading seminal articles to understand SmartPLS and its underpinnings, and watching YouTube videos to fine-tune my understanding of it. By this time, I had begun to use social media platforms as a learning tool. This proved very helpful to me as I started posting on forums such as those managed by academics and software developers and created valuable contacts online. I continue to use these contacts if I struggle with a particular analysis. Now that I have completed my PhD, as a gesture of giving something back and developing the academic community, I help budding researchers resolve their underlying issues online on these platforms.

Catherine: I knew that your eagerness and ability to learn is unbounded, and at that point I was also impressed how resourceful you are, Sameer! Now, let's talk more about your third research model. The research model and the ensuing hypotheses demanded that you demonstrate that the effect of one independent variable A on the dependent variable B (let's call it Path X) is greater than the influence of another independent variable D on the same dependent variable B (let's call it Path Y). Traditionally, researchers simply look at the regression coefficients of Paths X and Y, and whichever is greater is declared more powerful. You wanted to provide statistical evidence of the comparative strengths of the regression coefficients. What did you do?

Sameer: The problem I faced was again new, with few details about it widely available. Although a new consensus is building among experts that simply looking at the regression coefficients is not enough, little knowledge exists on how to statistically prove that one regression coefficient is stronger than the other. Solving this problem took me on a similar journey of discovery: reading and re-reading articles (e.g. Paternoster et al., 1998). Similar to the other challenges I had, there was a dearth of quality publications on the solution. Even when I found a solution, I realised that none of the software incorporated it. Thus, I was left with little option but to do all the complex calculations using Excel again. For the umpteenth time, I was finding how useful my decision was to learn the basic maths of what I was doing, rather than being satisfied with some software manuals. This made the learning of the complicated maths of statistically demonstrating Path X is greater than Path Y much easier. Ironically, I started with Excel and, after a detour of AMOS and SmartPLS, I am back to Excel.

Catherine: It was a few months' intensive learning and thorough data analysis, Sameer. Looking back at your experience, what lessons have you learned?

Sameer: Data analysis can be a messy business, and the only thing that kept me on track was perseverance and a knack for continuous learning. I have three key lessons from my learning journey:

1. *Never assume that you have learned all you need.* Every time I thought that I had learned what was needed to do the analysis, a new problem emerged from nowhere. After a while, I replaced the pretension of 'I know everything' with 'I know nothing'. This change in stand had a very positive effect on keeping my research on track. I approached every analysis, small or big, with an attitude that I might need to learn something new.
2. *Think outside the box when it comes to new-to-the-world problems.* When I encountered new issues for which solutions are not widely available in my areas of research, I made contacts with experts on social media platforms. This proved extremely useful. These experts not only helped me with ideas on how to tackle the problem but also pointed out newly published articles in journals beyond my core areas of research, which might be otherwise very hard to find or take up a lot of time and energy to find.
3. *Learn some of the mathematical underpinnings of user-friendly software.* The user-friendliness of the statistical software might lead us to believe that we hardly need to comprehend the mathematical foundations of

these techniques. However, my experience is that learning the theoretical underpinnings behind the techniques has proved extremely helpful. At times, we may need to do analysis that no software incorporates. At this stage, much time can be lost if we do not have a working knowledge of the mathematical underpinnings. Thus, the time we initially spend on understanding these mathematical underpinnings is worth it, and that can help us immensely to keep research on track at a later stage.

Catherine: Sameer, you did brilliantly in learning new analytical techniques and software packages along the way. You used them effectively to test your complex research models. However, I want to emphasise that every research project is different. As researchers we don't have to use very advanced analytical tools and software packages such as AMOS and SmartPLS. SPSS alone is sufficient to produce robust results that, together with a solid theory behind them and a sound research design, can push knowledge boundaries. Certainly, we shouldn't be put off by these advanced techniques, thinking that we cannot take on quantitative research. Even qualitative researchers can benefit from basic quantitative skills to enable the understanding of quantitative results in publications.

Like you, Sameer, I was a doctoral student and went through a sharp learning curve. I also taught myself statistical techniques and software packages, with the guidance of my supervisor. A few books were life savers to me as a doctoral student, and I often recommend them to my students and researchers new to quantitative methods. Below, I list them as recommended reading.

REFERENCES

Baron, R.M. and Kenny, D.A. (1986). 'The moderator–mediator variable distinction in social psychological research: conceptual, strategic, and statistical considerations', *Journal of Personality and Social Psychology*, **51**(6), 1173–82.

LeBreton, J.M. and Senter, J.L. (2008). 'Answers to 20 questions about interrater reliability and interrater agreement', *Organizational Research Methods*, **11**, 815–54.

Macho, S. and Ledermann, T. (2011). 'Estimating, testing, and comparing specific effects in structural equation models: the phantom model approach', *Psychological Methods*, **16**, 34.

Paternoster, R., Brame, R., Mazerolle, P. and Piquero, A. (1998). 'Using the correct statistical test for the equality of regression coefficients', *Criminology*, **36**, 859.

Podsakoff, P.M. and Organ, D.W. (1986). 'Self-reports in organizational research: problems and prospects', *Journal of Management*, **12**(4), 531–44.

Podsakoff, P.M., MacKenzie, S.B., Lee, J. and Podsakoff, N. (2003). 'Common

method biases in behavioral research: a critical review of the literature and recommended remedies', *Journal of Applied Psychology*, **88**, 879–903.
Preacher, K.J. and Hayes, A.F. (2008). 'Asymptotic and resampling strategies for assessing and comparing indirect effects in multiple mediator models', *Behavior Research Methods*, **40**, 879–91.

RECOMMENDED READING

Byrne, B.M. (2009). *Structural Equation Modeling With AMOS: Basic Concepts, Applications, and Programming*, 2nd edn, New York: Routledge.
Dancey, C. and Reidy, J. (2014). *Statistics without Maths for Psychology*, 6th edn, Harlow: Pearson.
Field, A. (2009). *Discovering Statistics Using SPSS*, 3rd edn, Thousand Oaks, CA, USA and London, UK: Sage Publications.
Hair, J.F. Jr, Black, W.C., Babin, B.J. and Anderson, R.E. (2009). *Multivariate Data Analysis*, 7th edn, Harlow: Prentice Hall.
Tabachnick, B.G. and Fidell, L.S. (2006). *Using Multivariate Statistics*, international edition, 5th edn, Harlow: Pearson.

22. When the words just won't come

Dawn C. Duke

I was invited to write this chapter not because of my research background in Neuroscience, but because for the past decade I have been working in Researcher Development, providing skills support for early stage research-ers. In this role, I have delivered workshops, writing retreats and coached many young writers through tough spots. The truth is that writing is hard. It is hard for everyone. The lovely newer researchers I work with often imagine that those of us that have been around awhile just sit down and magically write wonderfully flowing sentences that come together to create iron-clad arguments with amazingly interwoven ideas. The most important thing for you to know is this is just not true. We all struggle with writing from time to time, and none of us write perfect drafts the first time around, not even my emeritus professor friends. In this chapter, I will share with you stories of researchers struggling with writer's block and what helped them overcome this. For a bit of extra inspiration, I will sprinkle this chapter with quotes from famous writers who have battled with their own blocks and lived to tell the tale.

If I waited for perfection, I would never write a word. (Margaret Atwood)

The easiest thing to do on earth is not write. (William Goldman)

THE BLANK PAGE

There it is, perfect and white. Whatever goes there has to be just right. One word, two words . . . no, that isn't it. Delete, delete. More words. No. Delete, delete, delete. Every word down, taken away again to leave the lovely pure page. The words aren't worthy, they can't stay. I remember watching a young researcher, I'll call him Dan, do this over and over again at a writing retreat. It was painful to see; minutes went by, an hour, and everything put on the page, taken away again.

I sat down next to him and asked what was wrong. 'I just can't find the words', Dan said. 'I think of something, but it is just not right.' So I had him talk to me about what he wanted to write, about his wonderfully interesting research. His eyes lit up and out came words, not on the paper, but it was obvious he had a story to tell. His research journey was there, ready to come out and fill the pages of this chapter that was currently just a blank page.

So I asked Dan if he had written anything about this part of his research before. He had written an abstract for a conference – but that isn't the same as a chapter. I asked him to humour me and to copy the abstract onto that pretty white page of his, which he did, sceptically. After that I asked him to start writing underneath the abstract – but not to write the chapter. Instead, I asked him to write about what he would like to write about today. And then I gave him some very specific rules: (1) no backspace or delete buttons; (2) keep writing for 10 whole minutes, no stopping; (3) sentence structure doesn't matter, neither does grammar or word choice; in fact it doesn't even have to be in complete sentences; (4) suspend all judgement.

With an unsure look on his face, he agreed and started typing while I timed him and policed the delete button. After 10 minutes he had almost filled two whole pages. I asked him to read through and highlight parts that he thought were most interesting. From this, I asked him to pick a topic from what he had written that is important to that chapter and to start writing about that for another 10 minutes. At the end of those 10 minutes, there was a big smile. 'I think I have it!' he said. I told him to keep writing and then later he can go back and delete the bit at the top he didn't need any more. By the end of the day, when I went to check on Dan's progress he had a really good start to his chapter and was excited about what he was going to write the next day. There are two big take-home messages from Dan's story. The first is not to have a perfect white page in front of you when you try to start writing, and the second is to keep writing!

The first words on a page can be terribly intimidating. A really easy trick is to spoil the blank page from the start. Put something else on it, anything will work, but previous writing that is vaguely close to what you want to address is particularly beneficial. You can always take it away later, but psychologically, seeing words on the page already can help, especially for those with perfectionist traits.

> I love writing but hate starting. The page is awfully white and it says, 'You may have fooled some of the people some of the time but those days are over, giftless. I'm not your agent and I'm not your mommy. I'm a white piece of paper, you wanna dance with me?' And I really, really don't. (Aaron Sorkin)

> It is perfectly okay to write garbage – as long as you edit brilliantly. (C.J. Cherryh)

The other 'trick' I used with Dan was called 'free writing'. I love free writing and use it frequently in workshops and in my own writing. The idea is to let go of that inner critic and allow yourself permission to write poorly. I have seen it work time and time again, getting words down on paper works wonders. It even can lead to surprises. At times you can start freely writing and end up in a totally different place than you expected, sometimes with interesting new ideas. And even if you don't, you can always edit it later. Writing is like a hot tap, you have to let the cold water run before you get to the hot. Turning it off and then on again doesn't work. Writing and then deleting prevents you warming up. Sometimes you have to work through those poorly constructed sentences and unclear themes to get to the innovative ideas and eloquent arguments.

> What I try to do is write. I may write for two weeks 'the cat sat on the mat, that is that, not a rat.' And it might be just the most boring and awful stuff. But I try. When I'm writing, I write. And then it's as if the muse is convinced that I'm serious and says, 'Okay. Okay. I'll come.' (Maya Angelou)

NOT ENOUGH TIME

About a year ago, I was working with an amazing group of part-time PhD students; they were all professionals and teaching academics at the same time as they were working on doctorates. This was a group of very busy people! I had them all together for a session about developing the argument for their methodology. I used the start of the session to explore what they needed most from this session and the one theme that came out over and over was that they didn't have enough time to write. It wasn't that they didn't know what they wanted to write, it was that they had such busy days that carving out hours to sit down and write significant amounts of work was just impossible. They all felt the time slipping past and with it an increasing sense of urgency that something must be produced, but there was no time to do it in.

Once people start feeling that they are falling behind, the mountain they need to climb can look ever more daunting and the time needed can seem increasingly impossible to find. Therefore, what I did was introduce them to a time management technique, called the Pomodoro technique, founded by Francesco Cirillo (http://cirillocompany.de/pages/pomodoro-technique). 'Pomodoro' is Italian for 'tomato' and the technique is named after tomato-shaped cooking timers, because it is a task/time management technique that relies on strict timing of specific tasks. This technique is not something I made up, and if I am honest I don't always follow all the 'rules' either when teaching it or using it myself. However, the overall concept is extremely helpful for very busy people that have to get a lot done, and it can be used strictly as described on the above website, or more flexibly.

When using the Pomodoro technique to help you write, you decide on a specific writing task for that day and you identify at least one 30-minute time slot within that day that you can work on your writing. With your task in mind, you sit down and set a 25-minute timer and then you must focus solely on that writing task at hand. You do not look at emails, go on the Internet, or answer the phone or door. You do nothing but the writing task for the full 25 minutes. When the timer goes off, you stand up, stretch and have a five-minute break. If you are lucky enough to have another 30-minute slot, you can repeat the Pomodoro and write for another 25 minutes. A 25-minute session is referred to as one Pomodoro, and after each one, you should have a five-minute break. If you complete four Pomodoros in a row, it is suggested that you take a 15- to 20-minute break. The idea is to work in a focused way for short periods of time. Perfect for those of us who find we don't have big blocks of time to dedicate to writing.

I introduced this technique to these part-time PhD students during this half-day training session, by actually having them use the technique. In this case, I started the first Pomodoro in combination with free writing to help them get a lot of words on the page quickly. Then the next Pomodoro we used to edit and pull out ideas from the free writing, showing them that these periods can be used for different aspects of writing. The key is to identify what you are going to focus on and do just that during the Pomodoro.

Weeks later I ran into one of the ladies who was at this session and she said they had formed a Pomodoro group. They had signs up on their door or hanging on their computer when they were in the middle of a Pomodoro, so others would know not to disturb them. She and several of the students would try to plan their Pomodoros at the same time so they could have their breaks together. The most important thing was she now felt as if the task was now doable. This technique is great for breaking up a huge task, like writing a proposal or thesis, into smaller chunks. This helps you feel the progress you are making, and makes you realise you can achieve something, even if you only have short periods of time throughout the day to work on it.

> The secret of getting ahead is getting started. The secret of getting started is breaking your complex overwhelming tasks into small manageable tasks, and then starting on the first one. (Mark Twain)

FINDING FOCUS

Although for the last decade I have worked supporting other researchers with their doctorates, the first thing that came to my mind when asked to write this chapter was my own doctoral experience of authoring my first publication. It was very early on in my PhD, only six months or so; however, my supervisor was convinced that my first dataset merited publication and he suggested I work on getting a draft together. I remember staring at the data, and then determinedly sitting at the computer and putting words down, only to find myself waffling and winding and getting lost in the literature. Again and again I would try, but there was no direction.

I felt my data was rubbish, it didn't mean anything. How was I supposed to write? Weeks went by. I started to avoid my supervisor for fear he would ask for the draft. Then one day, I was just sitting there playing with the data, moving it around . . . not writing, when something clicked. An idea was forming, I could feel it. The patterns in the data were coming together. A story was emerging.

Knowing I needed to catch the idea before it vanished into the depth of my mind, I started scribbling down words, trying to bring the idea into focus, trying to crystallise the story. It was painful and took perhaps hours, but by the end of that day I had a sentence. Only one sentence, but a beautiful sentence that would guide that first publication. It was the paper's thesis statement, the heart of its story.

A thesis statement is a sentence (or a couple of sentences) that encapsulates the central 'argument' of your work. In academic writing this argument is your story. A good thesis statement lays out before you what you need to prove and how you are going to do it. It is your anchor that can bring you back when you get lost in the detail or pulled astray by interesting peripheral literature. A strong thesis statement should be an assertion that expresses a point of view that a reasonable person should be able to disagree with. In other words, no politician speak. Politicians often say things like 'I believe all children should have access to a good education' or 'People should be able to afford to heat their homes'. These are statements that have an opinion, but they are so broad and idealistic that it would be hard for a reasonable person to argue the opposite. Politicians do this on purpose, of course. They don't want anyone to be able to argue against their ideas. However, this is not academic.

In order to move our academic fields forward and develop academic thoughts, we must develop arguments that can be debated and push researchers on both sides of a debate to develop the body of evidence to further inform thought. Therefore, consider the thesis statement: 'Grammar schools provide increased school choice and expand upward mobility for children from low income backgrounds.' Or 'While expanding grammar schools may give the perception of increased school choice and diversity, they actually lead to fewer children having access to high quality education because they drain resources from local state schools.' People arguing either of these points care about high quality education, as do most people. The clear debate here is how to achieve this end. This is an area that can be debated and which can be informed by research. In fact, you can see the research question within those statements, but they go beyond the question to include the direction of the argument you will build within the piece of writing. With a statement like this you can outline a whole thesis.

The beauty of a good thesis statement is it grounds you, it is your focus. Once I found that sentence, it remained my light throughout the journey of that first paper. When I got lost in the detail of the data or in the vast amount of literature, I could look back and remember where it was I wanted to go with that paper. Side paths are for another day, perhaps another paper. That sentence lit the way so that I was able to figure out what I needed to write next.

> I always worked until I had something done and I always stopped when I knew what was going to happen next. That way I could be sure of going on the next day. (Ernest Hemingway)

WRITING COMMUNITIES

There are times when a doctorate can feel quite lonely, never more so than when you are in the final stages of writing your thesis. You are so close, but you are tired, your mind is weary and the worst part is you have entirely forgotten why your research is important anyway. I had a researcher who was in this state at the most recent writing retreat I delivered; we'll call her Maria. Maria had finished with all the analysis and had written the majority of her thesis, she just needed to write the final chapter to bring it all together, but she had lost the spark. She came into the writing retreat feeling that perhaps nothing she had done was worth a PhD and, therefore, was demotivated and almost physically unable to write.

In our writing retreats, we have writing groups and writing mentors. The writing mentors bring their groups together and everyone introduces themselves and their research and they say what they hope to get done over the course of the retreat. This builds a mini writing community and allows group members to support each other to achieve their goals. The mentor, in this case me, then goes around and talks to the participants in a bit more detail to see how we can best support them over the retreat. When I first talked to Maria, she seemed quite down and admitted to not having written anything for a while. She was concerned that she hadn't even read any of her earlier chapters for almost a year and feared they were not strong enough. Therefore, we decided she would take a bit of time to go through her different chapters and then come back to me to talk about what she saw as her major contributions to knowledge.

Just before our first break I sat with her and she told me all about her research (which was fantastically interesting!). However, she was still sceptical about the worth of the work. I suggested she chat about her work with some of her group members over coffee and biscuits. Throughout break I watched her having a quite animated conversation with a couple of her group members. I had to pull them away from each other to get them all back to writing at the end of the break. I suggested to Maria that she sit down and just start writing the different things she was explaining to her group members during their conversation. At this point, it was not important to worry too much about the idea of a 'contribution to knowledge' but to focus on what her group members found interesting about her research and to write that down. At lunch, I noted again she was very engaged with her group members and that there was definitely a true smile on her face, which hadn't been there when she first came in.

Over the weekend, Maria became more and more positive about her work. One of her group members was very interested in her methodology, commenting on how innovative it was, which really made her feel good. By the morning of the second day, she started really writing. She had seen her research through her writing group member's fresh eyes and that helped her recognise what was special in her work. At the end of the retreat, the group exchanged emails and vowed to keep in touch to motivate each other to finish this final year. I sure hope they do.

Over my years of working with researchers, I have come to appreciate the need for community more and more. Workshops and especially writing retreats that gather people in one place to write together in a supportive, encouraging community can act as a catalyst for creativity and a spark to reignite lost enthusiasm. With the wonders of modern technology, this can even be done virtually, through different forums or groups. We use Skype to deliver virtual writing retreats for our researchers who are off working across the world. This type of support can be a real lifeline when people are feeling stuck. There is no reason anyone couldn't make their own writing communities, either face to face or virtual. The most important ingredient is participants dedicated to writing and supporting each other, as well as biscuits . . . I do find those essential for writing, but that may just be me.

If you have other things in your life – family, friends, good productive day work – these can interact with your writing and the sum will be all the richer. (David Brin)

MAKING WRITING A HABIT

My final word of advice to all newer researchers out there is to make writing a habit. A researcher always has something to write. There are proposals, publications, conference papers and of course your thesis, but there is also writing for yourself. For your ideas to truly form, they need to become real; writing gives ideas shape. This allows you to clarify your ideas and to work with them, to mould them, to challenge them. Putting these thoughts on paper allows you to go back over them and see how they have developed over time. Just a bit of writing every day adds up significantly over time. If you do this, you will be amazed at the amount of material you have for your thesis or for publications. No writing is wasted. Always remember the best cure for writer's block is writing.

> Writing about a writer's block is better than not writing at all. (Charles Bukowski)

LESSONS FOR KEEPING ON TRACK

- Know that writing is hard for everyone, you are not alone.
- Allow yourself to write badly. You can always edit later.
- Don't start writing with a pure blank page, put something – anything – on it.
- Learn to break down your writing task and use short periods of time productively to help move your writing forward even when life is too busy.
- Craft a clear statement encapsulating your main position and argument to give your writing structure and prevent you losing your focus.
- Develop a writing community to maintain motivation and make the writing process more enjoyable.
- Make writing a habit. This is the best way to prevent writer's block in the first place.

REFERENCES

Angelou, Maya (n.d.). GoodReads.com. Retrieved 19 December 2016 from Good Reads.com website: https://www.goodreads.com/quotes/154213-what-i-try-to-do-is-write-i-may-write.

Atwood, Margaret (n.d.). BrainyQuote.com. Retrieved 19 December 2016 from BrainyQuote.com website: https://www.brainyquote.com/quotes/quotes/m/margaretat457937.html.

Brin, David (n.d.). Freelancewritinggigs.com. Retrieved 19 December 2016 from Freelancewritinggigs.com website: http://www.freelancewritinggigs.com/2015/04/15-encouraging-writing-quotes-for-when-you-feel-like-a-failure/.

Bukowski, Charles (n.d.). GoodReads.com. Retrieved 19 December 2016 from GoodReads.com website: https://www.goodreads.com/quotes/372045-writing-about-a-writer-s-block-is-better-than-not-writing.

Cherryh, C.J. (n.d.). GoodReads.com. Retrieved 19 December 2016 from Good Reads.com website: https://www.goodreads.com/author/quotes/989968.C_J_Cherryh.

Goldman, William (n.d.). BrainyQuote.com. Retrieved 19 December 2016 from BrainyQuote.com website: https://www.brainyquote.com/quotes/quotes/w/williamgol378655.html.

Hemingway, Ernest (n.d.). GoodReads.com. Retrieved 19 December 2016 from GoodReads.com website: https://www.goodreads.com/quotes/493513-i-always-worked-until-i-had-something-done-and-i.

Sorkin, Aaron (n.d.). BrainyQuote.com. Retrieved 19 December 2016 from BrainyQuote.com website: https://www.brainyquote.com/quotes/quotes/a/aaronsorki750752.html.

Twain, Mark (n.d.). Quotes.lifehack.org. Retrieved 19 December 2016 from Quotes.lifehack.org website: http://quotes.lifehack.org/quote/mark-twain/the-secret-of-getting-ahead-is-getting/.

23. I'm a paper person or maybe not?

Ilenia Bregoli

In my research career I started working with qualitative research during my PhD. At that time I did not have access to Computer Aided Qualitative Data Analysis (CAQDAS) software to help me in my coding, but from what I read in books and by talking to colleagues who were more expert than me, I understood how to work with pen and pencil. I highlighted the relevant pieces of interviews, gave them codes, kept updating my code book and then copied and pasted within a same file all the excerpts with the same code. It was time consuming, but the reality is that I always considered myself to be a 'paper' person. One of those people who when they buy a new book need to open it and put their nose in between pages to smell it.

During my PhD I really enjoyed coding manually, and for a few years afterwards I never thought that using CAQDAS software was necessary. If manual coding worked for me, why did I have to change? For this reason when I embarked upon a new research project I had one certainty: I would code manually, working on my printed interview transcripts.

However, I wanted to be more 'efficient' and for this reason one day I walked into a nice stationery shop where I bought myself a fancy, brand new set of 20 coloured pens; some with colour shades that I was not even able to name.

I set to work and started my coding. Each new code had a different colour: nice isn't it? Together with my coloured annotations and codes on paper I was also developing my code book in an Excel file: one column for the code name, another one for the code description and a third with an example of that code. However, at the second interview transcript I was already mixing my colours . . . perhaps my 'efficient and artistic' coding was not really so efficient. I had another ten interview transcripts to code, each of which consisted of 25 typed pages, so I was starting to worry a little bit. It was time to move on. I felt I was Robert Plant of Led Zeppelin (1969) singing 'Babe I'm gonna leave you'. I was betraying my manual coding for technology.

The first thing I did when using NVivo was to input the codes I had already developed manually. When I started I noticed that the list of codes was growing quickly and by the time I finished adding the codes from four interviews I found myself with 101 codes and I still had to code another eight interviews! Cleaning was the second task I embarked upon, but soon I realised how many duplicates I had and that I had not noticed this while I was coding manually. Although it took some time, at the end of this cleaning I started to understand my data better, and this allowed me to question my ideas more clearly. Furthermore, the fact that I could move easily from one code to another to check what I did, run queries, write annotations and keep memos, all in one place made me understand how crazy I was to do manual coding.

So what have I learned? Well . . . I still listen to Led Zeppelin, but apart from this I now recognise that CAQDAS software is helpful. However, before using such software, I believe that it is important to really understand the particular data analysis method. Indeed, my transition from paper to NVivo was smooth because I knew what type of coding I was carrying out and I knew how to do it. Thus, I did not have any particular trauma when I did it. I believe it helps to understand the basics of the data analysis and be comfortable with it and then use such software as a tool to help. Knowing a data analysis method means far more than just being able to use a piece of software.

Needless to say, I now usually code with NVivo, my 20 coloured pens being still used while reading journals. In the end I still am a 'paper' person, honest!

REFERENCE

Led Zeppelin (1969). *Babe I'm gonna leave you.* (CD track) 6 mins, 42 seconds. *Led Zeppelin.* London: Olympic Studios.

24. A mug of stress

Rohit Talwar

Cardigans aside, there are several clichés that most academics, regardless of their career stage, would agree with. One such cliché involves the reliance on warm beverages. Coffee, to be specific. It appears that an academic's life relies heavily on it. Coffee exists as one of the primary sources of magical inspiration that helps one stay up at odd hours, make small talk about writing, showing off that unknown brand of independent coffee . . . you get the picture.

It is surely only a matter of following tradition, then, that someone chasing an academic career would rely on a healthy supply of coffee, too. If you are like me, you have a coffee mug for all your work desks, including that compact tumbler (made of recycled material, no less) in your backpack to stay on top of your academic pursuits. Your academic training process involves learning all about research, building an argument, writing clearly, et cetera, but no one tells you about the level of caution needed to consume coffee while using your electronic devices. Probably because they expect you to have basic life skills. Well, not if you are me.

It was a rather warm night in July 2016, and I had been working on the world's best research paper in my field, when the cup of coffee on my desk met my hands, and then, in a completely unannounced fashion, slipped off my hands. Gulp. You may call me clumsy; I blame the mug. And my luck. I must have woken up my housemate, for it is quite unlike them to run to my room at 3 am, asking if I had seen a ghost. No, much worse. I had just learned that my beloved computer does not appreciate coffee the way academics do.

I know what you are thinking; surely I had made a back-up. Of course! Not as often as I should have, though. This is what not following the weekly ritual of backing up can do to you: over three weeks of data analysis and associated writing had gone missing, never to find its way back into my computer again. Nothing aside from the faint but glorious smell of coffee was left. In retrospect I should have been backing up all my work every day. No, every hour. Paranoia aside, my fellow researchers, please back up your work (aka your heart and soul) as often as you can. Things like that crucial argument you took days to articulate, that transcription along with notes that took more days than expected, those notes from that not-easy-to-access book . . . all deserve a lot more love. Time is money, they say, and I spent mine reconstructing documents from memory. Fun.

As I type, I have three hard drives, two cloud accounts, and a phone reminder to back up every night, collectively offering some kind of hope. Here's to never letting go of the habit and enjoying that mug of, er, coffee, and being more productive, stress-free.

25. Excuse me . . . should that comma be there? Dealing with awkward questions

Kenneth Cafferkey

Common convention suggests the PhD viva is the most daunting experience in any researcher's career. Students are constantly reminded of urban myths where an unnamed student in a distance university had a doctoral viva that went on for over a week. The reality, however, is very different; students are usually well versed, well supervised and largely ready for their doctoral defence. The same cannot be said for the first year progress review; this can be an altogether daunting experience for the PhD student in waiting. Emotions run high, sense of one's ability and self-worth plummets and long sleepless nights define the run-in to the moment of truth. The constant self-doubt is never far away: am I good enough? Is my idea good enough? Should I even be doing this? This all culminates in the first year progress review.

When the day of truth arrived I felt physically sick; no kind words of encouragement from my supervisor could help, I felt hopeless. My name was called. I entered. Game time!

I plodded through the early part, safe in the knowledge that questions were spared until the presentation was over; I would get to say my piece before being thrown to the lions. Then out of the blue I walked head first into the most bizarre exchange: a professor from a different department, sitting in the front row, abruptly interjected, 'Should that comma be there?' in relation to a definition. I turned around dumbfounded and read the definition a number of times to myself and responded, 'I don't know, it's not my definition', which seemed to infuriate the professor in question. A lengthy dressing down ensued regarding taking responsibility for my work and implying that my work was substandard (all because of a comma). I wanted to walk out and just quit there and then and the only reason I didn't is that I could tell the room was on my side. I proceeded; needless to say the professor in question had issue with absolutely everything, from what human resource management is, to methodological issues regarding the collection of worker perspectives. I finished the presentation and said with a wry smile, 'You're not a people person, are you?' I had survived the ambush. All in all it was a truly bizarre experience; I didn't really end up defending my PhD proposal – it felt more like I was defending myself.

Overall I was buoyed by the whole experience, and the encounter has become a staple in my research methodology teaching: 'Watch out for the commas.'

Note: I have intentionally misplaced a comma in this vignette; be aware if you decide to quote this work!

26. Finding the time to progress your research, and the big lie that you are part of!

Jennifer Kilroy

If this were just a two-line vignette, it would simply read: 'I finished my research project. (But) typed words revealed the hiding places of life's idleness and rhetoric.' It would be designed, first, to let the reader know that there is light at the end of the tunnel: yes, you can actually finish a research project! And secondly, it would evoke a moment of self-doubt, followed swiftly by a personal affirmation that *their* life surely has no idle space. And it is this lie, which many researchers tell themselves, that forms the gap for this small tale. One day I learned about this lie, and this is how.

Flashback to September 2013, my favourite GAA football team, namely County Mayo in Ireland, have progressed to the All-Ireland Final. This is akin to the Super Bowl of the NFL, or the Grand Final of the AFL, or the FA Cup Final at Wembley. Of course, as County Mayo had reached the final three times in the previous ten years and seven times in total since they last won in 1951, it was no surprise to me that they had reached the final. Winning on the other hand would be a surprise, as Mayo are rumoured to be cursed to lose until the last member of the 1951 winning team has passed on to the next world. As an evidence-based researcher, this nonsensical (and somewhat morbid) backdrop to the game only strengthens the hopefulness of the occasion for me. If you want to use Google, you can do your own research to find more on the nonsensical curse. Throw into the mix that the game was the usual 3.30 pm on an autumn Sunday, when 80 000 fans (that's a lot in Ireland, by the way) descend on Dublin city and Croke Park stadium. It is 3 pm, and I am just closing down my laptop in a car parking lot near the stadium.

I have just spent two hours analysing my interview transcripts in the comfortable office of my passenger seat (Tip: steering wheel is problematic for laptop use in driver's seat). Also, I should mention the virtual capabilities of my office. I am also communicating with my PhD supervisor via mobile calls and 'WhatsApp' messaging – although I did not learn that medium of communication and data transfer in any research methodology book. My supervisor, despite or perhaps because of being a (born) Everton soccer fan, is reading the summary of the research findings in his now local pub in Co. Galway, Ireland, awaiting to enjoy the tradition of an All-Ireland GAA game on the inevitable large screen television, just over the shoulder of a barman busily tending the Guinness taps. He seems as excited as I am about the transcript findings (though that might be the Guinness). Or it might be the theoretical themes of reciprocity, recounting Gouldner (1960) via WhatsApp, as emergent from the transcripts. Multiple employees give accounts on the interview tapes of going 'above and beyond', or applying discretionary effort (Purcell and Hutchinson, 2007) for the supervisor who treats them well. In addition, the individual variation in front line manager styles emerges stronger than expected for a single HR system (Kilroy and Dundon, 2015).

Yes, that Kilroy reference is me! The transcript findings found their way into my first journal publication. This moment of actual real-life connection with a literature review journey, as well as having it published, is, by the way, a pretty bright light at the end of that research tunnel! It has revealed some joys of social science research to me, a sort of reflective self-discovery and learning, advancing knowledge in a field for further inquiry, and the resulting practical implication to the lives of employees as we teach the next generation who may too become managers shaping the lives of others. In other words, those countless journal searches and late library nights are not in vain!

Meanwhile, as I close up my laptop, I am delighted with the ingenuity of my four-step plan. Step one was to depart five hours early for Croke Park, in order to miss traffic and to secure parking in the nearby school for the deaf which places me within sprinting distance of the stadium turnstiles. Step two, convert the car into an office to analyse transcripts for research findings chapter, listening to recordings on car radio and reading and typing on my laptop. Step three is to attend the All-Ireland final free of the never-ending researcher guilt. Step four, celebrate historic win! Simple. By 3 pm the entire plan had been a resounding success and all was on track, despite the odd stare off with the car parking lot attendant, as well as the gritty teeth stare to the opposing Dublin supporters, just to say I have got my game face on, laptop and all!

Here was the dilemma that had given birth to the plan. Any Mayo supporter will tell you, an All-Ireland is a full day commitment. You know, by the time you have the Irish breakfast, round up the flags and jerseys, hit the slow road train from west of Ireland to the east, mingle with fellow supporters on Jones' Road outside the game. However, the research deadline for my first ever publication submission was also looming and it seemed kind of important too. So the problem emerged. Miss the game and perhaps miss the most historic sporting event in the GAA for any self-respecting Mayo supporter, meaning I may never go home with pride ever again! Or, go to the game and risk delaying the pilot study beyond the submission date for my first publishable piece of research (in reality, that should read: miss 'another' submission date, again!).

Think, Jennifer, think! Queue the choir of gremlins that feed the lie of busy lives: 'you deserve to go to the game, as you've spent the last month doing data collection'; 'life is too short to be spending it in the library on your own'. The reality was, I had only spent one weekend in the previous month at data collection, and as for the library, it was a daily aspiration but only a weekly reality. In that moment I realised . . . I was lying to myself. I never actually spent the hours at research that I rhetorically attributed to research. Likewise, attending a Mayo game was never a full day event. The rhetoric of a full day event was in fact a reality of a three-hour drive and a 70-minute game. Uncovering this lie helped me to find four more hours on research on that special Sunday in September. There are always more minutes in the day. We are not perfect. In fact, we are often idly engaged in thoughts of how busy we are. Unfortunately, Step four didn't come to fruition that day, and not any day since. In fact, in 2016, Mayo competed once again and drew the All-Ireland final. The game went to replay, which they lost by a single point. The fans still have hope. That curse is still nonsensical.

REFERENCES

Gouldner, A.W. (1960). 'The norm of reciprocity: a preliminary statement', *American Sociological Review*, **25**(2), 161–78.
Kilroy, J. and Dundon, T. (2015). 'The multiple faces of front line managers: a preliminary examination of FLM styles and reciprocated employee outcomes', *Employee Relations*, **37**(4), 410–27.
Purcell, J. and Hutchinson, S. (2007). 'Front-line managers as agents in the HRM–performance causal chain: theory, analysis and evidence', *Human Resource Management Journal*, **17**(1), 3–20.

PART IV

Getting Finished

27. Authorship in action

Kate L. Daunt and Aoife M. McDermott*

INTRODUCTION

Research methods textbooks focus on the research process. This is both necessary and important. But for those aiming for or pursuing an academic career, the generation of published outputs is equally significant. Writing for publication is a core part of a sustainable research career – and a successful research project. Authorship informs appointment decisions, retention and confirmation in post, as well as progression and promotion. It can also inform funders' evaluation of the success of the project. Reflecting this, there are an increasing number of useful texts on academic writing and the publishing process. However, what are often neglected, but highly significant for academic careers, are the issues surrounding authorship. Regardless of the type of research relationship – which can range from the dyadic relationship between a student and a supervisor, to the multi-party (and often multi-disciplinary) relationships within large teams – similar issues arise: on what basis award authorship? In what order? And via what process? Addressing these questions also raises consideration of alternative strategies for acknowledging contributions that may not merit full authorship, and what to do when things go wrong. These can be awkward issues, often left implicit for this very reason.

We were prompted to discuss issues surrounding authorship earlier this year. Following attendance at a 'meet the editors' session at a conference, we shared lunch with a group of other delegates. The usual chit-chat followed: where are you from; what are you working on; and where are you sending it? All going well, until someone who turned out to be a junior faculty member piped up from the other side of the table: 'Mmm . . . I asked a colleague to read my paper. They did, and gave me some helpful comments. But now they keep talking about "our" paper. And now I don't know what to do. Is this normal? How do you know if someone should be an author?' A short period of silence – and some funny facial expressions ensued. They prompted, 'What do you do?' Cue more awkward looks.

'That's like asking someone to share their secrets' said someone down the other end of the table. What can we say – sharing ensued.

APPROACHES TO AUTHORSHIP

Our first contributor [we apologise for the absence of names – but we'd only just met these people, and the conference lanyards all faced the wrong way, as they do!] started by saying that their team worked on the basis of all names on all papers produced from a project. They explained that, in their team, all of the collaborators contributed to the design and conduct of the study – albeit in different ways – and therefore had contributed to the production of the publications. For them, authorship acknowledged the 'combination capability' inherent in getting a research project from early conceptualisation to a final, finished piece. In surprise, someone questioned, 'But what's the incentive to write?', noting that 'in my team, we only put the names of the people who write the paper, on the paper.' Their reasoning was that this led to better overall output – and was fair. The first speaker did recognise the benefits of this, and suggested that ideally all team members would take turns in leading a paper. But they explained that, in their experience, this is not always feasible in larger groups – where there may be more team members than potential papers within a project. They also noted that, realistically within a large group, not all papers come to fruition. As a result, in their view the combination capability, all names on all papers, approach was fair. Despite their debate, both delegates did agree that the lead writer should be the lead author. Happy nodding around the table on this point, from all but one.

The interjection of the dissenter shifted the focus of the discussion from who should be included as an author on the paper, to the order in which their names should appear. With a slight frown, this contributor explained that they took a different approach to the lead writer as lead author – with alphabetical acknowledgement of authorship. There were a few raised eyebrows at that one: 'Do you put in an asterisk to say that all authors make an equal contribution?' someone asked. The response was quick and negative, but accompanied by a laugh. Grinning, the speaker explained that their surname began with a letter earlier in the alphabet than their most common co-authors, so that by and large, this worked quite well for them. One individual noted that their team tried to support early career researchers to be high on the list of designated authors. But they flagged that whilst this was something they had historically done without much thought, they were increasingly aware that their efforts to support capacity-building made it look as if they were consistently a research collaborator, rather than a research leader. They felt that getting the balance right was important for people coming up the ranks.

An opposite approach was also mentioned: that of having the most senior individual – be it the project PI or supervisor – as the lead author. There was heated debate about this. Not just about the idea of seniority as premise for authorship, but also about the difference between a project PI and a supervisor. Inherent in this debate was concern about exploitation and the importance of recognising the intellectual property of PhD students, and balancing this with helping them to develop publishing skills and capacity. A side-debate ensued, with a continuum of supervisory roles in the publishing process evident. This ranged from a view of the supervisor as a paid overseer of a project that belongs to the student, who should be guided to publish in their own right, at one extreme; to a middle-ground perspective on the student as apprentice, who should work collaboratively to develop their publishing skillset; to a view of the student as employee, working as part of a larger (in this instance funded) project, with a need to negotiate their data versus project data upfront, to enable delineation of their contribution and publishing arena. Strong early career voices in the group emphasised the importance of learning how to publish, especially for securing post-PhD employment.

Whilst there was broad agreement (in our non-representative convenience sample!) that the lead author is typically the individual who takes the lead in drafting the paper, or the PhD student on whose data the paper is based, a range of models for allocating remaining places in authorship were evident. In effect, it seemed to be the case that allocating first authorship was relatively straightforward, but that subsequent ordering had potential to become a quagmire. The solution advocated by a majority in our small group was to order authors in accordance with the weight of their contribution. All sorted. Until our lovely early career colleague piped back up asking, 'Contribution to the paper or the project? And how do you know what counts as a contribution?' Collective groans all round. Someone pulled out their laptop.

After searching for 'authorship guidelines' they brought up a number of links. Both of us were interested that a number of those having lunch had never looked at such formal guidance. The guidelines brought up on the laptop included the British Psychological Society (BPS, 2011) statement of policy, the British Sociological Association (BSA, 2001) authorship guidelines, a briefing from the Committee on Publication Ethics regarding how to handle authorship disputes (Albert and Wager, 2003), and the University of Cambridge Authorship Guidance (2016). The owner of the laptop did note that there are a lot of medically oriented guidance documents – but that conventions vary across disciplines. The group were interested to see that themes raised across these documents echoed their earlier discussion relating to the premise and order of authorship. Three themes are worth emphasising.

First, the BPS (2011, 1) notes that its members should 'ensure that the contributions of others in collaborative work are accurately reflected in the authorship and other publication credits (including appropriate use of acknowledgements and footnotes)'. The issue of acknowledgements hadn't been considered in our discussion, and our early career colleague raised the potential of using this as a strategy to recognise the contribution of the individual who had reviewed their draft. Second, the BPS (2011) guidance explicitly notes that authorship credit should not be claimed on the basis of status or seniority, but rather on contribution. The BSA (2001, 4) echoes this, noting further that 'Participation solely in the acquisition of funding or general supervision of the research group is not sufficient for authorship. Honorary authorship is not acceptable'. The BPS (2011) also makes specific reference to PhD students, noting that authorship from doctoral work should normally be joint, with the student listed first. However, the level of supervision provided should justify the inclusion of the supervisor (with the implication that, at times, the exclusion of the supervisor may be merited). The BPS (2011) also draws attention to circumstances in which the supervisor may go first. Specifically, these relate to where the student lacks capability to progress the publication, or does not wish to write up their work for publication. Third, again raising an issue not previously noted, the BPS (2011) emphasises that initial agreed authorship may change during the publication process, to reflect different levels of contribution.

This causes us to return to the definition of a contribution – the initial reason our lunch companion began to search for formal guidance on authorship. Although definitions vary, some key commonalities are evident. Here we present and subsequently discuss three perspectives. For the BPS (2011, 1), a broad range of contributions can merit authorship:

> Authorship refers to not only the writing up of the work but also scientific contributions (origination and formulation of the research idea and hypotheses, design of the research, designing and conducting major analysis, and interpreting findings). Lesser contributions (such as designing or building research apparatus, recruiting research participants, data collation and entry, and other administrative duties) should not be considered to constitute authorship, but should merit formal acknowledgement. Where significant combinations of these tasks are undertaken, collaborators should ensure that agreement is reached as early in the research as possible as to whether authorship is merited and on what level (see Fine and Kurdek, 1993).

Within our lunch group, dismay was expressed by one member, who felt that playing a significant role in data collection should merit authorship.

Interestingly, this is an issue addressed within the BSA (2001) guidance. They argue that all those listed on a paper should have made a substantive contribution – explained as comprising intellectual responsibility and substantive work – to at least two of the four main components of the paper. For the BSA (2001), these are: (1) the conception or design of the project; (2) data collection and processing; (3) data analysis and interpretation; and (4) writing substantive sections of the paper. The guidelines further argue that all those listed as authors should have critical input at each point of the review process and should approve the final version of the manuscript. Similar themes are raised under the University of Cambridge (2016) guidance, which states that:

> Normally, an author is an individual judged to have made a substantial intellectual or practical contribution to a publication and who agrees to be accountable for that contribution. This would normally include anyone who has: a. made a significant contribution to the conception or design of the project or the acquisition, analysis, or interpretation of data for the work; **AND/OR** b. drafted the work or reviewed/revised it critically for important intellectual content.

Having noted formal guidance regarding the basis of authorship and the nature of a contribution, we return to insights provided regarding the order of authorship. Beyond noting that authorship should reflect the contribution made, and specific guidance regarding students, the order of authors is not explicitly addressed within BPS (2011) guidance. It is, however, within the BSA (2001). They note that the person who has made the major contribution or led the writing of the paper should be first author; that those who have made major contributions should follow (with the size of the contribution determining order); and that remaining contributors should be in alphabetical order. As noted by one of our colleagues, they also suggest that equal contribution by authors can be indicated by a footnote.

Also of interest to the group was the discovery of a document posted by the Committee on Publication Ethics authored by Albert and Wager (2003). In the spirit of prevention being better than cure, the guidance document, aimed at early career researchers, attempts to tackle the often politically charged and personally embarrassing scenario of authorship disputes. Recommending how authors might adopt proactive tactics so as to avoid authorship problems, three key principles are highlighted. These are: encouraging a culture of ethical authorship (and not blindly following precedent); starting to discuss authorship when you plan your research (and continuing these discussions throughout the life of the paper development, keeping written records of decisions); and deciding authorship before you start each article (including communicating and managing expectations). The document also condemns the use of 'gift' and 'ghost' writers. Gift writers refers to authors who are listed as so but have not fulfilled at least two of the four criteria listed above. Ghost writers by contrast are those who have made a significant contribution to the project but whose input is not acknowledged. Usefully, the document (see Albert and Wager, 2003) also provides insight into how to handle authorship disputes and misconduct.

Having reviewed the formal guidance, by way of summary one of the group members noted that the guidelines seemed to be a helpful way to depersonalise conflict. In their view, common to all was discussion about 'expectations, obligations, accountability and integrity'. They then directly addressed the early career faculty member, noting that there are different bases for awarding authorship. In the circumstances described, the speaker felt that the early career researcher's colleague hadn't made a sufficient contribution to merit authorship, although they could, if the feedback merited it, be given an acknowledgement. The speaker also advised that the author continue to refer to '*my*' paper!

AUTHORSHIP: EXPECTATIONS AND OBLIGATIONS

In our research we look at exchange relationships, respectively examining customer–employee interfaces and employment relationships. Like all relationships, including authorship ones, issues relating to the expectations and perceived obligations of all parties arise. Within authorship relationships, key points around which expectations are likely to occur are:

- the basis for inclusion as an author on papers;
- the premise on which the order of authors is determined, and by whom.

These expectations can arise and exist implicitly, if not formally addressed. Based on the experiences of those in our group, problems are likely to occur where expectations are implicit, and differences in perceptions don't become apparent, or resolved, early in the process. The longer it goes on, the harder it seems to be. Consequently, communication is key. Formal authorship guidelines provide a basis for discussion when starting new relationships or projects. For each project and paper, being upfront and honest regarding individuals' own expectations, time and ability to contribute is paramount – as is building in opportunities to revisit relative contributions and author ordering.

Like anything worth having in life, negotiating co-authorship isn't always easy. However, here we add a personal note to the discussion – and an advocacy of its benefits. We both really enjoy co-authoring. For each of us, co-authors have served hugely significant roles in developing our research skills, and our careers. Aspects of academic life can be lonely and trying. Working with others to see a project through from conception to completion can be a great source of fun and reward. A good co-author isn't just someone who you want to spend time with: they should challenge you. Co-authors provide deadlines that focus progression. They enable conversations about theoretical framing and data analysis – helping make tacit connections explicit. For us, co-authoring with others has developed our individual capacities to write, helped to enhance the quality of our work, and our enjoyment in the process. It has also enabled us, in turn, to mentor others in this process. Everyone, regardless of their level of seniority or time spent as an academician, can enjoy, learn and benefit from co-authoring. It is the fuel that propels academic and individual development. Being clear about expectations and obligations in this most common, and critical, of academic relationships can support enjoyable, enduring and productive writing relationships.

LESSONS

- Have a clear understanding of the basis of authorship at the start of a project and each paper within it.
- Contemplate who merits authorship and what order of authorship best represents each individual's contribution.
- Don't be afraid to communicate, discuss and debate. Ask questions and don't blindly follow authorship traditions or conventions.
- Revisit authorship and ordering of authors throughout the key milestones of an article's development, including the review and revision process. If needed, formally document any agreed changes.
- Be accountable. Authorship represents a responsibility. Ensure all co-authors sign off on the content of the paper at each stage of the writing and publication process.
- Leave egos at the door and actively manage your own expectations and the expectations of others. Who is responsible for what and by when? Agree on the process that needs to be followed by each co-author to bring the paper to fruition. It's good to talk.
- Use formal guidance notes to guide and depersonalise conflict. Don't let problems or misunderstandings fester, face them head on.
- Last and not least, act with integrity and enjoy co-authoring.

ACKNOWLEDGEMENTS

We acknowledge the input of our lunch companions to the ideas shared in this chapter. As they made substantive contribution to the development of the ideas therein, we would ideally have afforded them authorship – but we don't know their names.

NOTE

* Authors in alphabetical order. Each author contributed equally to the writing process. In addition, one contributed a packet of posh biscuits. The other ate most of them.

REFERENCES

Albert, T. and Wager, E. (2003), 'How to handle authorship disputes: a guide for new researchers', *Committee on Publication Ethics (COPE) Report*, pp. 32–4.

British Psychological Society (2011), *Research Board Statement of Policy on Authorship and Publication Credit* (July), accessed 10 November 2016 at http://www.bps.org.uk/system/files/images/statement_of_policy_on_authorship_credit.pdf.

British Sociological Association (2001), *Authorship Guidelines for Academic Papers*, accessed 22 November 2016 at https://www.britsoc.co.uk/media/21409/authorship_01.pdf.

Fine, M.A. and Kurdek, L.A. (1993), 'Reflections on determining authorship credit and authorship order on faculty–staff collaborations', *American Psychologist*, **48**(11), 1141–7.

University of Cambridge (2016), *Guidelines on Authorship*, accessed 11 November 2015 at http://www.research-integrity.admin.cam.ac.uk/research-integrity/guidelines-authorship.

28. 'They think I'm stupid': dealing with supervisor feedback

Amanda Lee

In this chapter I share my experiences of dealing with supervisor feedback and offer some thoughts, ideas, hints and tips on how you can turn this sometimes negative experience into something positive and useful. Writing is a skilled craft and it still takes me time, patience and practice (especially practice) to produce work of reasonable quality, but then, we all have to start somewhere. I remember thinking, 'What's the point in writing if I don't have anything to say?' However, I soon learnt that even if you don't think you have anything to say, write anyway. I found that once I begin writing I start thinking, creating, reflecting and critiquing, all of which ultimately contributes to and supports my writing. I have structured this chapter into three sections. The first reflects on my personal experiences of dealing with supervisor feedback at the beginning of my PhD studies. The second describes my experiences during the middle and latter stages of my doctoral research. Finally, I present the advice I would have liked to have had when I first embarked on my doctoral adventures in the hope that you find it of some help.

I'M NOT GOOD ENOUGH

My doctoral studies spanned six years and I had the added complication of being a part-time distance learner, working full-time in a different university. Six years prior to embarking on my PhD I had completed a Masters degree and considered myself to be reasonably articulate in respect of my writing skills. However, all that changed when I became a PhD student. I vividly remember the day I first received detailed written feedback from one of my supervisors. Even though the event was four years ago, I can still remember how utterly stupid and useless I felt. Furthermore, I was confused, because I had already received some encouraging feedback from my other supervisor. Luckily, I had a very close colleague in whom I could confide, so my first response was to call her up and tell her how I felt. She was also working full-time and studying part-time for her PhD, so I knew she would understand my situation. As a part-time student and researcher I found the support of colleagues, friends and fellow students was, and is, incredibly important. For me, the PhD road was long, often lonely and introspective and regularly all-consuming. The knowledge that someone else was going through the same trials and tribulations was certainly a comfort and reassurance to me. The first piece of advice my colleague offered was to write down how I felt at that particular moment in time, and so I did.

Since the beginning of my studies I had kept a reflective research journal in which I recorded observations, feelings, reactions and experiences. These related both to the subject of my research, as well as to my own personal reflections. This extract from my journal captures my feelings and state of mind on receiving this feedback:

> Feeling rather fed up this evening. Received feedback on my managerialism chapter in the post today and although comments were very constructive it made it clear to me that I have such a long way to go. I am getting so tired, work is very demanding at the moment, yet I am aware of how much more time I need to spend on my research. It isn't just time, it's useful time. It really struck me that work produced for my PhD can't be just good enough, it has to be much better than that, it has to make a difference and it has to matter. At the moment I feel as though it is all far beyond me and unachievable. I really hope this feeling passes soon as it is affecting my motivation and I am finding excuses as to why I shouldn't just get on with it.

Hopefully this extract will reassure you that, if you have been in this position, you are not alone. On the other hand, if you have not yet received feedback from your supervisor, it may help to prepare you for such an experience. The good news is, things will and do get better. It is all part of the steep learning curve synonymous with doctoral study. That journal entry was written towards the end of my first twelve months. Working full-time I found it incredibly difficult to juggle the demands of my job, PhD and family and I felt guilty that I was not devoting enough time to my doctoral studies. One of the things that struck me as I read through my supervisor's comments was the realisation of what is actually required to produce a body of work suitable to be considered doctoral level and especially important for me, how (and how much) to write. I had previously sent short pieces to my supervisors, but their feedback had been sparse. In all honesty, this was probably because I hadn't actually written enough for them to comment upon.

A few weeks after receiving this feedback I attended a conference where my supervisor was chairing a session. It was difficult, but I told him how I had felt when I received his responses and I was surprised at his reaction – in a good way. He seemed genuinely concerned that I had been so upset by his comments and explained that whilst my work was good, his aim was to help me make it even better. I was very appreciative of this and it helped me get things into perspective. He also told me I needed to write more, but as I have already intimated, I was already aware of that. Talking to my supervisor was really beneficial and I strongly recommend you do this, but maybe after a few days when you have given yourself time to fully digest their feedback and become a bit more objective. You might like to know that he has also told me he has tried to recognise this in the way he gives feedback, although his students still say his comments don't pull any punches!

When I reached the enviable final stage of writing up my thesis, I looked back on my journal entry and it seemed as though I was reading about someone else. It was only with the benefit of hindsight that I could see how far I had progressed. I felt as though I wanted to reach out to my earlier self and tell her everything would be all right in the end. The successful completion of my PhD is testament that it was. As my studies (and writing) progressed, I became more accustomed to receiving critical feedback and as a result was much better prepared. I also got to know my supervisors' own particular styles, likes, dislikes and expectations. This helped me develop a much clearer sense of what they thought I was capable of achieving. However, this was not always compatible with my own estimations of my capability. I have to admit it was not until I had written the first full draft of my thesis that I began to realise the extent to which my writing had improved. Had it not been for the frank, comprehensive and critical feedback received from my supervisors at the outset, and throughout my PhD studies, I do not believe this would have been the case. So, I suppose what I am saying is, it hurts like hell at the time, but it really is worth the pain!

ACTUALLY, I'M OK

By the time I was two to three years into my PhD I was receiving supervisor feedback on a more regular basis. I am also pleased to say I was writing more, but not necessarily as often as I would have liked. By this stage I had developed a strong relationship and bond with both my supervisors and in some cases I was able to anticipate their feedback. With this in mind I would often include my own notes and comments in my drafts to show them my thought patterns and plans for how I thought the writing of my chapters should progress. This process worked very well for me and it also made it much easier to respond to their feedback. The following are some journal extracts written when I was working on a peer-reviewed journal article on which my supervisors were second and third authors:

> Feedback received from first supervisor and main comments were that I needed to inject a more nuanced picture into my narrative. But overall, she felt it was a rich and interesting discussion. Obviously, feeling more anxious about second supervisor's comments.

A day later I received feedback from my second supervisor:

> Feedback received from second supervisor and the paper, together with both sets of comments, is pasted in my journal. Second supervisor wanted me to include more quotes/comments that I've observed and beef up the conclusion considerably.

What I find interesting to note in these journal extracts (as opposed to my earlier example) is that the focus is on summarising what I need to do, rather than how I was feeling. Nevertheless, the first extract above does reveal I was more apprehensive waiting for my second supervisor's comments.

Within the paper were numerous comments, suggestions, amendments, additions and deletions from both supervisors, but by now I was much better equipped to deal with and respond to them. I did this by systematically working through each point, making the necessary modifications and detailing my response in writing for my supervisors. I realised as I was doing this I was honing skills that would be needed to respond to other academic peer reviewers outside of the comfort zone of my own supervisors.

Ultimately, the paper we were working on was accepted for publication and this was a high point in my doctoral studies. As first author I had to respond to the journal editor's comments and I drew heavily on my experiences of responding to my own supervisors' feedback:

> Worked hard on getting the amendments done (with advice from my first and second supervisors). It was time-consuming, but a very worthwhile exercise and it was a learning curve for me as it was the first time I have written back to an editor with my responses. For my sake (as well as the Journal's), I sent back one draft with all amendments, another showing all the track changes and a separate document detailing all our responses to the copy editor's comments. I am really excited about seeing my first publication in print and it is a vindication that my PhD is worth doing.

The last eight months of my doctorate were spent analysing my data, revisiting, reviewing and updating earlier chapters and writing up later chapters and my introduction. By this stage I had begun to think of myself as a competent writer and this really struck home when I received feedback from my supervisors on my updated literature review chapters. In contrast to comments on my earlier work, they really didn't have much to say. My first supervisor responded only by email, pointing out a few typos, but was happy with the content and quality of my work. My second supervisor (the scary one) only made seven comments and most of these were for clarification. For the first time I didn't need to make any substantial changes or amendments in response to their feedback. I felt really good when my second supervisor told me in person that when he read my updated literature review chapters he could see that 'I had got it'. This gave me confidence and a real spur to get on with writing up the rest of the damn thing!

By the time I was in a position to send the first full draft of my thesis to my supervisors I was apprehensive about their feedback, but I was also incredibly relieved that this day had finally come. Furthermore, because I had been sending them written work throughout the whole process, they had already seen and commented on much of it. I can't stress enough how important it has been to send work to my supervisors for feedback and comment, and as I said at the start of this chapter, I have done this from the beginning. However, every supervisor/supervisee relationship is different and unique and learning how to manage your supervisors and nurture your relationship with them are other skills you need to develop. I consider myself very fortunate to have had the supervisory team I did, but this relationship is two-way and I was always ready to take their advice and act upon it.

After submitting my first full draft I was genuinely surprised by how quickly my supervisors came back to me, although I realise this may not be the case for all doctoral students. Nevertheless, I do recommend asking your supervisors how long you can expect to wait for feedback on written work. On this particular occasion, I can honestly say I was pleasantly surprised by their feedback. Yes, I still had work to do, amendments, additions and corrections to make, but their positive comments really gave me a lift. However, because this time the comments were few, and not in as much detail as I had been used to previously, I had several questions for my supervisors. I was now not afraid to ask for clarity or challenge my supervisors on the feedback they gave me. As I have mentioned previously, talking to them about my concerns, feelings and any difficulties I was having was essential. This is based on honesty, trust and respect for each other.

I responded to my supervisors by email, carefully going through each of their points one by one, explaining my rationale and asking for more information and clarity on the comments I was unsure of how to address.

I also followed this up with telephone and Skype conversations so I was absolutely clear about what it was my supervisors felt I needed to do. That was in July 2016 and I spent the summer (in between holidays and work) making the necessary amendments and adjustments to my thesis. By early September my amended full draft was sent to my supervisors.

The next few days I waited with bated breath. I was due to see my second supervisor at a conference the following week and I knew he would want to discuss my latest attempt. He was full of smiles when I saw him and he said, 'Have you read my email?' I hadn't, and for a split second I had a feeling of dread. This soon passed when he told me, 'Well, in my view it's ready to submit.' I felt euphoric, six years' work and I was nearly there! If you had told me I would be in this situation even one year ago I would have had difficulty believing it. Every doctoral student experience is unique, but for me, much of my thesis came together in the final six months. This was a culmination of previous years of work on my part, combined with the unstinting support, guidance and constructive criticism of my supervisors. I could not have done it without them and for that I will be eternally grateful. But, and there is always a 'but', it is *my* thesis and *I* had to do the work. This included sending regular drafts to my supervisors, accepting their feedback in the spirit in which it was offered and acting on their advice. I always asked if I didn't understand as I knew they were doing it to help me improve and enable me to make my work even better.

HINTS AND TIPS FOR DEALING WITH SUPERVISOR FEEDBACK

In this final section I present a list of Dos and Don'ts, based on my experiences. I have listed the Don'ts first, as from my perspective these were some of the feelings I experienced when first receiving supervisor feedback. From talking to other doctoral students, I now realise such feelings and reactions are normal, but it doesn't have to be that way.

Don't:

- Take feedback personally, even though it is intensely personal to you. Your thesis is your creation and it is a natural reaction to defend your work. Indeed, being able to defend your work is an important skill to develop.
- Ignore or dismiss supervisor feedback. Their comments are intended to help you and enable you to develop and improve as a researcher and writer.

- Use feedback as an excuse not to write.
- Use feedback to beat yourself up, or to think you are stupid, or not good enough. *You are not stupid* and *you are good enough*, but you have to learn how to do it.

Do:

- Write down, or audio/video record how you feel and why you feel this way. This can really help to consolidate and make sense of the situation and the feedback.
- Talk to someone unconnected with your thesis. This could be a fellow student, colleague, friend or family member. They will not be emotionally attached to your thesis in the way that you are.
- Sleep on it. Give yourself time to digest the feedback and go back to it a few days later. Make notes on the comments from your supervisor(s) and how you can address them.
- Arrange a meeting with your supervisor(s). Talk to them about their comments and your reactions to their feedback. Ask questions to clarify exactly what they mean and what you need to do.
- (Once you are clear about what you need to do to improve your work) systematically work through each comment and make the necessary amendments. Make a note of the amendments you have made.
- Keep earlier versions of your work, clearly labelled by date and version.
- Agree a timescale with your supervisor(s) for submission of your written work and stick to it.
- Write every day if you can – little and often soon mounts up. Some supervisors like to see small chunks of work on a regular basis, whilst others prefer complete chapters. Set the ground rules with your supervisor so you both know what is expected.
- After a period of time go back and reflect on your initial thoughts and feelings. With the benefit of hindsight you will recognise how you have developed as a researcher.

29. Grasping roses or nettles? Losing and finding ourselves in research projects

Kiran Trehan, Alex Kevill and Jane Glover

All the world's a stage,
And all the men and women merely players;
They have their exits and their entrances;
And one man in his time plays many parts . . .
(William Shakespeare, *As You Like It*, Act II, Scene VII)

INTRODUCTION

Developing, maintaining and sustaining research projects has become almost obligatory within research arenas. The aim of our chapter is to illuminate and explore the relationship between emotions, politics and disappointment in developing and maintaining research projects. We elucidate the lived reality of undertaking research projects as turbulent, volatile and an emotional endeavour. Using illustrations from our own experiences in the field, we develop three distinct in-depth accounts as 'scenes' to describe the dynamics that underpin research projects whilst also making connections between reflexivity, emotions and disappointment. We highlight how messy and complex keeping research projects on track can be. Our chapter is not written up 'straightforwardly' as a description of what happened but is an attempt to reveal the shadow side of finding, securing and maintaining research projects by three researchers at different trajectories in their academic careers. The illustrations illuminate how practice and experience in the field shape research endeavours.

SCENE 1: AN EARLY CAREER RESEARCHER'S MUSINGS

So there I was, sitting in a small plain meeting room, eating sandwiches and cakes, and celebrating my successful PhD viva with my supervisors and internal examiner. Four and a half years of blood, sweat and tears – and let's not forget the support of my wonderful supervisors – had got me to this point. Finally I was living the moment that I had pictured in my mind for so long! I had the ticket to my future career in academia and my mind basked in idyllic images of numerous journal papers flowing from my PhD study. I had successfully completed my first research project – my PhD – and it felt good! Now it was time to sit back and enjoy the fruits of all my hard work . . .

. . . Fast-forward eighteen months and here I am. A full-time lecturer, loving my job, yet frustratingly finding those journal papers are not quite as forthcoming as I had assumed. Time constraints have become my nemesis, intent as they are on starving me of my research endeavours. Exciting research ideas regularly give way to my increasingly familiar resignation that most of them will never materialise. My nemesis is winning the battle, it seems. And now, all of a sudden, I am being encouraged to get involved in my next research project! Furthermore, I sense that the more significant and impactful it is the better!

A small tremor of anxiety ripples through me and culminates in an overwhelming sense of exasperation. Surely I should be concentrating on getting publications from my previous research study, shouldn't I?! Why embark on another project when I don't even have time to make the most of the previous one? How can I possibly make time, within my already packed schedule, to undertake a new research project to the high standard I would demand of myself? Whilst such concerns flow through my mind though, they live awkwardly alongside a sense of enticement and excitement that I feel about embarking on a new challenge. After all, who wouldn't want to be part of an interesting, significant and impactful research project if they got the chance?

But where would I start? What would I, as an early career researcher, know about this? What, if anything, could I bring to the table? Will this be the point at which my self-perceived shortcomings as a researcher finally become evident to others? The thought of engaging and working with others in order to generate real impact both excites and terrifies me in reasonably equal measure. I feel lost in a sea of unknowns. I wonder particularly about how to establish links with relevant stakeholders outside of academic circles. This was challenging enough during my PhD study when trying to establish and maintain relationships with reasonably small numbers of research participants, each of whom had little vested interest in my research. A larger scale project, I am sure, would likely include a more diverse range of stakeholders – academic, organisational, governmental, interest groups and so on – each with different motivations and vested interests, and each needing to be satisfied and kept on board with the project. This seems to promise an unappealing labyrinth of politics and tension that require navigation: do I really want to be involved in this? How does one even start to navigate such politics and tensions in order to deliver impact from a project? And at a much more functional level, how do I even make contact with these stakeholders in the first place to bring them on board? Do I call them? Can I find somebody who can help get me a foot in the door?

And what about funding? Who do I seek funding from? How do I seek it? I know that funding applications require a thorough and well-considered research proposal, which is likely to require a lot of the groundwork – particularly bringing stakeholders on board – to be done before funding is even assured. And ultimately, all of that groundwork could surely be for nothing if funding is not gained. I wonder to myself how one possibly deals with the disappointment and anguish of facing such a rejection, knowing that all of the hard work and hours dedicated to the bid have essentially been futile.

My mind then switches to that word that we so often hear when talking about research projects: impact. What does impact really mean? Surely all research is impactful in some way, so is impactful research determined by achieving a certain threshold of impact? If so, what is the threshold and how does one go about achieving it? Surely different project stakeholders will have different perceptions of what impact means to them so is it really possible to achieve impact in all stakeholders' eyes or do the views and interests of some stakeholders matter more than others? Most frighteningly of all, what if I promise impact and then can't deliver it? That doesn't even bear thinking about!

These doubts and anxieties become lessened to some degree by the realisation that I could, first of all, seek an opportunity to work as a reasonably junior member of a large research project team. Yes, this sounds a promising compromise! It could surely help me gain much-needed experience whilst absolving me of some of the responsibility that I currently feel ill-equipped to take on. Yet nervousness begins to overwhelm my short-lived comfort. Do I really want to be subject to unequal power relationships with those leading the project? Could they drive my future research direction too much? Could I really bring myself to stand up to them if I feel that I need to? I also wonder about how one spots an opportunity to join a good research project team and how one initiates one's integration into the project. It seems obvious that I should join a project that I am truly interested in but what if such a project does not present itself? What impact would that then have on my career and, if that happens, should I just take part in any old project, whether I am interested in it or not?

Then my immediate next steps suddenly become clear to me. It's time to seek advice from colleagues more experienced in developing and maintaining research projects . . .

SCENE TWO: A POST DOC'S TRIALS AND TRIBULATIONS OF SECURING (OR NOT) FUNDED RESEARCH PROJECTS

In this section I share with you my reflective life experience of projects, and trying to move seamlessly from one project to another (quite the romantic dream when you read my story). I completed my PhD post changes to university funding in the UK so with little in the way of lectureships at the time I pursued a research career, I found I had more flexibility on research contracts, and because I was restricted to a specific location for family reasons, I found myself not actively pursuing teaching and research posts. My life working on projects started whilst I was doing my PhD; my supervisor at the time asked me if I would like to work on a project, and naturally, as I was self-funded I leapt at the opportunity to earn some money. I would, however, recommend this with caution as you become distracted from your PhD and get used to earning money and then there is a certain amount of willpower and dedication required to return to full-time studies again – but that's another story.

So I obtained my first working project and it was in an area related to my PhD: small business and innovation. I think I was extremely lucky with the person who was my line manager for this project; I was treated as an equal and, based on experiences I will detail later on, he was a total dream to work for. I learnt a lot on this project and improved my research skills. Having done this short stint, about eight months, I returned to my doctoral studies but managed to secure a few hours' work doing follow-up work on the project (I also took on teaching work to bolster my income).

A few months before finishing my PhD I secured another short-term project at the same university but in a different department. Maybe not the best decision, but you can't live off fresh air. I think this prolonged the agony of actually finishing my PhD along with the fact that three months before PhD submission we had a house fire, which resulted in turmoil. Anyway, this project, on innovation, was an enlightening experience. I was working for someone who could only be described as a lovely old-school professor (due to retire) and two younger, recently appointed academics. One was very quiet and relatively easy to work for, the other somewhat different from my previous experiences, his view of a researcher being someone to do all the hard work and write the papers so that he could be lead author and bask in the glory with minimal effort. This changed my previously somewhat romantic view that all line managers were like my first one. The key reflection is that when things go wrong, be careful in terms of the ideas you share as we have no way of securing intellectual property so ideas for funding research projects can easily get hijacked. . . . Only share these with someone you trust and someone with whom you really want to work and build a research agenda.

So by this point I was becoming quite adept at juggling many different projects but still hadn't got used to the fact that short-term projects are often intense (people seem to expect more in less time . . .) and no sooner have you started one, than you are trying to find the next one. This also has implications for creating your own research agenda and developing your own area of expertise so you may end up working on your own research in your spare time, which I did and found myself working 50 hours plus a week. I didn't mind at the time; I was younger, ambitious and I wanted to succeed and saw this as a way to do that.

Then with another stroke of luck a part-time position became available working with my original line manager. I was overjoyed and couldn't wait to start working with him again, and this was the start of a great role, working on different projects either full- or part-time for the next four years. These were four great years. I was able to take the lead in my area of expertise (qualitative research methods) and complement my line manager (who I would describe as a die-hard quants man), and it worked. I was allowed to manage projects freely so long as I delivered; I was encouraged to publish, to apply for internal departmental funds (which I managed to win twice), and to look for grants that we could apply for. To me this was what a working academic/researcher partnership should be like; we applied for two external grants, but sadly were unsuccessful. I was also heavily involved in his bid to create a research centre at the institution, which got funded. This was a highly productive partnership during which we had six publications and I had four publications from my own research (which I was encouraged to do) as well as having others under review. I have never been as productive again in my career, nor been as encouraged as I was by this line manager. But as the saying goes: all good things come to an end . . . and it did. . . . My line manager phoned me one day and said, 'I need to tell you something (deathly silence) . . . I'm leaving and moving to another institution. . . .' I was speechless, totally gutted; I felt as if my whole world had been swallowed up by a black hole and that I was about to be deserted for a life working for egotistical academics who are only concerned with their own ego and prestige. To be fair, my line manager did say that if I wanted to go he would try to take me with him, but I couldn't. So my academic knight in shining armour, a complete role model for all line managers, was leaving. I think for my career that was the single worst day: it changed my future direction.

The key thing to note about this working relationship is that I will happily work with him again (and we do currently have papers in review and also papers to write). He is the only line manager I have had who I would actively seek to work with in the future. The reason for this is that he helped me a lot in my early career, and I believe my path would have taken a different turn had he not left. The institution was not impressed that one of their best-performing academics (in terms of grants and publications) was leaving. Because I had worked solely with him they were not bothered about trying to keep me on so I was faced with a (short) spell of unemployment.

This very point signalled a change in my luck in terms of securing back-to-back projects, whether they were full- or part-time. I had to change my outlook and learn to cope with disappointment and with the stress of being unable to find projects that were longer than a couple of years. Whilst that sounds like a long time, it really isn't because you have to start looking for the next one at least nine months before your current project expires. I'm sure this would have been easier had I not been restricted to a particular location, but that was a life situation that I had to cope with.

I found part-time work again back at the institution for some of this time and I also worked part-time at other institutions to keep myself in full-time employment. I found some of this time quite stressful as at one point I was working on five different projects across two institutions. This was some of my least productive time and I often felt constrained and in some cases (unlike my first line manager) I felt that people didn't trust my judgement. For example, having spent months doing a literature review to identify gaps in the literature and a potential paper, this was ignored. When this happens you feel really deflated, especially if you put your heart and soul into something because it is interesting. As a word of caution, as a female researcher, my experience has taught me to be cautious and never, I really mean never, question a male professor who requires constant reassurance of his excellence – well, not if you want a good reference or a job somewhere else!

However, I did meet another academic on this project who reminded me of my first line manager and I have, over the years, developed a good working relationship with her and she is the only other person with whom

I have actively sought to secure funding and publish. Maybe one day we will secure that all-important large grant and I can bask in my own glory.

During my time of short-term projects I have been presented with obstacles and barriers when trying to apply for external funds, unless I have been lucky enough to have a supportive line manager. Even here, when we submitted two applications that progressed through stage one of review, and then after hours of hard work producing full proposals, we were not awarded anything. Over my somewhat erratic research career I have found there to be, in some institutions, a protectionist type philosophy where I think that young, ambitious researchers who question the status quo are not actually something that the institution wants (ironic, seeing as we are taught to be critical and reflective in undergraduate and postgraduate studies). I think that to be successful in securing external funding you need to have some luck and a very supportive line manager where your work resonates with theirs in such a way that you can legitimately make the suggestion that you should be a co-investigator! Otherwise, as someone on short-term contracts moving between institutions, unless you secure that all-important permanent position, I have found that it is virtually impossible to apply for external funds.

I'm still, now, stuck on short-term projects and would love to secure something full-time for three years or so just to have that bit of stability and security to allow me to pursue a particular research agenda and win funding for projects of my own! The best advice I can give to anyone is that I think you need to be prepared that life will throw many obstacles in your way; you may have luck on your side, but if you don't, you have to persevere. I've found the more you want something, the less likely it is you get it. I think you subconsciously put pressure on yourself, so as hard as it may be, try my philosophy of expecting nothing every time you try to secure a project and then you'll find one day you land a project totally unexpectedly. This may not be really what you wanted, but you end up enjoying it and it provides you with an opportunity.

In terms of managing projects themselves and trying to find the next one, all I can say is you have to know exactly what *you* (nobody else) want to achieve from that particular project. So by this I mean: if you see a project that you wish to work on, be clear about the reasons why. Is it the topic, the people you will be working with, the institution? And then where does this get you? (If times are desperate I appreciate anything will do . . . but even then you should carve out what the benefits could be for yourself even if it is simply to learn.) You need to be adept at spotting opportunity and being entrepreneurial.

In summary, my experience of projects, managing projects and looking for projects is one of ups and downs, of getting one's hopes up only to come crashing down again (and again). But my hope is that one day my strategy of being savvy, very selective as to who I will work with, and sheer grit and determination will mean that one day I *will* get that large grant and that 4* journal paper. I can look back and think: it may have been hard work, I may have been taken advantage of, but who cares if I achieve my goal . . .

SCENE THREE: RESEARCHER TURNED PROFESSOR: GRASPING ROSES, OR IS IT NETTLES?

And so to the final scene: how does the story end? Is it a tale of tragedy, like *Julius Caesar*, or is it a tale of triumph, such as *Henry V*? The next illustration illuminates the emotional and political labour required in securing and maintaining a research project.

I lie in bed, it's 6:30 am. Far too early to be getting out of bed on a cold morning, not quite winter yet, there's still a chill in the air. I spy out of the window, a dreary day. I haven't slept well, but there it was as I jumped in the shower, the familiar feeling in the pit of my stomach. I'm excited and anxious about a significant project meeting with a key stakeholder from the finance, business, policy and academic community. The stakes are high and we only get one chance to get it right! I feel out of my depth and the initial excitement turns to fear. I remind myself why I had said yes to co-directing the project; I wanted to learn and be part of an exciting opportunity. I muse as the warm water of the shower washes over me, not wanting to get out, but I must as I muster the energy for the meeting ahead with trepidation.

On the surface of it, all looks great and exciting – how often do you get the [highly influential] people together in the same room for 24 hours to work on a major research project. There is an edge of anxiety that I can feel and sense in the room between us (the team) – a conflictual edge that I have not experienced before. I'm intrigued and curious about what's going on but now's not the time to raise it so I stay focused on the task as we prepare for the arrival of our guests.

Our partners begin to arrive and we each play our part yet there is no script . . . It is interesting to observe the roles we take on . . . [Our administrator] does the meeting and greeting – checking everybody in – making them feel like old friends that have come round for dinner, introducing the newcomers so that they feel part of the group. Another colleague is warm and engaging. . . . There's a good buzz about the place. Dinner goes extremely well. . . . The newcomers are vocal and have made an impression; there is an interesting tension building behind the friendly and relaxed façade presented by some members and the challenges by new members.

The evening ends, we have a quick debrief in preparation for tomorrow. It's 11.45 pm, we are all tired; that edge I mentioned earlier is still there. We should be on a high. We have everyone's commitment and buy in. Actually we have much more than that, we have access to some of the most powerful resource holders and gatekeepers and they want to engage with us. It feels genuine, authentic and hugely exciting, so why is the team so flat? This is the thought I'm left with as I head to my room.

My reflections are that managing and keeping research projects on track requires particular types of collaboration, leadership and facilitation which are imaginative, passionate, experiential and action related. My own recollections are flooded with a myriad of emotions of fear, anxiety and excitement, and my limited understanding of all of the political processes was at the start anxiety provoking; however, the lived experience of enacting interdisciplinary research has been an incredibly rich endeavour. Extending the reach, reflecting and refracting light opened up my growing curiosity to not just talk about interdisciplinary research as an academic exercise but to endeavour to work with the struggle, fears and insecurities that come from a place of not knowing to a place of unlearning and re-learning. Working on the project has enriched my knowledge and my passion to stray from the narrow confines and alleys of the academic community to travel through wider streets and over borders, because when combined with passion, rigour, evidence and the commitment of others to make a difference, a difference that matters, nothing is more powerful than working in an interdisciplinary team with all its trials and tribulations.

CONCLUDING REFLECTIONS

Our collective narratives have attempted to offer a glimpse in the life of researchers attempting to broker and navigate their way through complex dynamics in the lives of research projects when things do not go quite to plan. What they do not do is tell the whole story: research projects are not without their risks, those big moments of self-doubt, frustrations and anguish alongside moments of laughter, hope, excitement and imagination. Our illustrations highlight the need for commitment, criticality, openness to risk, the ability to speak about the unspoken and question the systems, structures and institutions in which research is crafted, maintained and disrupted. . . . And as the journey begins:

- Always be true to yourself and what you eventually wish to be known for in the world of research.
- If someone looks after you, such as a line manager, then maintain that relationship, and in time you will be able to repay them.
- Be prepared for utter disappointment but master the art of bouncing back and learning from that experience.

- Try not to take things to heart if someone doesn't like what you've done: ask how it should be improved.
- Be opportunistic: always look for external funding, internal institutional funding, and projects to work on and don't be afraid to give it a go.
- Never settle for the path of least resistance.
- When you come close to selling out, reconsider.
- Do not be afraid to take the occasional risk.

30. Using social media to enhance your research

Angelique Gatsinzi

Academia may not be the most coveted career for the youth in the twenty-first century. The notion of an academic career has changed drastically over the last century and conversations with PhD students and early career researchers quickly reveal how difficult it is to establish yourself as an academic. This is not to say that academia or being an academic was better a century ago, it simply means that perhaps we need to embrace what the twenty-first century can offer. We are living in a fast-changing world, revolutionised by digital and information technology, an era where owning a smartphone and summing up your entire week in a single emoji is part of pop culture. How then can we make academia and research appealing to an emerging youth whose entire life is stored on a touch screen smartphone?

FINDING YOUR SOCIAL MEDIA NICHE

Long before I enrolled on my PhD programme, I considered myself to be a fashion and lifestyle blogger. Twice a week I posted articles about whatever trend was en vogue or I ranted about topics which had featured in my day-to-day conversations with friends, family or colleagues. In no time, I realised that I had a group of followers who eagerly awaited my posts and commented on them as soon as I hit the publication button. With that 'fame' came the requests from online newspapers and blogs to contribute thought pieces on social and international development issues. It was quite interesting to see how quickly I became known on this digital platform, all the while sitting comfortably in my bed recounting personal experiences to a faceless audience. When I applied for a studentship at my current university, I incorporated the use of social media in the research proposal. Most PhD students would know how radically such proposals can change once you are enrolled. In my case, once I familiarised myself with the ethical clearance procedures at the university, it became quite clear that justifying the use of social media would be very difficult, given the vulnerability of my participants. With my supervisor's consent, I decided to remove the social media aspect from the proposal and instead use social media to track my academic and personal development.

As you have already gathered, I did not use social media for the first time when I started my PhD; I had already accumulated enough experience as a regular Facebook, LinkedIn, WordPress and Twitter user in both a personal and professional manner. Deciding to stay connected was a result of my positive experiences and the useful connections I had made over the years via social media. Being as clueless as I was when I started my PhD, I knew that using social media would boost my confidence as an academic and perhaps even make me a better academic.

EMBRACING DIGITAL ACADEMIA

Using social media has allowed me to connect and engage with experienced academics in my field who, without social media I would probably only recognise in the references section in the last few pages of my thesis. Furthermore, it allowed me to connect with others worldwide who are finding their research paths like I am. Despite sharing an office with a dozen other students at different stages of their degree, pursuing a PhD programme can prove to be a very lonely experience. Most PhD students can relate to walking into the office with the aim of completing a chapter, only to struggle to begin a sentence. This becomes even more difficult when you look around you and everyone else seems to be busy doing something productive.

If you are reading this, then you probably belong to one of these three categories: (a) you are a regular social media user but have not really thought about how you can use it for your research; (b) you do not own any social media accounts but you are open to new ways of engaging with other researchers in your field; or (c) you don't have any social media and don't have any interest in starting social media but figured because you've paid for the book you might as well read all the chapters! The next section is my attempt to introduce you to two types of social media tools that I use and that have helped me to feel comfortable as an academic and, more importantly, give me a voice. There are several other platforms available but I can only guarantee the efficiency of the two mentioned below. In any case, the fewer social media accounts you have, the more likely you will find the time to consult your profile, upload content and engage with your network. Notice that the most crucial aspect of social media is the concept of engaging, or socialising, if you will. If you know that you're the type of person who will create an account, not bother completing some basic information about yourself and forget the login password after a couple of days, then perhaps this is not for you. Just like most things we apply ourselves to, some level of commitment is required to make social media work for us. Note: being committed does not mean being addicted – you will never get any research done if you are!

MICRO-BLOGGING

Micro-blogs allow you to 'exchange small elements of content such as short sentences, individual images, or video links . . . micro-blogs stand halfway between traditional blogs and social networking sites, and are characterised by a high degree of self-presentation/self-disclosure and a medium to low degree of social presence/media richness' (Kaplan and Haenlein, 2011, p. 106). Twitter has become the most popular platform for micro-blogging since it was established in 2006. The 140-character limit is what makes Twitter especially effective, and once you master the art it can benefit your research career.

Out of all the social networking sites I am registered to, Twitter is my go-to for most of my research-related queries and it is where I would usually spend some time if I were experiencing writer's block. I like using Twitter because of how instantly information is diffused, usually within minutes of an event happening. According to Kaplan and Haenlein (2011), on the day that Michael Jackson died in 2009, 100 000 tweets about the breaking news were exchanged per hour. As a millennial, I must admit that I am more likely to spend time looking for current news around the world on Twitter than to buy a newspaper or watch a news programme on television. If it is not trending on Twitter then it is probably not newsworthy – quite frankly as worrying as that may sound, this is where the world is heading. So how can you take advantage of this powerful tool?

At the end of the first year of my PhD programme, around the time I was due to submit my confirmation report things took a rather unpleasant turn. My research topic looks at modern theories of child labour and how they have potentially hindered the global abolition agenda. The topic is very sensitive and has garnered the attention of very passionate human rights activists. The general consensus is that child labour is bad and should be abolished, but here I was trying to say that the issue was far too complex to label entirely as negative. Having spent weeks writing and getting good feedback from my supervisor, I submitted my report and a week later I sat in a room with two academics from the department and my supervisor. From the minute I walked into the room, panic gripped my body and I felt like a fraud whose identity was about to be revealed in front of two respected academics. I would later find out that this feeling had a name: the 'impostor syndrome' (Martins and Anthony, 2007). As the questions flew around the room, I could feel my confidence slipping away. I had spent an entire year reading about this topic so how could two people who knew very little about it manage to make me feel so unprepared? Quite frankly, as I made my closing statement and walked outside the room so they could deliberate, I had already put an end to my academic career and had made a mental list of companies to send a speculative CV to. And even after they called me back to tell me I had passed, I knew that it would take a lot to get me back on track. Without confidence in your abilities, there is not much you can achieve.

With the above experience under my belt, the following weeks were a bit of a blur as I dragged myself around, regretting the day I submitted my proposal. Quitting felt like such a great idea and I remember writing an email to my supervisor a couple of times, declaring my intention to quit and pay the university back the studentship money I owed them – luckily the emails were never sent. Finally, after a pep talk from my parents I decided to stop feeling sorry for myself and to work out how to take the criticism I received and turn it around. Since going to campus evoked unpleasant memories, I chose to go to a library in a different university for some time. Once there, I would open my Twitter account and go through the tweets. I had silently followed a few accounts for some time but had never tested their efficiency. One gloomy day I tweeted, 'struggling to get back on my feet after brutal confirmation, need advice #PhdLife #PhdChat #AcWri'. Within a few minutes, people were responding with sympathetic tweets, assuring me that it was common to feel down after your confirmation. By using hashtags (#) in my tweet, I had increased my visibility and allowed people to find my tweets easily. In its support pages, Twitter (2016) says, 'a hashtag—written with a # symbol—is used to index keywords or topics on Twitter. This function . . . allows people to easily follow topics they are interested in.' In short, the support and advice I received from over twenty doctoral students who had had similar experiences helped to put things back into perspective. Feeling like a failure was sometimes part of the PhD process, and it did not mean that you were inadequate or stupid; it simply meant that you had to pick yourself up and try again. Armed with several resources that were tweeted to me, I could gradually get back on track with my PhD programme.

With Twitter, it is not just about sharing your thoughts and random ideas; it is also about engaging with an audience. Apart from posting tweets, you should dedicate some time to following other Twitter accounts. You can tell how popular a Twitter account is by how many followers it has and by how many more followers it has than it follows itself. Currently the most followed account on Twitter belongs to pop star Katy Perry, who has close to 95 million followers, while she only follows 245 accounts. Don't go thinking you are Katy Perry though; start small and work your way up. To get started upload your email contacts on Twitter and see who among them has an account. Once you have done that, follow your institution or workplace, your colleagues and if you know the full names of other researchers in your field, search them to see if they have an account and follow them. Eventually Twitter will make suggestions of accounts to follow based on your interests and activities when you are logged in.

I dedicate a few minutes a week to contributing to posts that appear on my timeline and often end up engaging with people in this way. I also click on relevant trending topics such as the Brexit campaign or American elections to read through what people are saying, then make my own contribution; this helps to raise your profile, especially if you are a naturally witty person. I also search topics that I am interested in and read through the first 100 tweets that appear; if I come across anything interesting I either retweet it or respond to it. I found that this technique also helped to increase the number of my followers. Twitter is a handy bookmark; if I come across a tweet sharing a link to a web page that contains information relevant to my research, then I 'retweet' or 'like' it to ensure that I can easily find it when I log on the next time.

Finally, Twitter is a great conference tool; many will probably agree that attending conferences the first time can be overwhelming. Sitting in a room with hundreds of people and not quite knowing how to get a conversation started is terrifying. Nowadays most conferences will have a hashtag, and once presenters begin their talks you can paraphrase key messages and tweet them, making sure to add the hashtag of the day, such as #ScienceConference2016. In your own time you can search the hashtag on Twitter and see what other contributions were made by those who attended and you can also use this as an opportunity to interact or even follow new accounts. It is highly likely that a person who attends the same conference will have similar research interests, so say hello and introduce yourself; who knows what this could lead to – a research collaboration perhaps?

My Favourite Twitter Accounts

@PhDForum
@PhDForum shares the successes and stories of PhD students worldwide. I tag them in every single PhD-related tweet – especially tweets which require answers – so that they can retweet me and make me visible to their 35 000 followers. If you are worried that only your cat will be excited when

you finally pass your viva examination, then why not let @PhDForum know and watch thousands of congratulations come through?

@WriteThatPhD

This is a good account to follow if you are struggling with writing techniques. What is great about this account is that rather than tweet links that will take you to a different website, they put the information in a picture file. You can easily save the pictures on your phone if you have the Twitter app and consult them on the go, which is very useful if you are not connected to the Internet when you are out and about.

@SUWTues

A virtual #shutupandwrite, which takes place every first and third Tuesday of the month. A shut up and write is pretty much what it says on the box. Find a room, bring a laptop or pen and paper, your essay or chapter outline, get rid of all distractions, Internet and mobile phones included, and then write. You can choose to write for twenty minutes and rest for five or work continuously for an hour and then take a twenty-minute break, it is up to you. If your university does not organise these or your work schedule conflicts with the ones available, then you can probably get involved in these virtual ones; you would be amazed at how much can be achieved in one session. I personally found these useful a month before a chapter or paper was due for submission because by then opening the document has become depressing and I have run out of words to say. Having that focus for 20 minutes with no distractions helps to get me back on track.

@AcademicsSay

This account I simply follow for academic humour, and based on how stressful academic life can get, this is a welcome distraction. You must be careful, though, because one minute can turn into thirty when you are browsing through their hilarious tweets.

BLOGGING AND VLOGGING

Blogs and vlogs (video blogs) are ultimately digital diaries; they can allow you to track the highs and lows of your academic journey in words, pictures or videos. Blogging is a great way to engage with an audience without a word limit like Twitter. You do not have to worry about referencing and using academic terminology – although if you decide to quote someone, it is always best practice to reference. With blogging, however, you should be extremely careful because once you click 'publish' that's it. Even if you delete the post later the Internet or that random follower will have a copy of it. In other words, do not use this medium to discuss or rant about issues that you probably would not have the guts to do in front of others.

A blog should be about discovering your true self, or at least your academic persona. What you blog about is entirely up to you, and you should make this clear in the 'About Me' section of your blog or in your very first introduction post. When I came across the impostor syndrome in one of my classes in the first year, I blogged about it and I found that writing about it helped me to figure out where my lack of confidence was coming from. Although I prefer to write most of my experiences in a personal diary, if I feel that what I am going through can benefit someone else I blog about it and share the link on all my social media accounts. If your blog posts are interesting, your audience often leave comments which can include topics they want you to cover in the future – this is very helpful in those weeks when you are lacking inspiration. It will take time to find your voice as a blogger, so don't give yourself a hard time if you're struggling to get into it. Just keep blogging, you will eventually get there. Having a blog requires a lot of dedication because it involves publishing fresh content daily or a couple of times a week. If, like me, you are juggling your PhD with parenting then perhaps you should consider guest blogging. You are unlikely to generate any pocket money from guest blogging but you will raise your personal and academic profile.

The best way to find out if you understand something is by explaining it to other people. If you want to make sure you understand the main argument of your thesis, sit behind a camera, record yourself explaining it, then upload it on YouTube. Of course, you can choose to be creative, and if you prefer to remain anonymous you can speak over presentation slides. I also found YouTube to be a great place to learn how to use various academic software applications such as NVivo, SPSS and EndNote, so if you have experience of using these you could upload tutorials explaining different functions of the software. Since becoming a parent, I do not have the luxury of signing up to training courses at my university because I would be met with childcare issues, so I use YouTube as a self-help tool. I recently uploaded my interview transcripts on NVivo, which I have never used before, and have been following beginner tutorials on YouTube to learn all its different functions. This is especially useful to those of us who are not computer whizzes – save the video and watch it as many times as you like. For YouTube, all you need is a room with good lighting, a quality video recording device and a few hours every week to record, edit and upload your content.

My Favourite Blogs

The Thesis Whisperer

This is a blog newspaper dedicated to the topic of doing a thesis, edited by Dr Inger Mewburn, Director of Research Training at the Australian National University. This is probably one of the best blogs available for guiding you through your PhD experience. I probably only consult it when I am a hair strand away from losing it. Dr Mewburn, with the help of guest bloggers, has produced a library of advice for the struggling or excelling PhD student or researcher. The blog posts range from how to parent while PhDing, to how to manage a supervisor who suddenly becomes your adversary.

Times Higher Education and Guardian Higher Education websites

I thoroughly enjoy reading the articles/blog posts on both the Times Higher Education and Guardian Higher Education websites. They are well written and often include important and country-specific information about various issues such as equality in universities, employment and pay debates and so on. It is important to stay up to date with higher education news; you never know how changes in politics or law could affect you. If you don't have the time to run your own blog but are passionate about an issue, you can submit articles/blog posts to either of these websites; if it is relevant it will get published.

Explorations of Style

I recently discovered this blog run by Rachael Cayley at the School of Graduate Studies, University of Toronto. It is entirely dedicated to academic writing, which is very relevant to me right now since I am at the writing stage of my PhD. Writing is probably a nightmare for many researchers, so having a free resource like this should not be taken for granted. She covers pretty much everything including drafting, revision, audience, writing challenges and productivity.

James Hayton PhD

When I discovered I was expecting a baby two months before my initial date of submission, the idea of writing a thesis in three months, like he did, seemed like something I had to master. When my maternity leave ends, I will have about four months to submit my thesis before having to register as a continuing student and I absolutely do not want to drag my PhD any further than it already has, so I have been absorbing James Hayton's advice like a keen pupil.

TIPS TO KEEP YOU ON TRACK

- Before registering with any social networks, get to know the social media policy of your institution. Memorise the dos and don'ts of your institution's social media policy to avoid trouble.
- Once it is released into the digital world there is no rewind button.
- Share slides from your conference presentation on Slide Share and tweet the link.
- If you are in a conference presenting or simply attending, make sure you take a note of the official hashtag of the event. Use it to track the event and people's live thoughts.
- Add your social media information – such as your Twitter username or website – to all presentation slides and business cards for visibility.
- Be realistic about the time you can dedicate to social media; being popular can distract you from your academic goals.
- Tweet or blog about your recent publication to increase readership; get your friends to retweet the post or share it on their Facebook pages.
- If you want to be a successful blogger, producing/creating content must be on your priority list. It should not be seen as a hobby but rather as part of your work routine.
- You can schedule your tweets or blog posts so they are sent out automatically at a specified time; this means that if you have lectures/classes all day/all week you don't have to worry about the fact that your Twitter account or blog is inactive.
- Just because you found it on Twitter or on a blog does not mean it is yours to use as you please; the rule of respecting intellectual property is valid on social media too.

REFERENCES

Kaplan, A.M. and Haenlein, M. (2011). 'The early bird catches the news: nine things you should know about micro-blogging', *Business Horizons*, **54**, 105–13.
Martins, R. and Anthony, L. (2007). 'The impostor syndrome: "what if they find out I don't really belong here?"', in J. Scevak and R. Cantwell (eds), *Stepping Stones: A Guide for Mature Aged Students at University*, Camberwell, VA: Acer Press.
Twitter (2016). 'Using hashtags on Twitter', accessed 12 December 2016 at https://support.twitter.com/articles/49309.

Blog Website URLs

https://thesiswhisperer.com/
https://www.theguardian.com/education/higher-education
https://www.timeshighereducation.com/
https://explorationsofstyle.com/
http://jameshaytonphd.com/

Twitter URLs

https://twitter.com/PhDForum
https://twitter.com/WriteThatPhD
https://twitter.com/SUWTues
https://twitter.com/AcademicsSay

31. Organisations, clients and feminists: getting in, coming back and having fun

Marian Baird

This is an account of doing organisational-based research as engaged scholars and feminists and about how relating to 'the client' is crucial to the process. The story begins some time ago, in fact over a decade ago now, so that gives some indication of the time it can take to make, build and maintain relationships with case study organisations. The title of my chapter is derived from a chapter I found to be very useful in my PhD research: 'Getting in, getting on, getting out, and getting back' by David Buchannan, David Boddy and James McCalman (in Bryman, 1988). In the case I'm relating here, I did get in, didn't always get on with the client, got out, but did come back!

There are some points to make before getting underway: first, it can be seen that the authors of the chapter in Bryman's text were all men and that's important to note, because gaining access to and doing research in organisations can be hard enough (as many of you may already know), without approaching it as feminists and from a feminist perspective – a point I will return to later. Second, the times are important, and the times, well, 'they are a-changin' when it comes to research. In some ways it's harder to do research in organisations because so many researchers want access to them, but on the other hand, if you are doing the research they are interested in, then access is easier, and it may even come in the form of an invitation from the organisation! Third, the astute reader will already have noticed that I have reified 'the organisation' as giving access, when, in fact, what we usually mean is a manager or person who has some authority to let you do research in his or her company, be it in the private sector, not-for-profit sector, government departments or unions. This relationship with a person is critical to doing organisational-based research.

I first cover the two phases of my research and then conclude with some reflections on the lessons I've learnt as a researcher, starting from naive beginnings to gaining, hopefully, a more mature approach and perspective on relating to clients and undertaking organisational case studies.

THE FIRST PHASE

After I completed my PhD in greenfield sites and high commitment work systems, my attention turned to a completely new research area: that of women in the workplace. One thing leads to another and soon I found that I was becoming totally engrossed with what was happening in the policy arena in terms of women and work, and in relation to both organisational and government policy, at that time, specifically, paid parental leave. The feminist researcher in me also had a chance to emerge, following the calls from other researchers in industrial relations (see Baird, 2003). I turned to work being done in the USA on the gendered organisation and practical ways to bring about positive change for women and the workplace by being more gender equitable.

This led me to a methodological approach that was firmly grounded in the theory of the gendered organisation: Collaborative Interactive Action Research, or CIAR (see Bailyn and Fletcher, 2003). In this rather long title, each of the words means something purposeful about the research process: the research is 'collaborative', in that researchers work with managers and workers to improve both gender equity and organisational efficiency (known as the dual agenda); the research is 'interactive', as it involves multiple phases of data gathering and feeds back ideas to managers; and it is 'action research', in that it is recognised that the fact of the researcher's presence brings about changes and the researcher is therefore engaged with the making of the outcomes. A foundational aspect of the CIAR methodology is to unpack the underlying assumptions about male and female work and workers and in this way the research has a feminist angle. It is also important to recognise that resistance from participants is likely because the status quo is being challenged. In this regard, for example, being explicit about gender relations, rather than, say, the more generic 'work–life balance', can become a challenge.

My intention was to test the CIAR methodology in Australian organisations. I teamed up with a wonderful researcher and colleague in another state and we won an Australian Research Council (ARC) Linkage Grant to study the possibilities of the 'dual agenda' in two organisations: a public sector utility in one state and a private sector manufacturing company in the other. This way each of us could focus on one organisation each, although we constantly consulted with each other and visited both workplaces. We gained agreement from and access to both organisations through people we knew in each of them and through their support we managed to attract interest in our research. This is important to remember, because the interest didn't come from the managers in the organisations initially, although both organisations did have problems that could be addressed by our research – they were both very male-dominated organisations with ageing workforces. Because the methodology had an action research element, it meant our approach needed researchers to be embedded in the organisations and we also expected a lot of interaction with managers and workers. We managed to organise for a research assistant to work onsite for 2–3 days per week in each organisation and in effect these research assistants became 'insider/outsider researchers'. The first lesson is that getting gender on the research agenda can be difficult, and keeping it there is time consuming for both sides. It can also be confronting (Charlesworth and Baird, 2007).

The essence of the CIAR approach was to use skilful interviewing and observing of management and employees to identify and bring to the surface the characteristics of the 'ideal worker' in that particular workplace. That is, it wasn't necessarily a male worker or manager who was being targeted, but rather who and what was needed to do the work. But when the characteristics were brought to the surface rather than left assumed, it was frequently seen that males were more identifiable as 'ideal workers' – they typically didn't request leave to care for others or want part-time work, they could do overtime or take on other work when requested, they didn't need special uniforms to fit pregnant bodies or separate toilet facilities, and it was generally assumed they could drive trucks, lift heavy loads and shovel dirt – because they were males. In addition, in the process of the research, the work itself is closely observed and documented, including aspects such as hours of work, what skills are required, when it is done and how it is done. This information about underlying assumption and the nature of the work itself is then fed back to the management, and with consultation between the researchers, managers and workers, new ways of organising work are suggested in order to identify a solution to a problem that could then be a 'small win' for the organisation and for women in that organisation. That is, it meets the 'dual agenda'. By doing this it can be shown that the approach is sound and that it lays the groundwork for other beneficial organisational and gender equitable change.

The process requires feedback to the client, which is built into the methodology. My experience in one of the organisations proved difficult. In this case the 'client' was the almost exclusively male management team who had virtually been co-opted into the research. They hadn't asked to have their processes and policies investigated through a gender lens, they hadn't asked to have the 'ideal worker' concept interrogated in their organisation, and perhaps not surprisingly and in hindsight, they didn't like the message I as the researcher gave them in our feedback sessions. But we had gathered all the statistics about the pay, positions and promotions of women in the organisation, we interviewed women at management levels through to low administrative grades, we ran focus groups of women, and interviewed many male workers and managers. In that process we uncovered many problems about the assumptions, work allocation, behaviours, employee entitlements and job design. The research assessment we fed back to management was critical of their workplace, of how they managed women, of their lack of facilities for women and low levels of consciousness of female workers' needs in a largely male workplace. It was a very icy meeting when I fed back the research findings. I had made life quite difficult for them, and although the relationship did recover to a degree, I certainly didn't think I'd be invited back. In retrospect, I think I had not had enough experience working with an organisation, and particularly with managers, essentially the clients, and had overstepped the mark. The second lesson here is that the experience taught me that I had to learn to provide feedback and information to the client in a way that is useful but still maintains the academic integrity of the methodology and, in this case, a critical, feminist lens.

This was engaged research; we were deeply engaged with the organisations and we did bring about small changes, or wins, that benefited women. But it was also very resource intensive, in time and people. When I look back on that experience, I realise there are many elements that are rarely mentioned when today everyone gets excited about 'engaged' research. The truth is, engaged research activities and working with organisations, or clients, can be hard and time consuming and one has to be constantly prepared to answer the client's needs and in their time frames.

I didn't leverage the outcomes of that research for another round of research and in some ways (and in truth) may have even been relieved when the project was over and I could return to the safety of my own office, teaching students and thinking about organisational and public policies from afar.

THE SECOND PHASE

Some twelve years later, however, I received an invitation to speak about women and the workplace at a senior managers' workshop at the same utility company I had studied all those years ago. This time they were explicitly interested in why there were so few women in their division. The senior manager was serious about finding out why this was the case and how they could rectify the situation. The new director of HR was also committed to increasing diversity in the organisation. In the time since we had undertaken the earlier research, there had been a massive shift in consciousness about women at work, not only in that organisation but also more broadly in society. The social context was completely different and being invited back was a delight.

This time the client invited us in to do the research. The brief from the (male) divisional manager was clear. He wanted to know what were the attitudinal, behavioural and job characteristics that might attract or repel women from working in his division. He also wanted numbers – that is, a survey. To his way of thinking, qualitative research would not provide enough evidence. This time I invited a feminist colleague in my own department to join me, and while we agreed to a survey (not our speciality at the time) we convinced the manager that gathering some qualitative data would be useful to give meaning to the survey results. At this point it should also be noted that we were not being asked to examine the whole organisation, but to study one division, where the work was not white-collar or desk-based, but was work in the blue-collar area, done outdoors or on large plants, often requiring round-the-clock attention. The work was historically very manual in nature, and while it still involved hard labour at times, it had also become more automated in some areas and required relatively complex computer skills in other aspects. As you, dear reader, can imagine, actually being invited to research this type of work (and be paid, I should add) was quite an exciting prospect as such opportunities don't come along that often.

This time, however, as opposed to last time, we stayed as outside researchers, and did not have a researcher embedded in the organisation. We did, however, employ a statistically trained research assistant to help with the survey and other aspects of the project, and we had very good administrative support within the organisation. This time the middle managers we dealt with were welcoming, and although still mainly men, they were very cognisant of contemporary debates about women and work. So too were the vast majority of the blue-collar workforce, it must be said. The time frame was also much shorter than the usual ARC or similar grant. We were originally commissioned to do the research between January and June, but the end date was pushed back and we completed the gathering and reporting of the data and our suggestions for action (recommendations) by the end of November.

It doesn't matter if one is a feminist or not, there are certain phases of the research process that must be done, even when approached and contracted by a company or client. In essence there are really no short cuts, but when doing contracted research we have to ensure that agreed delivery dates are met and the turnaround time is usually quick, by our academic standards at least. This can be difficult for the academic working in a slow-moving institutional setting and used to long lead times, compared to the client who is used to quick responses. The research with a client begins with making contact, settling on the scope of the research and organising a contract, and this contract making can be the most difficult and time-consuming process unless your university is well set up to help – and it seems very few, if any, are! After a frustrating beginning I eventually 'made friends' with a person in my university's research office who I could pick up the phone and talk to. This relationship was invaluable in getting the contract settled and having speedier responses to questions like owner-ship of the data, publishing from the research and establishing a dedicated research account code.

Once the contract is finalised, there are then many other parts to action. In this case, it involved gaining human ethics approval, doing the literature review, developing a customised survey instrument and also questions for focus groups, doing the research including going into the field, collecting, collating and analysing the results, and finally, reporting the results back to the client. We then prepared a final report and presentation for manage-ment and a poster summarising the results for the employees. This was all completed in a period of eleven months.

What we bring as feminists is arguably a more acute sensitivity to the issues around women and men at work – and this is exactly what the client desired. In addition, as female feminists, we were also entering an almost all-male domain, which raises other questions and dilemmas. For example, we pondered whether or not to bring in a male colleague in order to give us more legitimacy and perhaps make the largely male respondents more open to us as researchers. In the end, we didn't and I am confident it made no difference. In fact, being female researchers in male workplaces might even have given some of the men more opportunity to talk about issues they wouldn't raise by themselves under normal work circumstances. For instance, in giving the surveys out at the team briefing sessions, the male respondents were often eager to discuss the issues. We also had feedback from some of our male respondents that they took the surveys home and discussed the issues and questions with their wives, partners and daugh-ters. In our fieldwork too, we certainly seemed to enjoy open conversations about how women would cope in the workspaces and witnessed first-hand how these male workers responded to customers. For instance, the male workers asked questions about how women would go to the toilet when they were working outdoors all day, and what they would do about changing clothes. In one event when I was out in the field, the next job was at a brothel where one of the utilities that the company serviced had broken. The male supervisor I was observing was very careful to respect my interests but also to show me the sort of unusual situations his workers might find themselves in. His interest was in repairing the fault for the customer, and this came through very clearly.

In this research we kept in close contact with the client throughout the life of the project and discussed all steps. For example, we discussed with the client what questions to ask in the surveys of managers and workers (based on our literature review and their interests), the best way to actually gather the survey data (online or paper form), and how to get an understanding of the work and what managers and employees would think of the survey results (interviews and/or focus groups).

In the end we developed a survey instrument by scouring the literature on research on the attitudes, behaviour and job design in masculinised blue-collar workplaces, only to discover there were few surveys to guide us. We utilised what was available and consulted with the client in developing and piloting the survey questions. We also consulted with them about the optimal length of the surveys for managers and employees. The client's advice was to keep the survey to a maximum of ten minutes and to make the language very clear for the workforce, many of whom were from non-English-speaking backgrounds. This meant the survey had to be carefully designed to meet these requirements and some questions, which we as researchers would ideally have liked to have asked, were discarded. We used a paper survey for the field-based workers and an online version of the same survey for the office-based, more technical workforce. For all the managers we used an online survey. The response rates were high (72 per cent for managers; 59 per cent for employees), and we suspect we were fortunate in distributing the paper-based survey in team meeting time where it could be answered and collected there and then. We also gave out university pens to answer the survey, which most of the respondents loved and chose to keep.

After the results were collected and collated (we outsourced the data entry of the paper forms), we met with the client team to discuss the first analysis of the results. There were more than 30 questions on each of the surveys, so we had a wealth of data to work with. At this point our initial contact, the senior division manager, had unexpectedly moved on to a higher position in the organisation and we were assigned to a new HR project officer, who had not been involved in the origins of the research. Her focus was somewhat different and we had to adapt. In addition, the organisation had embarked on a flexibility project, so she was very interested in the managers' and employees' views of flexibility. Unfortunately, many of our original flexibility questions had been removed from the survey in the interests of space and time. But this is where the focus groups came in very handy. A number of focus groups were then held with male and female managers, and male and female workers, and in these we were able to pursue some more flexibility questions. Additionally, the focus groups really did bring to life the issues about the work itself, and the behaviours and attitudes of the workforce and the managers. The old CIAR project was also very useful here because using questions to uncover those taken-for-granted assumptions about who is considered to be an 'ideal worker' was what provided insights into other aspects of the workplace not canvassed in the survey. These unexpected findings went to rostering and performance issues.

We drafted a report that included the summaries of the key survey findings and feedback from the focus groups. An element of judgement is called for at this stage because not all of the data can be included in the report – and it wouldn't be read in any case. Our report used a colour coding to indicate in the survey responses where the warning signs were. This was intended as a guide to where management might want to investigate more closely, and was not set as directions for the client. That is, we maintained a very consultative and open process through to the end. We also developed an extensive list of suggestions for action, rather than a list of recommendations. One of our suggestions was to continue undertaking focus groups at regular intervals to test where change or resistance to women entering the division might be occurring in the future – and where we might be able to continue to play a role, and play to our strengths!

REFLECTIONS: THEN, NOW AND LESSONS LEARNT

The time between the two rounds of research in the same organisation was a significant factor in shifting the context in which the research was done and presented an opportunity for our research interests. By the time we commenced the second project, discussions about women at work and barriers to women's progression had become very popular in the public and business media. Not only had the debates moved on, but I had also aged – and had gained more experience along the way. This second time in, I'd probably have to admit that I wasn't as purist about the research process as I had been the first time. However, with my colleague, I still kept the feminist voice and critical sensitivity to the issues alive, and in fact, this is what the client wanted.

Coming back by invitation was also comforting. I was not as defensive about being there or worried about being asked to leave. We had a negotiated contract with the client so knew exactly what had to be delivered, and the project wasn't as open ended as the first round of research I had done with the organisation. But the timing was much tighter than one would normally do in 'traditional' academic research and this is the reality of contracted research. While the timing is much tighter and 'deliverables' are expected, there are benefits of working directly with the client. For example, the support provided by the organisation is greater. Interactions were facilitated by the organisation, and we were assisted by an interested and smart young female manager who provided contacts for distribution of the surveys for workers and managers, organised for us to visit team briefings at 7 am in far-flung parts of the city, set up focus group meetings and organised field trips.

A fair question to ask at this stage would be: did this commissioned research and close contact with the client 'bias' our results? My answer is that it certainly didn't bias the survey but it was something we were conscious of in the focus groups. We were conscious of the need to state our independence from management and feel, given the very open conversations we had and the breadth of issues covered, that we managed that.

It sounds almost ideal, doesn't it? It's true that it was an enjoyable if not at times pressured research experience, but it wasn't all plain sailing. We had to find a way to reconcile the quantitative versus qualitative debate and adapt quickly to meet the needs of the new manager who wanted a focus on flexibility. We also had to plan our many other work commitments carefully to ensure we could meet the timing needs of the client, and we had to maintain a friendly relationship with all parties during an industrial dispute that emerged in the course of our research and our attendance at team briefing meetings. Unfortunately, the original manager who invited us in moved to a more senior and different role and sadly we didn't see him again. Our results went to a new generation of male line managers – younger, enthusiastic and open to considering gender and job changes, but it's yet to be seen if more women will work in these male-dominated areas. In terms of the research, the first time around I was almost constantly worried about the research relationship with the client, the second time around it was, largely, a pleasure.

In reflecting on the whole experience I would summarise the lessons for me as follows:

- Lesson 1: Context is important to facilitating a good working relationship with the client. In my case, making gender an explicit research focus was hard the first time round but much easier the second time, because the social and organisational debates had shifted so dramatically in the intervening period.
- Lesson 2: Learn to provide feedback that is relevant and sensible to the client at the same time as maintaining academic independence

and rigour. It's important to remember that this academic integrity is often as important to the client as it is to us.

- Lesson 3: Clearly articulate and record the scope and timelines of the research you are doing for the client as these will become your navigation instruments through the research journey. They may need adjusting, but you will have the baseline from which to work.
- Lesson 4: Never underestimate the importance of building a research relationship with the client; after all, you never know when they might come back to you!

REFERENCES

Bailyn, L. and Fletcher, J.K. (2003). 'The equity imperative: reaching effectiveness through the dual agenda', *CGO Insights*, No. 18, July.

Baird, M. (2003). 'Re-conceiving industrial relations: 2003 presidential address', *Labour and Industry*, **14**(1), 107–15.

Bryman, A. (ed.) (1988). *Doing Research in Organizations*, London: Routledge.

Charlesworth, S. and Baird, M. (2007). 'Getting gender on the agenda: the tale of two organisations', *Women in Management Review*, **22**(5), 391–404.

32. Born to . . . write, rewrite and rewrite again

Mark N.K. Saunders

I'm sitting in my hotel room and have taken a break from reading Bruce Springsteen's (2016) autobiography *Born to Run*. I'd just got to a bit where he's talking about how he writes his songs, or rather about how he writes and rewrites his songs, sometimes leaving partially honed lyrics for a while and then coming back to work further on them and refine them. When listening to the recordings of Springsteen's songs I've never really thought much about how they were written but, having just finished reading the chapter where he talks about writing, I'm beginning to think of my own and my students' trials with writing.

Conversations with colleagues and students, past and present come to mind. These seem to focus on how difficult they all find it to write and, for many, how they will spend hours or even days staring at their laptop screens: typing a few words, editing these words, re-editing these words, thinking they are rubbish, and sometimes even deleting them. They then comment, seemingly accusingly, 'It's all right for you, you can write really well', the implication being that I don't understand what it's like to find writing difficult. If only that were true.

Earlier on this week Keith (the co-editor of this book) and I were discussing the chapters and vignettes that had been submitted for this book when we met up in Singapore. I was also teaching students in the daytime for my university and he was also meeting with a doctoral student for a supervision. Our conversation turned to the amount of rewriting and revising that we had undertaken on a recent paper.

This paper, now published in the *British Journal of Management* (Saunders and Townsend, 2016), had begun life as a conversation over an early morning cup of coffee. During our conversation we both bemoaned the seeming lack of advice about the number of qualitative interviews that were likely to be sufficient when conducting research, a question our students often asked us. On the basis of this conversation we had decided to undertake a small piece of research both to critically review the extent and nature of advice actually available in the literature (rather than just moaning about an apparent lack) and, if we found relatively little had been written, establish what the norms were for published organisational and workplace research articles.

During our conversation we began to realise the amount of drafting and redrafting our paper had gone through – we went back through our records and it was 22 versions before we had even submitted it to a conference. We consoled ourselves that although this seemed a great deal of work, each version had represented a significant improvement on the previous one, and that through our rewriting we had begun to get our ideas clearer. Although the paper had been accepted by the conference, the reviewers had made useful suggestions for improvement and the audience at the conference found a few flaws in our arguments. We decided we needed to address these before submitting the paper to a journal and, in doing so, realised that we actually had written responses to some of these flaws in our earlier drafts. Fortunately we had kept all 22 drafts!

Following four further versions, the paper was submitted and we were relieved that the editor considered it worthy of sending out to review. Our three anonymous reviewers and the editor, however, felt that the paper still required substantial revision. We worked through eight further versions, showing our penultimate version to two colleagues who we hoped would be constructively critical. Believing we had now addressed the reviewers' comments, we resubmitted the paper. Whilst one of our reviewers now appeared to be happy with our revised paper, the other two felt more work was needed. After a further seven versions we felt ready to resubmit the paper. This time the reviewers' comments were more favourable, but more revisions were still needed. We both worked on the paper, exchanging five further versions, again asking colleagues for critical feedback. The version we resubmitted was accepted.

Keith and I, despite (or probably because of) the number of years we have been academics, have learned that for our arguments to be clear and our writing to reach the standard required by journals we need to redraft our work numerous times. In writing the paper we had exchanged and commented on 41 versions. So a total of 41 drafts – not bad for a couple of academics whose students think that it's easy for us to write! Secondly, we have learned that constructive critical feedback by others improves our writing, our paper having been commented upon by conference reviewers, colleagues, three journal reviewers and the journal editor. Finally we have learned to keep earlier versions of our papers as we never know when we might need to go back to them.

And, in case you are wondering ... this vignette has gone through at least six versions during its rewriting. It has been discussed and critiqued by a class of postgraduate students and Keith has given his constructive (and critical) comments.

REFERENCES

Springsteen, B. (2016). *Born to Run*, New York: Simon and Schuster.
Saunders, M.N.K. and Townsend, K. (2016). 'Reporting and justifying the number of interviews participants in organisation and workplace research', *British Journal of Management*, **27**(4), 836–52.

33. 'I'm over it . . .'

Peter J. Jordan

This is a phrase I have often heard repeated by students and less so by academics. It emerges in a number of situations, with the most common being prior to the submission of a Doctoral thesis. That said, I have also heard it said during data collections, when writing articles for journal submission and (surprise, surprise) sometimes from supervisors when supervising research students.

So what does this mean?

I think there are plenty of interpretations, from 'I have done the best I can', to 'I am sick of this project', to 'close enough is good enough', to 'I am not going to be told that this work could be improved any more' (fragile ego), to 'there is nothing wrong with my work' (narcissism), to 'I am never working with these people again'.

I used to have a view that Doctoral students were never close to the submission if they did not tell me they were 'over it'. Then I would keep them working at it for a few more months to achieve a quality they were proud of and suggest they submit. I have never had a student fail or require anything other than minor revisions on this basis.

That said, there are only a couple of times in around twenty years in academia when I have actually said this myself. When submitting my Doctoral dissertation, my memory (which probably gives me a false heroic status to protect my ego) is that there were times when I said, 'Let the examiners find any mistakes and I will fix them' – but I can't remember a time during my PhD when I was 'over it'. This is the same with my current research streams. I am never 'over' my research. Indeed, I find it a bit weird (or lucky) that someone pays me to do something I love doing and find endlessly interesting.

'Over it' denotes to me a loss of passion about the topic or the task. If you say it too often, it might mean an alternative profession is in the offing. Indeed, in preparing this piece, I reflected on the students who I have supervised as Doctoral students and those who were most prone to the 'I'm over it' statement. All of them have taken career paths outside academia. Some have had very successful careers, in a broad range of professions, but not as a researcher who is passionate about or who simply enjoys their research and writing.

So next time you tell your supervisor or colleagues that you are 'over it', take a step back and figure out what you mean. You might want to be a bit more specific about what you are over. If you say it all the time to the point where those you work with are 'over' hearing you're 'over it', enjoy taxi driving or whatever you are passionate about. Life is too short to spend time doing things we are constantly 'over'.

Index

academic writing
  assisting students in process of 29
  different genres of 33–4
  Explorations of Style website 181
  journal articles 34, 35
  student accountability for quality
    of 30
  writing groups for practising 29
  see also authorship; theses
academically ranked journals 33, 34
@AcademicsSay 179
Academy of Management Journal 11
access, *see* cognitive access; research
  access
accuracy, of purchased databases 65
achievability (project) 35
acknowledgements 152
advice
  on literature reviews 27
  on research questions 46–7
advisory panels, systematic reviews
    24–5
advisory teams, research projects 77–8
agreement, about next steps in research
    107–8
Albert, T. 153
Alvesson, M. 12, 114
American Association for Public
    Opinion Research 65
AMOS 124, 126, 127
Angelou, M. 131
ANOVA 122
applied research, data collection 5
approval (organisational), of research
    107
arguments, development of 133–4
assumptions
  about knowledge, *see* epistemology
  about learning 126
  questioning theoretical 12
Atwood, M. 129

author relations 154
authorship 149–56
  approaches to 150–54
  as core part of a research career 149
  evidence of 83–4
  expectations and obligations 154–5
  familiarity with rules governing 83
  guidelines 151–4
  issue of contributions 149–50, 151,
    152, 153, 154, 155
  lessons learnt 155
  order of 149, 150, 151, 152, 153, 154
  problem avoidance 153–4
awkward questions 142–3
axiology 51, 52

back-up plans, Internet questionnaire
    64–5
back-ups, of work 140–41
balance
  in advisory teams 41
  in negotiating access 92
Baron, R.M. 123
Baruch, Y. 61
beliefs, about knowledge, *see*
    epistemology
bending approach 95–6
bias(es)
  directed participation and potential
    for 94
  incentives and potential for 105
  in organisational-based research 192
  see also common method bias;
    desirability bias; non-response
    bias; personal biases
bibliographies 35
blogging 179–80, 182
blogs 181
Boddy, D. 184
body language 69, 75, 76
bounce back (email) 61, 62

British Psychological Society (BPS)
    151, 152, 153
British Sociological Association (BSA)
    151, 152, 153
broad review questions 25
Buchannan, D. 184
builders (theory) 11

case research 87–97
    alignment of interests 90–91
    cross-sectional designs 97
    finding suitable research sites 89–91
    gaining respondent participation
        and involvement 93–4
    in-depth 97
    involvement as interference 94–5
    readjusting research instruments
        95–6
    research access 87–8, 91–2
Cayley, R. 181
Cherryh, C.J. 130
Cirillo, F. 131
clarity, about research needs 106
clients, negotiating with 82–4
co-authorship, negotiating 154–5
coding 116, 138–9, 191
cognitive access 59
cold-calling 89
collaboration 35, 84, 172
Collaborative Interactive Action
    Research (CIAR) 185
colleagues
    advice and feedback on research
        questions 46–7
    advice on literature reviews 27
    importance of support from 158
colour coding 116, 138, 191
Colquitt, J. 11, 12
Committee on Publication Ethics 153
common ground 90, 93
common method bias 122–3
common understandings 72, 76
communication
    of responsibilities 85
    talking to supervisors about
        feedback 159
    of value of research 107
    see also body language; English as a
        second language
competitiveness 34, 78, 83, 84

completion dates, addressing missed 31
comprehensiveness, of systematic
    reviews 22
compromised research 93, 95, 96
Computer Aided Qualitative Data
    Analysis Software (CAQDAS)
    138, 139
computer program courses 30
computer-based technology 113
'conclusions' sections, theses 34
conferences 178
confidence 177
confirmation (examination) 37
conflicting evidence, find the truth
    amongst 67–76
contacts
    finding 102
    and research access 32, 64, 65, 92
context
    and meaning construction 67
    in organisational-based research 192
    in qualitative research 117, 119, 120
contextualisation, of research evidence
    25
contingency plans 65, 66, 78
continuous learning 126
contracted research 189, 192
contributions
    authorship 149–50, 151, 152, 153,
        154, 155
    to knowledge 32, 52, 53
controlled environments, working
    outside 79–82, 85
covariance-based SEM 123–4
creativity 135
credibility 67, 88, 90, 91, 92, 96, 113
credits (authorship) 152
'critical appraisal' component,
    systematic reviews 22–3
critical assessment 39, 40, 43
critical feedback 159
critical reading 31, 33
critical realist epistemology 54
criticality 21
cross-sectional quantitative designs 98
customer value proposition (CVP) 107

daily goals 31
data, trustworthiness of 105
data analysis

in developing ideas (FMS study) 14–16, 18
in field research 81
section, in theses 33–4
in systematic reviews 26
see also qualitative data analysis; quantitative data analysis
data collection
applied research 5
and authorship 152–3
criticality to high quality theses 33
experimentation 120
in field research 80–81
in qualitative data project 115–16
understanding potential research sites before 76
see also Internet questionnaires
data extraction forms 25
data screening 122–3
databases (purchased) 64, 65
decision-makers
building trust with 107
seeking permission for access 106–7
deductive logic 11
Denyer, D. 22
desirability bias 79, 88
director of studies, *see* thesis advisors
directories, for gaining physical access 65
'discussions' section, theses 34
drafts/drafting 129, 195
dual agendas 185

early career researcher's musings 165–7
email bounce back 61, 62
empirical evidence 13
employability, enhancing 34
EndNote 30, 180
engaged research 187
English proficiency 30
English as a second language 29–30, 33
epistemology, finding 51–7
evidence
of authorship 83–4
contextualisation of 25
finding the truth amongst conflicting 67–76
see also empirical evidence
exaggerations 70, 75
examination (confirmation) 37

Excel (Microsoft) 116, 123, 126, 138
expanders (theory) 11
expectations
authorship relations 154
non-compliance of ideas with 11
experience(s)
colouring of memory and interpretation 69
industrial relations researchers' focus on 114
learning from others' 85
in literature reviews 20
experimentation, data collection 120
experts, approaching/contacting 27, 47, 57, 126
Explorations of Style website 181

facilitation 172
feedback
from colleagues, on research questions 46–7
in organisational-based research project 186–7, 192–3
see also supervisor feedback
feelings, feedback and dealing with 158
fellow researchers, *see* colleagues
feminists 189
field research 79–82
examining prevailing ideas (FMS study) 14
and impact of research 83
making additional notes 110
flattery 90
flexibility 84–5
in access negotiation 92
in interviews 109–110
in research designs 102
'flirting' negotiation method 91
focus, finding 133–4
focus groups 34, 60, 93, 95, 96, 187, 189, 190–91, 192
focus point, in systematic reviews 24
formative second-order constructs 125
foundation skills 30
fragmented literature 22
free writing 131, 132
funded projects 82, 83, 84
funding, securing 167–71
funding applications 166

gatekeepers 71, 73, 76, 100, 101, 102
generalisability 122
generalisation 60–61
ghost writers 154
gift writers 154
goal setting 31
Goldman, W. 129
grammar support 33
Guardian Higher Education website
    181

Haenlein, M. 176
hard bounce back 61
Harman's one factor test 122
hashtag function (Twitter) 177
Hemingway, E. 134
hidden agendas 76
Holtom, B.C. 61
humans, as autonomous individuals
    17–18
hypothesis testing 123

ideas
    caution in sharing 168
    developing (study) 11–18
        data analysis 14–16, 18
        familiarisation with the literature
            13–14
        fieldwork 14
        ideas informing 12–13, 14
        illustrating argument 16–17
        theory generation 16
    non-compliance with expectations
        11
'I'm over it' statement 197–8
immediacy, of word association
    technique 114
impact of research 53, 83, 85, 166,
    175
impostor syndrome 177
in-depth case research 97
incentives
    internet questionnaire 63, 64, 65
    too lucrative 104–5
inductive logic 11
inference 17, 54
insights
    from systematic reviews 23
    in quantitative studies 122
integrity 88, 92, 94, 96, 107, 154

intellectual property 83, 86, 151, 168,
    182
inter-rater agreement, calculating 123
interactive research 185
interference, involvement as 94–5
Internet questionnaires, using 59–66
    assumed response rate 61
    back-up plans 64–5
    lessons learnt 65–6
    research context 60–61
    research difficulties 61–3
    threatened legal action 63
interpretation
    factors colouring 69
    individual autonomy and 17–18
    social sciences and potential for
        different 12
    see also qualitative data analysis
interviewees 93, 113
interviewers, and non-truthfulness of
    participants 69–70
interviews
    finding the truth amongst conflicting
        evidence 67–76
    flexibility in 109–110
intraclass correlations 123
introductions (theses) 33
involvement (respondent)
    gaining 93–4
    as interference 94–5

James Hayton PhD (blog) 181
Jesson, J.K. 21
journal articles
    noticing structure and pattern in
        29
    plans and spreadsheets of key 34–5
    refereed 35
    using as templates for writing 29
    writing 34, 35
journals
    importance of reading the best 33
    plans and spreadsheets of key 34–5
    writing for 29

Kaplan, A.M. 176
Kenny, D.A. 123
knowledge
    contributions to 32, 52, 53
    criticality regarding 21

in normal and revolutionary science 11
and power 17
see also epistemology; management knowledge
Kuhn, T. 11, 12

language, *see* body language; English as a second language
large projects 77, 82, 83, 84, 86, 166
large teams 83, 84, 149
latent constructs 124–5
lead authors 150, 151
leadership 172
learning, assumptions about 126
legal action (threatened) 63
lies 75
list errors 61–2
listening, to interview transcripts 98
literature
    creating summaries of 30
    drawing together fragmented 22
    familiarisation with, in developing ideas 13–14
    reading to establish a gap in 31, 32–3
    taking a systematic approach to reading 34
    tendency to focus on preferred pieces of 21
literature reviews 20–27
    deciding which to use 20–21
    experience in 20
    lessons for keeping on track 26–7
    section, in theses 33
    see also systematic reviews
long-term thinking 85
longitudinal qualitative studies 115
lucrative incentives 104–5

management disciplines, additions to theories in 11–12
management knowledge 12
manual coding 138–9
manual observation 79–81
marketability 35
master–apprentice relationship 28–35
mathematics, in statistical data analysis 122, 123, 124, 126–7
matrices, in data analysis 15, 18
McCalman, J. 184

meaning construction 67
mediation model, testing 123–4
meetings, planning staff–student 31
meta-analyses 21, 26
methodological approaches 33
methodological pluralism 55
micro-blogging 176–9
Microsoft Excel 116, 123, 126, 138
mindset, for academic writing 29
miscommunication 74
misinterpretation 116–17
misunderstandings 72, 74, 75
mixed methods research 33, 60, 79–82
monitoring, questionnaires 66
multiple mediator mediation model 124
multiple sources, using 96
mutual gains approach 91

naivety, in believing others 68
narrative analysis 26
narrative literature reviews 21
narrow review questions 25
negotiation
    with clients and partners 82–4
    co-authorship 154–5
    research access 90, 91–2, 93–4
networks/networking 51
    encouragement of, in academia 77
    for gaining physical access 64–5
    about research questions 47
    in team work 78, 83, 86
non-response bias 122
normal science 11
note-taking 30–31, 34
NVivo 34, 138–9, 180

objective data 122
objectives 77, 82, 90
objectivity 53, 79
observation templates 81
observational research 79–81
ontology 13, 51, 52
optimism 18
organisational filters 96
organisational reality 88, 93, 96
organisational-based research 184–93
    attracting interest in 186
    CIAR methodology 185, 186
    clarity about research needs 106

derailment of projects 84
engaged nature of 187
feedback sessions 186–7
gaining access 184
lessons learnt 191–3
survey 188–91
usability/tangibility 87–8
outside researchers 188
over-eager managers 94–5

paranoid managers 95
paranoid researchers 67
paraphrasing 30–31
part-time work 168, 169
participants
    caution in rewarding 104–5
    checking and double-checking 94
    gaining participation and
        involvement 93–4
    hidden agendas 76
    involvement as interference 94–5
    non-truthfulness
        incidents in PhD research 70–75
        interviewer shortcomings 69–70
        possible reasons for 68–9
    survey research for finding suitable
        89–90
partners, negotiating with 82–4
partnership(s) 77, 83, 84, 85, 168
pattern exploration 15, 18
pattern observation 80
patterns, noticing, in journal articles 29
performance, in advisory teams 78
permission, for access 106–7
perseverance 100, 126
personal biases 69
personal contacts 21
PhD students
    accountability for quality of writing
        30
    homework on supervisors 29
    key lessons for 35–6
    selection of high quality 28–9
@PhDForum 178–9
philosophies, researchers 52
photographic techniques 80
physical access
    sales skills needed for gaining 106–8
    using Internet questionnaires 59–66
pilots 98–9

planning
    failure in 78
    importance of 2
    large projects 83, 84
    process of 77
    staff–student meeting times 31
    work–life balance 31
plans
    of key literature journals and articles
        34
    see also back-up plans; contingency
        plans; publication plans
plants (interviewee) 93
PLS-SEM 125
politician speak 133
politics 166
Pomodoro technique 131–2
Popay, J. 26
positivism 53, 56
positivity 76, 78, 86, 95
power 17
power distance cultures 96
power imbalance
    in access negotiation 92
    accounting for 109–10
practice 56, 57
practitioner community 56, 57
pragmatism 56, 57
pragmatist epistemology 54, 55, 56, 57
pre-determined outcomes,
        organisational involvement and
        93, 94
preconceived idea 69
preparedness 78, 84–5, 110, 170
procedural methods 122
proficiency, in English 30
project management skills 84
projective techniques 114
protectionist type philosophy 170
psychometric meta-analyses 21, 26
publication plans 83
publishing
    from theses 34, 35
    knowing the rules of the game 86
    strategy and goals 34
purchased databases 64, 65

qualifiers (theory) 11–12
qualitative data analysis
    interpretation (study) 113–20

data collection approach 115–16
developmental problems 118–19
identifiable problems 116–18
lessons learnt 120
positive aspects 119
word association technique 114,
  118–19
quantification in 120
software 34, 113, 138, 139
qualitative research 33, 55–6
bending approach 95–6
longitudinal 115
value of 114
quantitative data analysis
statistical method 121–7
use psychometric meta-analysis 26
quantitative research 33, 55–6, 60
in case studies 93
cross-sectional 97
good research designs 121
robust 122
questioning assumptions 12
questions
dealing with awkward 142–3
systematic reviews 23, 25–6
quotes, cherry picking 117

rapid evidence assessments/appraisals
  21
rapport building 91, 103, 104, 115
re-drafting 195
reading
to establish a gap in the literature
  31, 32–3
to establish theoretical framework 33
see also critical reading
readjustment, of research instruments
  95–6
realist ontology 13
realist reviews/syntheses 21
reality(ies) 67, 95, 114
refereed journal articles 35
reflection
epistemological 52, 57
on interviews/observations 76
on one's chosen path 86
reflective research journals 158
regression coefficients 125–6
rejected hypotheses 123
reliability 33, 122

reluctant interviewees 93
reporters (theory) 12
representative samples 60–61
reputation 44, 78, 85
research
competitive nature of 84
see also individual methodologies
research access
case studies 87–8
and the diminishing dissertation
  101–2
negotiation 90, 91–2, 93–4
organisational-based research 184
precarious nature of 100
research sites 32, 71–2, 89–91
see also physical access
research assessment 187
research assistants 63, 82, 186, 188
research design(s)
flexibility in 102
quantitative 98, 121
researchers' philosophies 52
using pilots to test for weakness in
  98–9
research findings
contextualisation of evidence for
  explaining 25
from pilots to strengthen main
  projects 98
non-confirmation of prevailing ideas
  18
systematic reviews and confidence
  in 22
research instruments, readjusting
  95–6
research projects
achievability and simplicity 35
advisory teams 77–8
communicating value of 107
data, *see* data analysis; data
  collection
developing research ideas 11–18
doubts and anxieties about 165–7
dynamics underpinning 164–73
emotional and political labour in
  securing/maintaining 171–3
finding the time to progress 144–6
'I'm over it' statement 197–8
knowing when to give up 103
making back-ups 140–41

managing/securing funding
(personal account) 167–71
marketability 35
need for pilots 98–9
organisational derailment of 84
PhD students' starting point 32–3
planning, *see* planning
research questions
advice and feedback from colleagues
46–7
approaching experts 47
creating literature summaries for
thinking about 30
finding common ground between
organisational objectives and 90
integrity 92
principal 32–3
using multiple sources to answer 96
research relationships 149
importance of building 193
interviewer memory and
interpretation 69
see also authorship relations;
partnership(s); supervisor/
supervisee relationships
research sites
accessing 32, 71–2
finding suitable, in case research
89–91
understanding before data collecting
76
researchers
paranoia in 67
philosophies 52
sales skills 106–8
see also colleagues; interviewers
response rates (questionnaire) 61, 65
responsibilities, outlining/
communicating 85
'results' section, in theses 33–4
revolutionary science 11
rewriting 195–6
robust quantitative research 122
rules of the game, knowing 86

sales skills, for researchers 106–8
sample selection (questionnaire) 60–61
Sandberg, J. 12
Saunders, M.N.K. 115
scepticism 67

science, distinction between normal
and revolutionary 11
scope of research, articulating and
recording 193
scoping study, systematic reviews 24
second-order constructs 124–5
selection, of high quality students 28–9
self-discovery 51, 145
Shakespeare, W. 164
Shaw, G.B. 67
short-phrase approach, in data
collection 117
short-term projects 167–8, 170
simplicity (project) 35
simplistic research models 121
skillset, for academic writing 29
SmartPLS 125, 126
social media 174–82
blogging and vlogging 179–81
engaging and connecting with
academics 175–6
finding one's niche 174–5
knowledge of institutional policies
182
micro-blogging 176–9
platforms as learning tools 125, 180
and reputation 44–5
tips for keeping on track 182
social reality 114
social sciences, variety of thinking in
12
software
data management 30
learning from YouTube 180
qualitative data analysis 34, 113, 138,
139
statistical data analysis 22, 123–4,
125, 126–7
Sorkin, A. 130
specific review questions 23
'speed dating' negotiation method 91
spreadsheets
of key literature journals and articles
34–5
use in qualitative data analysis
project 116
SPSS 122, 123, 127, 180
statistical construction 124–5
statistical data analysis 122–7
statistical difference 123

statistical software 122, 123–4, 125, 126–7
structural equation modelling (SEM) 122–3, 123–4, 125
structured approach, of systematic reviews 22
structured observational technique 79–80, 81
study habits 31, 136
subjectivity, of narrative literature reviews 21
summaries
in data analysis 14, 26
of literature topics 30
supervision, key issues and challenges 28–31
supervisor feedback 157–63
hints and tips for dealing with 162–3
personal account
during middle and later stages of research 159–61
reflections on dealing with 157–9
supervisor/supervisee relationships 28–35, 161
supervisors
in authorship 152
key lessons for 35–6
selection of high quality students 28–9
students' homework on 29
support
from colleagues 100, 158
as a mutual process 86
in writing 33, 135
survey research, finding participants 89–90
@SUWTues 179
systematic reviews
advantages 22–3
definition 21
disadvantages and challenges 24–6
origin and popularity 21
scoping study 24

task/time management technique 131–2
Taylor, F.W. 13
team-based approach, English as a second language 29, 33
telephone questionnaires 62–3

testers (theory) 12
theoretical framework (theses) 33
theory(ies)
generation 11, 16
in management disciplines 11–12
questioning underlying assumptions of 12
theses
blogs 181
contributions to knowledge 32
different sections within 33–4
publishing from 34, 35
statements 133–4
understanding process and appearance of 30
using to build future careers 35
see also academic writing
thesis advisors
lessons for keeping on track 43
personal account
finding 36–7
keeping 41–2
losing 37–41
to complement one's strengths 37, 43
transferring between 42, 43
The Thesis Whisperer (blog) 181
thinking
epistemology as a mirror of researchers' 55
like an academic 29
long-term 85
variety in 12
thinking outside the box 6, 126
time management 27, 131–2
'time to market' approach 97
time-off 31
timelines, articulating and recording 193
Times Higher Education website 181
topics, finding and choosing 32, 35
Townsend, K. 115
Tranfield, D. 22
trust/trustworthiness 91, 105, 107
the truth, unearthing 67–76
lessons for keeping on track 76
participants' non-truthfulness
instances in PhD research 70–75
interviewer shortcomings 69–70
possible reasons for 68–9

Twain, M. 132
Twitter 176, 177–9, 182

understatements 70, 75
uninterested interviewees 93
universities
    computer program courses 30
    differences in requirements,
        expectations and procedures 42
    encouragement of partnerships 77
    writing groups 29
University of Cambridge 153
university libraries
    computer program courses 30
    helping with literature searching 34
unpredictability, dealing with 79–82
untruths 71, 73, 74, 75
user-friendly statistical software 124,
    126–7

validated scales 88, 95
validity 33, 90, 113, 122
value of research, communicating 107
vlogging 179–80

Wager, E. 153
word association technique 114,
    118–19

work–life balance 31
working relationships 77, 83, 169,
    192
workshops 135
world views 18
WrapPLS 125
writers' block 129–36
    dealing with the blank page 129–31
    finding focus 133–4
    lessons for keeping on track 136
    making a habit of writing 136
    Pomodoro (time management)
        technique 131–2
    writing communities 134–6
@WriteThatPhD 179
writing
    making a habit of 136
    see also academic writing; free
        writing; rewriting
writing communities 134–6
writing groups 29
writing mentors 134–5
writing retreats 134, 135
writing tasks, breaking up 132

YouTube 73, 124, 125, 180

Zapata-Phelan, C. 11, 12